Entering the Frame

ITALIAN MODERNITIES

VOL. 10

Edited by
Pierpaolo Antonello and Robert Gordon,
University of Cambridge

PETER LANG
Oxford · Bern · Berlin · Bruxelles · Frankfurt am Main · New York · Wien

Entering the Frame

Cinema and History in the Films of
Yervant Gianikian and Angela Ricci Lucchi

Robert Lumley

PETER LANG

Oxford · Bern · Berlin · Bruxelles · Frankfurt am Main · New York · Wien

Bibliographic information published by Die Deutsche Nationalbibliothek
Die Deutsche Nationalbibliothek lists this publication in the Deutsche National-
bibliografie; detailed bibliographic data is available on the Internet at http://
dnb.d-nb.de.

A catalogue record for this book is available from the British Library.

Library of Congress Cataloging-in-Publication Data:

Lumley, Robert.
  Entering the frame : cinema and history in the films of Yervant
Gianikian and Angela Ricci Lucchi / Robert Lumley.
      p. cm. -- (Italian modernities ; 10)
  Includes bibliographical references and index.
  Includes filmography and installations.
  ISBN 978-3-0343-0113-8 (alk. paper)
  1. Gianikian, Yervant--Criticism and interpretation. 2. Ricci Lucchi,
Angela--Criticism and interpretation. 3. Experimental
films--Italy--History and criticism. 4. Motion pictures and history.
I. Title.
  PN1998.3.G5L86 2011
  791.43'658--dc22
                          2011009919

Cover image: Yervant Gianikian and Angela Ricci Lucchi,
Visions du désert (2000).

ISSN 1662-9108
ISBN 978-3-0343-0113-8

© Peter Lang AG, International Academic Publishers, Bern 2011
Hochfeldstrasse 32, CH-3012 Bern, Switzerland
info@peterlang.com, www.peterlang.com, www.peterlang.net

Printed in Germany

To Martin Chalmers

Contents

Acknowledgements

This book probably has its origins in a distant past when I was on the edges of a London independent film world that I found in equal measure fascinating and mysterious. Just out of university and a little lost, I used to go to screenings with friends at the Slade School of Art. I remember seeing Ken Jacobs's *Tom Tom the Piper's Son*, and half-following the subsequent animated discussion in the smoke-filled student bar with Paul Marris, Simon Field, and Deke Dusinberre. They were studying on the new Film MA, a pioneering course at the time, which was foolishly discontinued a couple of years later. I was taking a free ride. Similar screenings took place at the Royal College of Art where I recall seeing films by Kurt Kren. At the London Filmmakers' Coop you could sit on the floor and watch films. A festival of the avant-garde at the National Film Theatre showed Michael Snow's *Région Central*. I worked collecting tickets for a few months at the Electric cinema in Portobello Road, one of London's oldest. The air was the same colour as the seats and carpet, and the substances in it meant that inhaling made you feel slightly giddy. *Time Out* magazine contained reviews by Tony Rayns. The British Film Institute was at once abuzz with Continental theory and cinephiles. I sometimes ask myself whether I didn't write this book in order to try and make sense of the inchoate mix of sensations and ideas left over from that time. Who knows! What I have found is that the names, films, and places that I first encountered in early 1970s, resurfaced during my research. The first time I saw one of Yervant Gianikian and Angela Ricci Lucchi's films was at the Millenium, one of the holy places of the New York independent film scene. When I looked into the possibility of getting *Prigionieri della guerra/Prisoners of the War* shown in London, I found myself contacting the film curator of the ICA, who happened at the time to be Simon Field. Gianikian and Ricci Lucchi re-filmed and manipulated found footage in ways reminiscent of Ken Jacobs's work. They were very much part of a film scene, bubbling with energy and invention.

When I embarked on writing this book, I was (and am) very much aware of not being a film scholar or a filmmaker. My limited knowledge of different film stocks or tinting processes and similar technical questions means that I frequently fail to ask the right questions. I would still like to get a better understanding of the use of colour in the films, an aspect given too little attention by critics. The scope to the project has been enormous in that it involves not only the filmmaking of Gianikian and Ricci Lucchi but that of the found or archival footage on which it is based. In other words, the ideal study calls for familiarity with the history of silent cinema as well as with the independent cinema of the late twentieth century. Those who have helped me learn about film language and to grapple with the technicalities of filmmaking have therefore played a particularly important role in the writing of this book, though any errors in this regard are my own. I attended courses at no.w.here, the artist-run project and workshop, which keeps alive skills and technologies used for 8mm and 16mm filmmaking as well as holding courses on the historical and theoretical legacy of independent cinema. I would like thank Karen Mizra, Brad Butler, and Maxa Zoller not only for what I learnt from the ideas-filled sessions that they hosted – I am thinking especially of the course 'The Cinematic Body' – but also for the encouragement to write about films which they showed me resonate for contemporary practitioners.

In doing the research, I found I had to explore many areas connected to the contents of the films. I read Theodor Adorno on Mahler, accounts of Armenian history and culture, Surrealist writings on film and ethnography, and studies of colonial cinema and post-colonial theory. The First World War features significantly in Gianikian and Ricci Lucchi's *oeuvre* as the 'event' to which so many of the disasters of the last century can be traced. When I was researching the war trilogy made between the early 1993 and 2004, I received a great deal of help and advice from Diego Leoni, who acted as historical consultant on the films. I am grateful too for access to his private archive. I would also like to thank Camillo Zadra, director of the Museo Storico Italiano della Guerra in Rovereto, and Gabriella Belli, director of the Museum of Contemporary Art of Rovereto and Trento.

I have received help from innumerable people during the writing of this book and if their names are not listed here they are likely to be acknowledged in the footnotes. My thanks go to those who invited me to conferences that helped me relate Gianikian and Ricci Lucchi's work to Futurism. Particularly important for me in this respect was the conference 'Futurism at 100' organised by Claudio Fogu, Ara H. Merjian, and Lucia Re, and the conference 'Shock and Awe: The Troubling Legacy of the Futurist Cult of War', organised by Emily Braun, at Hunter College, CUNY, both held in 2009. Sections of the book, especially in Chapter 5, will be recognised by organisers of seminars and symposiums where I delivered papers on the films of Gianikian and Ricci Lucchi, occasions that gave me the opportunity to rethink my analyses – I am thinking here of Marina Spunta, Charlotte Brunsdon, and Maud Bracke, respectively of the universities of Leicester, Warwick and Glasgow. The various papers and essays may never have led to a book without Robert Gordon and Pierpaolo Antonello, the editors of the series 'Italian Modernities'. I hope that they are as pleased with this new addition as I am to join their impressive list. During the months in which I was busy writing several people hunted down articles and sent me photocopies including Giuliana Adamo, Jacopo Benci, Elena Dagrada, John Foot, and Rod Stoneman. Marta Petrusewicz made me feel at home in New York during various research trips.

I am particularly grateful to Martin Chalmers, Matilde Nardelli, Clare Coope, and Robert Gordon, who read and commented on the manuscript. It would be difficult to enumerate the instances in which they have corrected serious errors, suggested ways of recasting material, or offered interpretations subsequently adopted. Their aid was vital in shaping the book in the final stages. I want to thank Ruth Ben-Ghiat for the clarity and many insights of her Preface, and also for encouragement over the years for a project she witnessed from the very beginning.

Enormously important, in a different way, has been life beyond the book in keeping the author relatively sane. Laurence and Matthew have kept a benevolent if quizzical eye on proceedings in the top room. Clare has watched many of the films with me and has generously shared ideas about them over several years. She has also tolerated the habitual carpeting of any and every surface with papers.

My thanks go to Gemma Lewis, Mette Bundgaard, Hannah Godfrey and Isabel James of Peter Lang for their helpful and conscientious work on producing this book. I am grateful also to Hazel Bell for her excellent index.

The book is dedicated to Martin Chalmers, a good friend and long-time admirer of the filmmakers, whose encouragement and ideas have been invaluable.

I have not yet mentioned my debt and gratitude to Angela Ricci Lucchi and Yervant Gianikian. They have always been generous in giving me their time and attention over the years. I greatly appreciate their friendship and hope that they find things in the book of some interest and value. Apart from being the makers of films of exceptional artistic quality, they provide an example of artists who have maintained an ethical and political integrity that is rare in these dark times.

Sources of Images

RUTH BEN-GHIAT

Preface

In 1996, I suggested to my colleague Bob Lumley, who was visiting New York from London, that we see the American premiere of a film about World War I that seemed promising but which neither of us knew anything about: *Prigionieri della guerra/Prisoners of War* (1995), by Yervant Gianikian and Angela Ricci Lucchi. I remember shifting about on the rather uncomfortable chairs until the movie began and I was swept into a celluloid world of the likes I had never seen before. This was no documentary, but a shaky, hallucinatory rendering of the human casualties of war, composed of scenes of bodies plodding through city streets and ruined natural landscapes, bodies motionless and mutilated in death and in life, bodies going everywhere and nowhere, advancing only to retreat. I drew on my historical training to find some larger logic or narrative to interpret these images, only to surrender in the end to the spectacle of humanity and despair presented to us by the filmmakers, to the strangeness of the folk songs and the beauty of the tinted frames, and to this enigmatic and spectral world which conveyed more truths about the meaning and consequences of war than many conventional historical documentaries. I also recall feeling upset at several points by the imagery – a not uncommon reaction to the work of Ricci Lucchi and Gianikian – and wanting to ask Bob to leave. Today I am very glad that I did not make that request, for the present book by Bob Lumley is, in small part, a result of staying the course through that screening, at which the filmmakers were present.

Although Gianikian and Ricci Lucchi are famous, even cult figures within the world of experimental film, Lumley's book is the first English-language monograph on them and their work. It guides us through the evolution of their films, working methods and critical reception from the 1970s onward, while investigating, through themed chapters, the concerns that recur throughout their *oeuvre*: death and cinema, history and memory, the body and embodiment. Film scholars have paid much attention of late to such questions, and the movies of Gianikian and Ricci Lucchi will speak strongly to those with an interest in the relationship of cinema and history, the corporeal, sensual and material nature of film and its makers and spectators.[1] Indeed, the filmmakers have been pioneers in the creation of cinematic experiences that mobilise the senses, enchanting and discomfiting the spectator. This is one dimension of their emphasis on the tactile and material nature of film as a material and medium – they highlight, rather than obscure, the scratched and worn nature of the decaying footage they work with, made still more textured by their own hand-tinting of individual frames. The sensory world is also, for them, an avenue into the kinds of histories and memories that have little to do with the written page and the realm of institutional or governmental record. It is central to the effectiveness of their poetics of contrast and to their searing investigations of the everyday as lived within contexts of natural beauty and extreme brutality. A case in point is *Catalogo N.3. Odore di tiglio intorno alla casa/ Catalogue No. 3. The Smell of Lime Trees Around the House* (1976), one of their 'scented cinema' (*cinema profumato*) works which featured an 'odour track' of essential fragrances released in the theatre during the screening. Here, flowering lime scent and the sweet title introduce a display of quotidian objects of a family of militant Fascists: the Mussolini portraits and colonial 'trophies' (pictures of military service in North Africa, half-naked African women) that were objects of desire in those years. By recreating the same smell as that enjoyed by the house's long-dead owners, the filmmakers unsettle the neat divide between past and present, spectator and subject, pleasures of then and pleasures of now.

---

1   Such as: Vivian Sobchack, *Carnal Thoughts. Embodiment and Moving Image Culture* (Berkeley: University of California Press, 2004); Laura U. Marks, *The Skin of the Film: Intercultural Cinema, Embodiment and the Senses* (Durham, NC: Duke University Press, 2000); Belinda Smaill, *The Documentary: Emotion, Politics, Culture* (New York: Palgrave, 2010); David MacDougall, *The Corporeal Image: Film, Ethnography, and the Senses* (Princeton: Princeton University Press, 2005).

Gianikian and Ricci Lucchi are best known for their 1985 work *Dal Polo all'Equatore*, which has had a double impact in the worlds of film and Italian studies for the interest it has generated in the documentarian Luca Comerio. Based on Comerio's 1929 documentary of the same title, which contains footage shot by Comerio and others over a period of twenty-odd years, *Dal Polo all'Equatore* is a tour de force of experimental and found footage filmmaking. Re-photographing hundreds of thousands of frames, colouring them, slowing down the images, and removing the intertitles and other original framing and contextual devices, Ricci Lucchi and Gianikian turn a Fascist documentary into a film that comments critically on rhetorics as well as representations of history and on the entanglements of cinema, imperialism, and Fascism. Lumley discusses the film extensively and here I want to mention just a few salient points. First, the filmmakers' reworking of Comerio's footage highlights that in Italy, no less than in France, Germany, and Britain, cinema played a central role in the culture of empire. We see the camera as weapon of war and imperialism –seeing as an integral part of the act of killing – ; violence as inevitable and a masculine rite; the ability of modern technologies to tame and vanquish nature, performance as a lens on the essence of the 'primitive'; the privileged position of the cinematic apparatus and its operator in registering all of this. Yet there is also the positing of a chain of prosthetic sight – repeatedly the camera aims at the targeter, with the lens pointed at the back of his head – which implicates the camera in what is being filmed – which occupied ever more importance as a gloss on Fascist schemes of political visualisation. This relay of gazes ends, of course, with Mussolini, who is not present in *Dal Polo all'Equatore* but figures in many other Gianikian and Ricci Lucchi films as an icon of imperial aggression.

Second, *Dal Polo all'Equatore* reminds us that both the history of cinema and the history of war and imperial expansion have depended on technologies of movement. No less than the train operator or pilot, the cameraman was an emblem of a mobile modernity. The qualities of a peculiarity modern temporality based on 'assault, acceleration, and speed,' which are also those of the battlefield, were a hallmark of Futurist aesthetics and came to define Fascist-era non-fiction film productions by Comerio

and others.[2] Gianikian and Ricci Lucchi's *Dal Polo all'Equatore*, like their
subsequent 'war trilogy' of *Prigioneri di guerra, Su tutte le vette è pace/On
the Heights all is Peace* (1998) and *Oh! Uomo/Oh! Man* (2004), engages
polemically with cinema's enmeshment in this martial matrix. As Lumley
writes, in the film's opening sequence of a train travelling through the Alps,
the slowed and tinted footage and the absence of any commentary give a
sensation of suspension, which after a while brings acknowledgement that
time it is subject, along with the act of looking. At times this suspended
gaze seems endless, as in the scenes of violence against animals by explorers
and imperial adventurers. As Crista Blümlinger has noted, Ricci Lucchi
and Gianikian slow the action of a hunter killing a polar bear twelvefold,
forcing us to experience its agony. As Gianikian has commented, 'the slow
motion of our version is the opposite of the extremely fast movement of the
original [...] Slow motion becomes emphasis, the rhythm of memory.'[3] A
direct line links the triumphalism of the early expedition and exploration
documentaries by Comerio and others to the manic pace of Fascist imperial
documentaries. In this regard the filmmakers' interventions in the sphere
of filmic temporality might also be taken as exhortations for us to examine
the timelines we draw, especially those which allow Italian imperial aggression to be confined only to the years of the Fascist dictatorship.

I return here, by way of conclusion, to the ways that the filmmakers'
manipulations of archival and found footage in *Dal Polo all'Equatore* and
their war trilogy represent a radical rewriting of not merely of Fascist history but of a postwar tradition of documentary representations which is
represented in Italy by the Istituto Luce (itself an institution with Fascist-
era origins). In movies like *Prigionieri di guerra* and *Su tutte le vette è pace*,
the slowed down pace and isolation of details through enlargements allow

2   Mary Ann Doane, *The Emergence of Cinematic Time: Modernity, Contingency, and
     the Archive* (Cambridge, MA: Harvard University Press, 2002), 33.
3   Yervant Gianikian, in Scott MacDonald, *A Critical Cinema 3: Interviews with
     Independent Filmmakers* (Berkeley: University of California Press, 1998), 279; Crista
     Blümlinger, 'Inside the Frame from the Pole to the Equator', in *Cinema Anni Vita:
     Yervant Gianikian and Angela Ricci Lucchi*, ed. Paolo Mereghetti and Enrico Nosei
     (Milan: Il Castoro, 2000), 93.

a universe of human and intimate moments to emerge from the backdrop of industrial warfare, exposing what Michael Zyrd calls 'the history behind the image.' As the opening intertitle of *Su tutte le vette è pace* proclaims, their aim was

> the search for the individual, for the 'man-soldier' in the archive that depicts anonymous masses. In the details, in the particulars, in the expressions, in the microphysiognomies, in the behavior of the single person. [The film was] Shot through the 'wounded body' of nitrate material. On the Alps.

These individual glances rebuke the eclipse of the person through aerial and long-range warfare that has marked the twentieth century. Stripped of their original propagandistic context, they offer up 'layers of speculation, subjective evocation, and poetic ambiguity,' – things Fascism suppressed but which also had little place in any modern war machine. Teshome Gabriel has argued that film, unlike historiography, can represent 'emotion, loss, the past, relying not so much on full or completed narratives but on collections of fragments.'[4] The cinema of Ricci Lucchi and Gianikian is a cinema of fragments, of traces; theirs is a history cinema which paradoxically proclaims its ephemeral and incomplete nature, not least by calling attention to the parallel processes of human and cinematic decay. Lumley writes eloquently that 'archival images are not curiosities of purely antiquarian interest. They are themselves survivors and bear traces of the history of which they are fragmentary remnants.' His book opens up the world of those scarred images, as given new life by Gianikian and Ricci Lucchi over thirty years of filmmaking.

4   Teshome Gabriel, 'Ruin and the Other', in *Otherness and the Media: The Ethnography of the Imagined and the Imaged*, ed. Gabriel and Hamid Naficy (Chur: Harwood Academic Publishers, 1993), 7; Michael Zyrd, 'Found Footage Film as Discursive Metahistory: Craig Baldwin's *Tribulation 99*', *The Moving Image* 3.2 (Fall 2003), 40–61, 42. See also Robert Rosenstone, 'Introduction', in *Revisioning History: Film and the Construction of a New Past* (Princeton: Princeton University Press, 1995), 3–14.

Introduction

There is a sequence in a film by Yervant Gianikian and Angela Ricci Lucchi that I find myself 'watching' as I walk down the hill, as I sit on the top deck of a London bus, as I lose concentration on what I am reading or writing. I am in a tunnel, then I emerge into a red-tinted Alpine landscape, and once more I am in a tunnel, and now I can see the train winding in front of me as well as the valley below. I remember many images as if they were freeze-frames but movement takes me onwards and downwards. Everything is in slow motion.

The sequence opens *Dal Polo all'Equatore* (*From the Pole to the Equator*, 1986), which is the filmmakers' best known work and a masterpiece in the genre of archival or found footage films. It lasts about eight minutes. The original footage run at normal speed would have flashed by, unremembered. But re-framed, tinted, stretched and edited, it has left indelible traces in my memory. Nor is this simply the result of multiple viewings for the sake of study. Nor am I alone in having this experience; the critic Philippe Azoury states unequivocally of *Dal Polo all'Equatore*: 'Anyone who has seen it will always remember it'.[1] Why exactly certain sequences – what Victor Burgin has called 'sequence-images'[2] – are remembered depends on any number of variables independent of the film itself. But it is also true that certain films are *conceived* in mnemonic terms; they are made to be remembered long after they have been seen, and are made for the viewer to remember through them. Such is the case with the work of Gianikian and Ricci Lucchi. For them, the tunnel is a tunnel of memory through which to travel back in historical time and back in cinema history.

---

1   Philippe Azoury, 'Sur "certaines radiations encore loin d'etre claires"', *Trafic* 38 (Summer 2001), 59.
2   Victor Burgin, *The Remembered Film* (London: Reaktion, 2004).

Edwin Carels, in an essay entitled 'The Politics of Recollection', portrays Gianikian and Ricci Lucchi as time-travellers who 'use the power of the cinematographic device to travel into the past [...] They act like inventors, as if the Lumière brothers had never managed to impose a standard, and follow instead the example of Marey and the tradition of the magic lantern show'. He compares them to 'authentic alchemists', masters of 'occult powers' hidden in the banal transformation whereby the still frames of a film strip move and come alive.³ In a similar vein, the filmmakers are pictured by Marco Belpoliti in their 'magic cavern', devotees of their art, 'secular monks, shy, mild in manner yet very severe, they have worked in silence for almost 30 years'.⁴ Gianikian and Ricci Lucchi are cast in the role of Orpheus, moving between the worlds of the living and the dead. Ara Merjian associates their practice with that of ragpickers: 'Many frames – as well as ellipses between them – conjure something of the conception of the filmmaker as ragpicker, homing in on otherwise ignored or overlooked fragments of reality that illuminate larger historical development'.⁵

Gianikian and Ricci Lucchi appear as liminal figures standing at the doorway between past and present, explorers and inventors, alchemists and apothecaries, magicians and shamen. While these characterisations are sometimes fanciful, the recurrence of certain tropes emphasises the extraordinary powers of the filmmakers and their remoteness from the routines of the cultural industry. Indeed, Gianikian and Ricci Lucchi are held in the highest regard, if not revered, by leading critics and historians of film internationally, even if they remain unknown to the average filmgoer.

Interestingly the language used to speak of them and their films is reminiscent of that of the writing on early cinema at the beginning of the twentieth century when cinema was a novelty likened to magic and ascribed

3   Edwin Carels, 'La politica del ricordo/The Politics of Re-collection', in *Cinema Anni Vita. Yervant Gianikian e Angela Ricci Lucchi*, ed. Paolo Mereghetti and Enrico Nosei (Milan: Il Castoro, 2000), 105–14.
4   Marco Belpoliti, 'Così filmiamo la Storia cancellata', *La Stampa* (13 February 2006).
5   Ara Merjian, 'Bodies of Evidence', *Artforum on-line*, artforum.com/film/id=21962, dated 2 February 2009; accessed 20 May 2010.

the power to preserve the living in moving images in perpetuity.[6] Indeed, Gianikian and Ricci Lucchi have been celebrated for making films that return to the experimentation of early film before Hollywood established its dominance. For Raymond Bellour, their work opens up new ways of thinking about the history of cinema: 'Without doubt there will come a day when, faced with the need to see the history of cinema as part of a wider adventure, people will seek to understand it through an inventory of the modalities by which continuous attempts have been made to counteract its movement, to arrest it, and, above all, to create speeds different from the norm of the "natural" typical of analogical montage (or based on the analogy of movement)'.[7]

The return to the pre-history and early days of cinema is noted by Scott MacDonald as a route taken by a number of filmmakers whom he groups under the category 'critical cinema'. Looking to Muybridge and Marey, 'virtually every filmmaker I've introduced', he writes,

> has focused on the study of motion, whether it's physical motion of bodies in space (Rose Lowder, John Porter, Arthur Peleshian) or in previously recorded film imagery (in the 'recycled cinema' of Martin Arnold, Yervant Gianikian and Angela Ricci Lucchi, Raphael Ortiz and many others).[8]

However, when MacDonald asked Gianikian and Ricci Lucchi whether they considered themselves 'cine-archeologists', they replied: 'Somebody might define us that way [...] Something is missing [...] We are interested in an ethical sense of vision. A project is usually born from our reading of film images'.[9]

---

6   'Curses and ghosts, the evil spirits that have cast entire cities into eternal sleep, come to mind', wrote Maxim Gorky, 'and you feel as though Merlin's vicious trick is being enacted before you'; Lynda Nead, *The Haunted Gallery: Painting, Photography and Film c. 1900* (New Haven and London: Yale University Press, 2007), 104.

7   Raymond Bellour, 'Il retromondo' in *Cinema Anni Vita: Yervant Gianikian e Angela Ricci Lucchi*, ed. Paolo Mereghetti and Enrico Nosei, 75.

8   Scott MacDonald, *A Critical Cinema 3: Interviews with Independent Filmmakers* (Berkeley: University of California Press, 1998), 5.

9   Ibid.

The filmmakers' own self-representations and conception of their work departs in significant respects from the image of them constructed by others, of which examples have been cited. They baulk at the idea that their films might be considered formal exercises or historically motivated excavations of the past. Instead, they stress the primacy of ethical purpose and the part of interpretation – what they bring to the images. In interviews, they draw attention to the meaning of the images in the contemporary situation: 'The relationship between Then and Now is always a dominant concern in our films', they tell MacDonald.[10] History preoccupies Yervant Gianikian and Angela Ricci Lucchi because they see the past not as over-and-done-with but as a spectre, a constant possibility of recurrence in the form of colonialism, fascism, war, persecution, genocide, mass deportation, and other disasters with which twentieth-century Europe was rife. Archival images are not curiosities or of merely antiquarian interest. They are themselves survivors and bear traces of the history of which they are fragmentary remnants.

There is a photograph of Yervant Gianikian and Angela Ricci Lucchi, used in catalogues, that is emblematic in this respect. They are shown sitting in the kitchen of their apartment in Milan. On the table in front of them a basket holds pears and apples, plates and a glass remain from a meal, and they look intently to camera – a portrait with still life. This photograph has often been cropped however. The original image had a small travel radio on the table in the foreground with its antenna extended. Its removal makes for a more balanced composition, but the object that stands for modernity and connection to the wider world is lost. Insignificant in itself, this edit points to the importance of keeping the contemporary world in the frame when considering the filmmakers and their work. News of what is going on today whether in Afghanistan or Zanzibar is for them a reality that is ever present, not something external to or irrelevant to the films.

It should be added that the filmmakers are always photographed together. All their films are jointly authored and they constitute a fine example of a partnership in art and life. Interviews and the majority of

10   Ibid.

texts are undertaken jointly. Gianikian and Ricci Lucchi have invariably spoken of their work as a totality in which every phase and aspect of the filmmaking is discussed and agreed, even if some division of labour is entailed. Gianikian, for instance, can be considered the technician and plays the leading role in handling the film, while Ricci Lucchi is responsible for most of the research on the historical and literary contexts in which the original films were made. Commentators and critics have speculated on their different personalities as artists.[11] At the MoMA retrospective in New York in 2008 the programme, in a symbolic gesture, reversed the alphabetical order, putting Ricci Lucchi's name first. This study acknowledges the joint-authorship of the films and only refers to individual contributions where indicated or relevant for a particular reason.

Gianikian and Ricci Lucchi are often referred to as 'Italian filmmakers' but this identification requires some qualification. It is true that they describe themselves as 'living and working in Milan', and they have used Italian as the principal language in their films – in titles and inter titles, for example. However, Gianikian always states in biographical notes that he is 'of Armenian origin', while Ricci Lucchi sees herself as coming from Romagna rather than Italy. He speaks of not really feeling at home anywhere and sets great store by origins that make him a second-generation member of a diaspora that stretches across continents. Ricci Lucchi dwells on an attachment to locality that bypasses the national, while identifying herself as a citizen of the world. Their outlook represents a current of 'critical cinema' emerging in the 1990s; MacDonald writes of this as 'simultaneously

11   Morando Morandini writes: 'How does the symbiosis – syntone, synergy, synderesis, sympathy – work between Angela and Yervant? It's no use asking them. They answer with a smile that they cannot and don't want to end their collaboration together: they do everything together, with two pairs of hands – from the conception of the project to the selection of materials, from *mise-en-scène* to editing, from music to post-synchronisation. Those who know them well might hazard a conjecture or hypothesis. Between the two, Yervant is East and Angela is West. He is Platonic, she Aristotelian. He is the eye, she is the ear: he paints the pictures, she is more attentive to the sound'; Morando Morandini, 'The Eye and the Ear: Some Things I Know about Angela and Yervant' in *Cinema Anni Vita*, 133.

multinational and transnational, multi-ethnic and inter-ethnic, not simply
in the sense that various filmmakers identify themselves with a considerable
range of locations and heritages, but because all the filmmakers see their
work as the product of many and varied interests and influences'.[12]

Gianikian and Ricci Lucchi have developed a philosophy and strategy
that cuts across notions of 'national cinema'. They occupy a unique and
rather isolated position within Italian cinema. It is not that they dismiss
feelings of belonging and attachment to place and culture – to what in
German is called *Heimat*. On the contrary, loss of home, negation of identity, denial of language and other acts of violence feature strongly in their
films. In contrast, the situations that preceded the onslaught of war and the
turning of neighbours into enemies are affectionately documented. In the
trilogy of films they made on the First World War, they carefully sourced
the footage from different national archives and used multiple languages
to avoid privileging any one national experience.

Within Italy, Gianikian and Ricci Lucchi have been acknowledged as
important filmmakers. The publication in 1990 by the Museo Nazionale del
Cinema of a collection, edited by Sergio Toffetti, of essays and interviews
dedicated to their work,[13] and in 2000 of another volume, this time edited
by Paolo Mereghetti and Enrico Nosei for the Fondazione Cineteca Italiana,
marked significant moments of recognition. Leading cinema historians,
such as Alberto Farassino and Antonio Costa, critics, especially those writing for the newspaper, *Il Manifesto*, and the influential presenter of RAI 3's
film programme, Enrico Ghezzi, have consistently followed and supported
their work. However, Italian state bodies have done little to help with the
financing of projects, whereas regional organisations, on the one hand,
and European ones, on the other, have proved much more enlightened.
Critical recognition and commissions from outside Italy have undoubt-
edly played a key part in enabling Gianikian and Ricci Lucchi to make and
make known their work. The part played by French film critics, historians,

---

12   MacDonald, *A Critical Cinema 3*, 3.
13   *Yervant Gianikian, Angela Ricci Lucchi*, ed. Sergio Toffetti (Turin: hopefulmonster,
      1992). Texts are in Italian and English. However, I have mostly translated texts from
      the Italian myself for the purposes of this book.

and museum curators has been especially important in this respect, as has been the role of American counterparts.[14] Gianni Comencini observed that 'the two Italian filmmakers living in Milan enjoy considerable fame outside Italy (in Paris and New York their films are often featured in major cultural events) but are as yet little known in this country'.[15] Recognition has taken several forms, from nominations in the Cannes Film Festival to screenings at international film festivals around the world. The filmmakers recall the enthusiastic support of Harald Szeemann, the inspirational curator of contemporary art. Szeemann commissioned installations that allowed the artists filmmakers to develop their practice in a new direction. Their installation *La marcia dell'uomo* (The Walk of Man, 2001) for the Venice Biennale of 2000, for example, opened the way for several projects for museums and galleries in Europe and North America.

The position of film within contemporary art has changed radically over the decades in which Gianikian and Ricci Lucchi have been working. When they started making films in the 1970s, they were frequently shown in galleries. Subsequently, especially after the success of *Dal Polo all'Equatore*, they were screened in cinemas and film festivals. Then, from 2000, they returned to showing their films and installations in contemporary art environments once more, mostly in public museums, as well as screening their films in festivals. The changes in exhibition venue corresponded in part to changes in Gianikian and Ricci Lucchi's practice but it also reflected transformations in the nature and position of film within the visual arts and the wider culture. These can be tracked in relation to particular genres, such as the documentary. Gianikian and Ricci Lucchi have long been known as makers of documentary films and recognition of their work at the prestigious Flaherty Seminar in 1986 was a watershed for them.[16] But what exactly was meant by 'documentary' and how it was understood was increasingly problematic, its uncertain status as a visual

14   The journal *Trafic* has followed their work with exemplary scholarship and encouragement.
15   Foreword by Gianni Comencini in *Cinema Anni Vita*, 5–6.
16   Bill Sloan, then film librarian at MoMA in New York, was bowled over by the film. He subsequently organised the distribution of Gianikian and Ricci Lucchi's titles through the museum's circulating film and video library.

language explored by many artists as a means of both producing a critique of the art world and engaging with contemporary realities. Analogous shifts occurred in the use of 'found footage'. Writing in the catalogue of the 2005 exhibition *Film as Found Object*, Rob Yeo noted: 'The practice of using earlier film from a variety of sources – found footage – as the raw material for new works of art has a history that dates back almost to the origins of cinema and is currently considered *a* if not *the* dominant critical procedure in independent film and video making.'[17]

As filmmakers who made documentaries that were simultaneously found footage films, Gianikian and Ricci Lucchi anticipated trends and helped to create what was to become a sub-genre, the archival documentary. However, it is more interesting and productive to view their films without slotting them into genre categories. As pioneers who have seen themselves first and foremost as artists, they worked across institutional and genre boundaries. Their films, as a consequence, have been open to reading and appropriation by different audiences and constituencies. It is this hybrid quality that has been one of its strengths and distinguishing features. These genre considerations should, at the same time, be put into the wider framework of the massive technological revolution that has made cinema into a chapter within the longer history of the moving image.[18] From the 1990s, the introduction and diffusion of the digital has changed what constitute images – how they are produced, distributed, viewed, and understood. The significance attributed to the films of Gianikian and Ricci Lucchi has as much to do with the historicisation of cinema itself as with their treatment of historical subjects. They stand at the beginning of the new millennium as witnesses to the twentieth century seen through the history of cinema, and as witnesses to the history of cinema seen through the history of the twentieth century.

17   Rob Yeo, 'Cutting through History: Found Footage in Avant-garde Filmmaking' in *Cut: Film as Found Object in Contemporary Video*, ed. Stefano Basilico (Milwaukee: Milwaukee Art Museum, 2005), 13.
18   For a remarkable study of the historical turn in avant-garde filmmaking, see Jeffrey Skoller, *Shadows, Specters, Shards: Making History in Avant-Garde Film* (Minneapolis: University of Minnesota Press, 2005).

The contemporary circumstances of 'permanent war'[19] in which the films have been made and viewed at the beginning of the twenty-first century have sharpened the political and ethical edge of their artistic project. By 'war' is meant not single battles or events but the cumulative process of framing and redefining whereby human beings are attributed value and are treated as worthy of life or dispensable. If dispensable they can be killed, left to die, or reduced to mere survival. Statistics on the historically low rates of military casualties and ever-higher casualties in the civilian population are but one stark indicator of this new type of war.[20] Such an understanding of war informs the films of Gianikian and Ricci Lucchi – mostly obviously the trilogy made from footage of and immediately after the First World War, but also in their films about colonialism. Through images they have assembled a body of work in syntony with the idea of a 'new bodily ontology' delineated by the philosopher Judith Butler.[21] War provides the condition with which to think through the question 'What is a life?' and on what makes loss, injury and death have meaning. The films of Gianikian and Ricci Lucchi mount a coherent resistance to the 'frame' that enables power to deem some lives 'grievable' and others not. They work with footage by 'stepping into' the cinematic frame, and by taking apart and putting together again frames that are at once material, formal, and ideological. A description by Judith Butler of the instability of the frame and its vulnerability to counter-strategies could be a description of the potentialities realised in the filmmakers' practice:

19   Paul Virilio, 'Impure War', in *Pure War* (Los Angeles: Semiotext(e), 2008), 7; for a discussion of this concept in relation to politics and culture in the early twentieth century, see *Zones of Conflict*, ed. T.J. Demos (New York: Pratt Manhattan Gallery, 2008).

20   'Although numbers cannot tell us precisely whose lives count, and whose deaths count, we can note how numbers are framed and unframed to find out how norms that differentiate livable and grievable lives are at work in the context of war'; Judith Butler, *Frames of War: When is Life Grievable?* (London and New York: Verso, 2010), xx.

21   Ibid., 2.

The frame is always throwing something away, keeping something out, always de-realising and de-legitimating alternative versions of reality, discarded negatives of the official version. And so, when the frame jettisons certain versions of war, it is busily making a rubbish heap whose animated debris provides the potential resources for resistance.[22]

***

The idea for this book took shape in 2006. But I first met Yervant Gianikian and Angela Ricci Lucchi on a very cold February night ten years earlier at the Millennium in New York after seeing the American première of *Prisoners of the War* (1995).[23] We kept in touch over the intervening years during which I did not lose an opportunity to see their films on those rare occasions when they were screened in London. Since the book project got going, I have had many discussions with the filmmakers about their work. But it is not only talk about film that informs this study. Impressions, sensations and half-formed thoughts experienced when with Yervant and Angela – walking or having a meal or travelling in the car – have filtered into the writing in ways that I find it hard to pinpoint.[24] I particularly remember one time when I visited them in Italy. It was outside their house at Pavo. I took a photograph of them. Yervant had just told me about the crab apple that had saved the life of his father, Raphael, when he was a young boy at the time of the Armenian genocide. He was sick and the family to whom he was enslaved was planning to get rid of him. Raphael Gianikian ate the apple found in a coat pocket and recovered. He asked Yervant and Angela to plant a crab apple tree in his memory. In the photograph they are standing next to the tree and the evening light is shining through its leaves.

Whether a book like this can ever be adequate in the eyes of its subjects is doubtful, but I hope it achieves some of what it sets out to do. In

22   Ibid., xiii.
23   It was Ruth Ben-Ghiat who suggested we see the film. I remain very grateful for the idea.
24   A heightened awareness of history in the landscape might be one sign of a change of perception I experienced when with Yervant and Angela. To give an example, on a visit to the pretty little Piedmontese town of Moncalvo, they pointed out the synagogue now closed and without a community, a mute reminder of genocide in the midst of everyday life.

the first instance, the aim is to provide information about the films and installations made by Gianikian and Ricci Lucchi over the thirty-five-year period, from the mid 1970s to 2010. In that time, they were responsible for about fifty films – of which nine of feature length – and several installations for museums and foundations. The earliest works were 8mm shorts. Unfortunately, few of these have yet been transferred to either 16mm or DVD. It has, therefore, been particularly difficult to write about them, a difficulty augmented by the fact that they were originally shown as part of performances. I have relied on contemporary accounts to reconstruct this work. Most documentation on the *oeuvre* deals with single films and is dispersed, so one of the aims of this book to gather this information in one place and summarise the main arguments and analyses. Writings have appeared, moreover, in several languages – in Italian and French above all – and in a variety of journals, catalogues and film programmes. Again, anyone reading this text should form a fairly comprehensive idea of the literature on the filmmakers.

A second, more ambitious, aim is to describe and analyse Gianikian and Ricci Lucchi's work as it has evolved over the better part of a lifetime. With this intention, I have divided the book into two main parts. In the first part, the majority of the five chapters are organised on a chronological basis, and in the second part, the final chapter, the films are discussed thematically.

Chapter 1 starts with the films of the 1970s when Gianikian and Ricci Lucchi made performance-based films using scents – what they called *cinema profumato* or scented cinema. After the discovery of a collection of old 9.5mm films in a shop, the filmmakers began to make found footage films and to work exclusively with images and, later, sound. This experience is put in the context of the independent filmmaking in America and Europe at a time when it was still possible to speak of 'avant-garde cinema'. Chapter 2 examines the transition to a more history-conscious use of found footage in the early 1980s. It looks at how Gianikian and Ricci Lucchi moved from working with 9.5mm films to working with the 35mm of an important collection of documentary films that once belonged to a pioneer of documentary films in Italy. This footage provided the material for the making of *Dal Polo all'Equatore* (From the Pole to the Equator, 1986), which is analysed in detail. In Chapter 3 the focus is on the films that deal with the

Armenian massacres and deportation that resulted in what has been called the first genocide of the twentieth century. Yervant Gianikian's father, Raphael, who was one of very few survivors, bears testimony to the events in a video, *Ritorno a Khodorciur. Diario Armeno* (Return to Khodorciur. Armenian Diary, 1986). A subsequent film, *Uomini anni vita* (Men Years Life, 1990), revisits the genocide in a journey through film archives. Chapter 4 addresses the films now called the 'War Trilogy': *Prigionieri della guerra* (Prisoners of the War, 1995), *Su tutte le vette è pace* (On the Heights All is Peace, 1998), and *Oh! Uomo* (Oh! Man, 2004). The three films, which were released between 1995 and 2004, are based on archival footage shot during and immediately after the First World War. In addition, Gianikian and Ricci Lucchi produced installations for museums that further developed their meditations on the wars and catastrophes in the twentieth century, exploring analogies between the physical wounds sustained by the old film frames and by the men at the front. Chapter 5 deviates from the overall chronological structure by analysing a series of short films made in the first half of the 1990s, which are grouped together on account of their common preoccupation with Italian Fascism. It also looks at films dealing with war in the Balkans in the 1940s – *Inventario balcanico* (Balkan Inventory, 2000), and again in the early 1990s – *Nocturne* (1997). Finally, it surveys Gianikian and Ricci Lucchi's longstanding interest in colonialism and the exotic, looking at a variety of short films collected under the heading 'Fragments', and at the longer *Images d'Orient, tourisme vandale* (Images of the East, Vandal Tourism, 2001). In this chapter, as in previous chapters, attention is paid to the tendencies, such as the new exploitation of documentary forms by artists or the interest in a 'third cinema' informed by post-colonial thinking, that led to greater interest in and recognition of their work. The commission of an installation for the Venice Biennale proved an important step.

The last chapter, Chapter 6, seeks to review and assess Gianikian and Ricci Lucchi's *oeuvre*. While the previous chapters aimed to give as much useful information as possible and to describe the films, the aim here is to stand back from the detail and consider them in the light of three themes indicated by the subheadings 'History and Memory', 'The Body and Embodiment', and 'Death and Cinema'. The writings of Walter Benjamin on a range of questions, notably on history and memory, are shown to be an essential point of reference for such an assessment. Benjamin provides analytic concepts that help us to think about how, for example, the filmmakers use 'outmoded' cultural phenomena – in their case old film footage – to reprise artistic strategies first developed by the surrealists. But Benjamin, in turn, needs to be brought into the frame as someone who has influenced if not the filmmakers, then the reception and interpretation of their work. The theme of the body raises issues to do with craft and the making of the films, and with the connection between the materiality of the film and its subject matter – practices and concerns that have been associated with currents emerging in what Scott MacDonald calls 'critical cinema' since the 1990s. It also relates to shifts in film criticism away from notions of 'reading' and 'text' and towards a phenomenological approach that considers ways in which the spectator's whole body is caught up in responses to film. Gianikian and Ricci Lucchi, whose films dispense with plot and verbalisation, invite such an approach; in the words of one critic, theirs is a cinema that 'constructs its discourse not from a story but from the immediacy of the look that first registers and then (re)thinks reality'.[25] Finally, there is the theme of death. Here death is understood above all in terms of debates about the dying out of analogue technologies of visual reproduction and their replacement by digital. The films of Gianikian and Ricci Lucchi belong uncompromisingly to the domain of old technologies. They can even be said to stage a process of mourning in which the dead are remembered through images that are slowly degrading. The sudden and rapid changes that have come with the end of the twentieth and beginning of the twenty-first century should not, however, be seen simply in the negative. Commentators, such as D.N. Rodowick and Laura Mulvey, point to the way that digitalisation has had the paradoxical effect of heightening our awareness of what is special and different about analogue images. As filmmakers, Gianikian and Ricci Lucchi are perhaps among those who have contributed most to our understanding of what we are losing when we lose this cinema.

25   Aldo Spiniello, '*Diario 1989. Dancing in the Dark* di Yervant Gianikian e Angela Ricci Lucchi', 24 November 2009; www.sentieriselvaggi.it/articolo.asp?sezo=1&sez1= 256&art=34776; accessed 14 December 2009.

CHAPTER 1

Cinema profumato and Independent Filmmaking in the 1970s

We saw in the cinema a lyrical substance simply waiting to be hauled in *en masse* with the aid of chance. I think that what we valued most in it, to the point of taking no interest in anything else, was its power to disorient.

— ANDRÉ BRETON[1]

How many colours are there in a field of grass to the crawling baby unaware of 'Green'. Imagine a world before the 'beginning was the word'.

— STAN BRAKHAGE[2]

After the Second World War, European and American culture began to be dominated by the ideologies of mainstream cinema, television, saturation advertising and mass distraction. In this new situation speed lost much of its critical edge and most of its artistic credentials. To be radical was to be *slow*.

— DAVID CAMPANY[3]

When Angela Ricci Lucchi and Yervant Gianikian met in 1972, he was already making 8mm films and had shown work at a gallery. At university in Venice he did a degree in Architecture for which his thesis had

---

1   André Breton, 'As in a Wood', in *The Shadow and its Shadow*, ed. Paul Hammond (Edinburgh: Polygon, 1991), 81.

2   Stan Brakhage, 'Metaphors on Vision', in *Film Theory and Criticism*, ed. Leo Braudy and Marshall Cohen (Oxford: Oxford University Press, 1999), 228.

3   David Campany, 'Introduction: When to be Fast? When to be Slow', in *The Cinematic*, ed. David Campany (Cambridge, MA and London: Whitechapel and MIT Press, 2007), 10.

included close analysis of silent films. His interest in images, however, was not exclusive to cinema, and he made multi-media objects, usually in the form of boxes in which different materials were assembled into tableaux. Ricci Lucchi was showing work in a gallery in Ferrara with a catalogue presentation by the critic Renato Barilli. She had studied painting with Oskar Kokoschka in Vienna. She too was now engaged in multi-media experiments. It was at this time that she undertook a survey that consisted in putting a seemingly simple question to a wide range of people, namely 'What is a rose to you?' The screenwriter Cesare Zavattini wrote back a 'wonderful letter'. Another respondent was Yervant Gianikian, to whom she put the question shortly after meeting him. In an interview of 1991, she remarks: 'It all began there'.[4]

There is little information about what the two artists did in the pre-partnership years. Their public statements avoid giving more than a minimum of autobiographical detail and they restrict themselves to providing information on their joint productions. Both were born in 1942, and they were entering their thirties when their working partnership began. Arguably it was another decade before they established themselves as artists/filmmakers with a consolidated signature style and international reputation. However, the research and practice of the 1970s already showed them to be single-minded and independent in their thinking and strategy, and gave rise to a distinctive body of short films. Yervant Gianikian and Angela Ricci Lucchi became known as the practitioners of *cinema profumato* (scented cinema). Sadly, this cinema experience is now closed to us. The filmmakers gave their last performance in Paris in 1995, and have said that they do not intend to re-enact the work. It is important nonetheless to describe and analyse *cinema profumato* not only as an interesting experiment in its own right, but as the matrix from which their subsequent films originated.

4   'Cataloghi della memoria: Conversazione con Yervant Gianikian e Angela Ricci Lucchi (Sergio Toffetti e Daniela Giuffrida)' in *Yervant Gianikian, Angela Ricci Lucchi*, ed. Sergio Toffetti (Turin: hopefulmonster, 1992), 8.

Cinema profumato (Scented Films)

The first example of scented film was *Erat-Sora* (1975). In the words of a catalogue entry: 'In May the air smells of roses. In the countryside people pray to the Madonna of Fatima, of Lourdes, of Pompeii. Metamorphoses, transformations, miracles, mystic dances and rosaries'.[5] Shot in colour in 8mm and lasting 10 minutes, it was accompanied, as one would expect, with the scent of rose essences. However, this film had its roots in an earlier project. Angela Ricci Lucchi had undertaken a project of recording images of the *pilastrini* that were scattered through the countryside of Romagna in the area near her home town of Lugo. The *pilastrini* were (and are) small structures, often in brick, that house devotional figures – 'miniature theatres'. Some go back to medieval times, but many were put up in the nineteenth century and early twentieth century at cross-roads, on the edge of fields, and similar sites, marking places where popular religion and everyday activities meet. It is striking that the artists should have been drawn to a cultural form that was humble, on the margins, and under threat at a time when the peasantry was abandoning agriculture for the city. While conservation organisations worried about the survival of artistic monuments, lesser forms, such as the *pilastrini*, were overlooked. It is also interesting to note the initial association between religious images and scents. Flowers would have been placed at the *pilastrini* on appointed days, such as the festival of the Ascension. Incense was a regular accompaniment to the rites of the Roman Catholic and of the Armenian Churches with which Ricci Lucchi and Gianikian would have been respectively familiar from childhood.

The significance of the sense of smell in the films of Gianikian and Ricci Lucchi is linked above all to a preoccupation with memory. Gianikian was a habitual frequenter of fleamarkets and bric-à-brac shops, and collected objects such as old postcards and toys that were second-hand. For him, collecting and making work went hand in hand. Objects were collected as potential components for tableaux, not for their own sake. They were

---

5　'*Erat-Sora*' in *Yervant Gianikian, Angela Ricci Lucchi*, ed. Toffetti, 64.

objets trouvés destined to be re-cycled. Possession was important because it allowed for intimate knowledge: 'There is an encounter with the object: possessing it means studying it in depth and in detail, and having all the time to do so'.[6] The object, as the Surrealists maintained, was full of unsuspected potentialities: 'In isolating objects, magnifying them and recombining them in new ways, new things were revealed – and *reveiled* – as Breton demanded – in all their hieratic mystery'.[7] Gianikian's tableaux, however, anticipated aspects of his filmmaking; he notes: 'I filmed the objects and made long catalogues of them. I made "boxes" already structured like film "sequences"'.[8] In his films, moreover, he experimented with superimposition and other devices using the possibilities for editing in the camera that were available with 8mm. He recounts that he re-worked the footage of the *pilastrini* shot by Angela Ricci Lucchi, 'partly cancelling images with superimposition', thereby giving material form to the desacration described in the words taken from a poem by Corrado Costa.[9] If the smell of roses and evocation of the Madonna were elements of *Erat-Sora*, the intentions of the filmmakers were far from religious in the traditional sense.

The discovery and purchase of a trove of letters, toys, and other artefacts that once belonged to four sisters living in Mühlbach provided Gianikian and Ricci Lucchi with a major resource for their inquiry into the relationship between image, memory, and the sense of smell. Mühlbach, now in Italian Alto Adige, had formerly been part of the Austro-Hungarian Empire and the sisters had been children in the early part of the century. They had accumulated an extraordinary quantity of things, amounting to some 10,000 items. The filmmakers wrote of its importance for their work:

> For a number of years […] we have been engaged in cataloguing and making associations that arise from within the material and that can be put into various categories.

6   Paolo Mereghetti and Federico Rossin, 'Il magazzino della Storia. Incontro con Yervant Gianikian e Angela Ricci Lucchi', *Lo straniero* 110–11 (August–September 2009), 121.

7   Paul Hammond, 'Available Light' in *The Shadow and its Shadows*, ed. Hammond, 8.

8   *Yervant Gianikian, Angela Ricci Lucchi*, ed. Toffetti, 9.

9   The title *Erat-Sora* is an anagram of a poem by Ezra Pound; conversation with the author, 8 December 2009.

So far, we have concentrated on everything connected to the childhood of the four sisters of whom there remain portraits in wax along with a multitude of children's objects that constitute an accumulation, as opposed to a collection proper, with many multiple versions of the same item. Another category comprises objects commonly used in daily life, and yet another photographs not only of the family but of the village, travel, the countryside and so on. Analysis of the archiving, listing, and cataloguing that we have done up to this point shows us forms of representation that are fairly typical and taken-for-granted at the time.[10]

They go on, however, to describe the new element that supplied them with the 'key to the task of reconstructing the story (*racconto*)', that is the 'introduction of a web of sensory images in which the sense of smell plays an important part'.[11] They discovered letters by one of the sisters, Katerina, in which she assumes, on various occasions on entering the garden, the form of a flower or a plant in the belief that she was sometimes one scent and then another. The idea excited Gianikian and Ricci Lucchi who found parallels in the Treatise of the French Enlightenment thinker, Condillac, according to whom the sense of smell had to be understood independently and as the first of the senses.[12] They observe: 'Many of the objects belonging to childhood are often nothing but fictions of the real or of other images and situations that lead back to particular smells or scents'.[13] The Mühlbach 'collection' represented for them a kind of 'illustrated encyclopedia' and a source for deriving new images – images that 'pushed them to formulate other associations and allusions in a "montage of voices" in which the "voice" smell/scent offers its physicality in parallel to the images with their "other" presence'.[14]

10 Yervant Gianikian and Angela Ricci Lucchi, 'Profumi' in *Yervant Gianikian, Angela Ricci Lucchi*, ed. Toffetti, 55.

11 Ibid.

12 Ètienne Bonnot de Condillac, 'A Treatise on Sensation', in *Philosophical Writings of Ètienne Bonnot, Abbé de Condillac*, trans. Franklin Philip (Hillsdale, NJ: Lawrence Erlbaum, 1982); see also Lorne Falkenstein, 'Ètienne Bonnot de Condillac', plato.stanford.edu/entries/condillac/; accessed 14 September 2010.

13 Gianikian and Ricci Lucchi, 'Profumi', 55.

14 Ibid., 55–7.

The notion of 'catalogue' is indispensable for understanding the films of Gianikian and Ricci Lucchi. Alberto Farassino noted that one of their films actually has the title *Cataloghi* and that 'the whole body of work can be summed up in the figure of the classification, of orderly and serial accumulation'.[15] The everyday or administrative ordering and storing of things – creating, for instance, a category of childhood objects – is a necessary procedure but the significance of the Mühlbach find lies in the mysterious connections and associations that await exploration. The use of the word *trama*, which can be translated as 'plot' and as 'woof and weft', suggests the narrative in the fantasies of little Katerina (K) together with the material qualities of things that appeal to the sense of touch and smell. A brief description of one of the films goes as follows: '*Vladimir Propp – Smell of Wolf*, 8mm, colour, silent, 10', 1975. Raspberry scented. In an Alice-like dream three fairy tales are rolled into one. Snow White, Little Red Riding Hood, and Hansel and Gretel, the fairy and witch are the smell of wolf, which is the essence of wolf similar to raspberry'.[16] The link derives from reading a letter by K who was reminded of a fairy tale about a wolf told her one day by Doctor Gartner as he was extracting essence from raspberry with a still in his chemistry laboratory.[17] A complex of threads run from the Mühlbach children's writings, folklore and stories, to literary and art appropriations of these sources. The filmmakers are wilfully obtuse and playful in their descriptions. And the titles are intriguing: *Klinger e il guanto* (Klinger and the Glove, 1975) refers to a work seen by Gianikian in an exhibition of Surrealism in Turin, but the smells used are 'disguised smells' (*odori mascherati*).[18] The term catalogue, which recurs in titles, sometimes has bureaucratic connotations, bringing to mind filing cabinets and index-cards, as in *Di alcuni fiori non facilmente catalogabili* (Of Certain Flowers Not Easily Catalogued, 1976). Precision of language can ironically

15   Alberto Farassino, 'Cataloghi e profumi', ibid., 25.
16   Yervant Gianikian and Angela Ricci Lucchi, 'Profumi' in *Yervant Gianikian, Angela Ricci Lucchi*, ed. Toffetti, 65.
17   Yervant Gianikian and Angela Ricci Lucchi, 'Cinema profumato', in *Yervant Gianikian, Angela Ricci Lucchi*, ed. Toffetti, 59.
18   '*Klinger e il guanto*', ibid., 68; Max Klinger, a Symbolist artist whose work prefigured Surrealism, produced a series of etchings on the theme of the glove in the 1880s.

assume a scientific tone, while on other occasions the attempt to catalogue is overwhelmed by the lack of definition of what is being catalogued, as in *Cataloghi – Non è altro che odori che sente* (Catalogues – Nothing but the scents you smell, 1975). This leads to a situation in which language is shown to be powerless. Smell is pre-linguistic.

Gianikian and Ricci Lucchi seem to call into question the primacy of vision and to open up an area of investigation into the relationship of the visual and the olfactory that is unparalleled in cinema. As Laura Marks has written, this attention to senses other than the visual corresponds to shifts in thinking found in Horkheimer and Adorno, for whom the unmediated sensuous response through smell acted as a reservoir of non-alienated experience. It counteracted the tyranny of the optical and preference given to detachment and distance as opposed to nearness and engagement. With smell, the subject yields in an act of mimesis.[19] *Cinema profumato* reveals an interest in synaesthesia and the subversion of a hierarchy of the senses that goes back to the Symbolists and early twentieth-century avant-gardes. The poet Paul Valéry had written: 'We may inhale the smell of a flower whose fragrance is agreeable to us for as long as we like; it is impossible for us to rid ourselves of the fragrancy by which our senses have been aroused [...] He who has set himself the task of creating a work of art aims at the same effect'.[20] The work of Gianikian and Ricci Lucchi was presented in the form of performances that excluded the use of spoken or written words. The writing was done by other means: 'our films want to write through objects; they want to discover relationships between the things represented that go far beyond the usual associations, beyond empirical reality. The series of films with *Catalogue* in the title, for example, are a mini symphony of objects. And then the scents want to widen the range of experiences, to create a "total moment"'.[21] For them, the sense of smell is to do with psychological and emotional reactions that are connected with the hitherto unexplored aspect of this sense, not the chemical-molecular

19   Laura Marks, *The Skin of the Film: Intercultural Cinema, Embodiment, and the Senses* (Durham and London: Duke University Press, 2000), 140.
20   Paul Valéry, quoted in Walter Benjamin, 'Some Motifs in Baudelaire' in Walter Benjamin, *Illuminations* (London: Fontana Books, 1973), 189.
21   Gianikian and Ricci Lucchi, 'Profumi', 57.

and neuralgic level that has been fully studied. Their screening/perform-
ances were designed to elicit reactions that escaped the expectations or
preconceptions of participants.

Alberto Farassino, a critic and film historian who closely followed the
work of the filmmakers, gives a description of a performance of *cinema
profumato*:

> It is a cinema of scents, a 'perfumed cinema' [...] But the fragrances that accompany
> the screening of their films don't come from nowhere. The notion of total cinema had
> repeatedly proposed the addition of this hidden olfactory track to sound and visual
> film. Such an addition would reinforce the illusion of realism. These scents, however,
> come from precise and visible sources. They are enclosed in glass bottles. They drip
> through tubes and pipes into metal cups heated by the flame of a spirit-stove. Here
> we are in the presence of a ritual priest who, during the screening, manoeuvres the
> machinery, the scents. The perfumery, a place where opium, incense, benzoic, and
> carnation are burned in order to develop mnemonic associations, to increase the
> involvement of the senses and the emotions. But scents also have the effect of trans-
> forming and illuminating the space of the darkened room with flames and movements,
> thereby involving the spectator more in techniques generating scents and language
> than in the illusion of what is on the screen. '*Pro-fumeria*' or, in English, perfumery
> might be read as '*fumeria*' or a smoking house.[22]

This description of the spatial aspect of the experience brings to mind
Vivian Sobchack's comment: 'Smell occupies space rather than a point
in our experience and its diffusion and concentrations are extraordinarily
subtle'.[23] Altogether Gianikian and Ricci Lucchi made some nineteen short
films of *cinema profumato* over a five-year period. As such, it represents a
sustained experiment, not a passing fad. In doing so, they took the writings
of little K on her garden flowers and plants as a guide, examining them
as seriously as any treatise by Condillac. They also became highly knowl-
edgeable collectors and distillers of the smells and scents they then used
for their performances, compiling a growing catalogue of at least eighty
different essences.[24]

22   Farassino, 'Cataloghi e profumi', 25–7.
23   Vivian Sobchack, *The Address of the Eye: A Phenomenology of Film Experience*
      (Princeton: Princeton University Press, 1992), 185.
24   Raphael Gianikian, father of the filmmaker, worked as an industrial chemist. His
      work in the laboratory may have influenced his son.

Gianikian and Ricci Lucchi made a film with olfactory accompaniment in 1976 that they retrospectively see as a turning point in their work. *Cesare Lombroso. Sull'odore del garofano* (Cesare Lombroso. On the Scent of Carnation, 1976) grew out of *cinema profumato* but led towards more historically-minded filmmaking and a preoccupation with forms of power and violence in society exercised in the name of science. I will therefore look at this film in greater detail.

The way in which the filmmakers initiated the Lombroso project gives an insight into their working methods. In the words of Ricci Lucchi: 'you just follow a path and then come across something. Sometimes you engage in provocation so as to make a discovery'.[25] In this instance, they stumbled on a text by a certain Strassman, a follower of the Italian criminologist, Cesare Lombroso. In it, Strassman describes tests carried out on criminals with respect to variations in the sense of smell in different sections of the prison population. The text, of which an extract was subsequently used as a caption at the beginning of the film it inspired, describes the procedure whereby criminals were exposed to gradually increased concentrations of the essence of carnation. Their reactions were recorded and measured, and the findings translated into statistics. These demonstrated a notable impairment of the sense of smell among female criminals, who were said to be three times more likely to show this condition than their male counterparts.[26] The filmmakers, who were struck by the uncanny parallels with their own work, started research for what was to be a new film. In Turin, in the Cesare Lombroso Museum, they discovered similarities between the types of artefact they had retrieved at Mühlbach and those collected by the celebrated criminologist – between, for example, the toys featured in their *cinema profumato* and the objects made by criminals and the insane. Likewise, the methods of cataloguing and displaying items were analogous. Above all, Gianikian recalls, they could identify with the collector in Lombroso:

25　'Cataloghi della memoria: Conversazione con Yervant Gianikian e Angela Ricci Lucchi (Sergio Toffetti e Daniela Giuffrida)', 13.

26　For the ideas of Cesare Lombroso and his followers on female criminality, see Mary Gibson, *Prostitution and the State in Italy, 1860–1915* (New Brunswick and London: Rutgers University Press, 1986).

What linked us to Lombroso was collecting. Because in reality he was a collector of criminal objects who had exhibits sent from all over the world. The mechanism was similar to that of the postcard collector, except that Lombroso, instead of swapping postcards from Egypt, had people send him photographs of Japanese prostitutes, of the bodies of murder victims in the Far East, and so on. Then there were plants, criminal plants [...] The whole world catalogued in accordance with an obsessive criminological vision. To the point that to us the real deviancy seemed to be this excess of collecting.[27]

One work, shot in 16mm, with the title *Catalogo n. 2* (Catalogue No. 2, 1976) was based on a comparison between the two sets of materials – those of the filmmakers and those of Lombroso. But the important film that emerged from this work was based entirely on the footage that recorded the contents of the museum. Over 12 minutes, each shot lasts about five seconds. Objects placed against a white background are mainly filmed from directly above or at a slight angle. The images are not steady, suggesting the shake of a hand-held camera. The image goes in and out of focus, sometimes making it hard to read labels. As in the previous films, Gianikian and Ricci Lucchi present catalogues of objects and images on screen. The matter-of-factness of the presentation – the format reminiscent of an illustrated lecture (without speech) – is belied by the content of what is presented and by the cumulative effect of the display. In order of appearance, the following objects are shown:

1 Embalmed heads, each with a handwritten label giving the name of the crime committed by the criminal and a number: 141 *corruttore* (corrupter); 121 *falsario* (counterfeiter); 79 *uxoricida* (wife-murderer). These are filmed one by one, and then in groups on shelves, frontally and in profile.
2 A sequence of photographs from an album showing women criminals, mainly prostitutes, and portrait photographs organised in grids.

---

27 'Cataloghi della memoria: Conversazione con Yervant Gianikian e Angela Ricci Lucchi (Sergio Toffetti e Daniela Giuffrida)' 13.

3 A sequence of objects, some single, others juxtaposed to form *tableaux*. These include *lavori dei pazzi* (works by the insane): a bottle containing a miniature figurine, toys and dolls, playing cards; items associated with crimes and criminals: hand-made knives, tiny saws, spent cartridges, a piece of cloth with bullet hole. And items displayed in combination – for example, a mask, weapon and photograph placed together and linked to a particular crime.

4 A sequence with the title *Anatomia comparata* (Comparative Anatomy), which includes dried vulva and foetuses. The final image of the film shows the head of Lombroso himself preserved in a jar for posterity.

Cesare Lombroso. Sull'odore del garofano can be interpreted in many ways. It can even be seen as a documentary that records the contents of a museum just prior to its closure and dismantling. By 1976 the museum was a monument to a science that had fallen into disrepute and was in the process of being consigned to oblivion.[28] In fact, Lombroso represented an aspect of Italy's history that many wished to forget. It is not by chance, therefore, that Gianikian and Ricci Lucchi, whose film research was to dig deeply into the hidden and the repressed of twentieth-century history, made him an object of inquiry. There are two respects in particular in which Lombroso can be seen as a significant figure for the development of their filmmaking. First, Lombroso's theories elaborated ideas of Social Darwinism in which notions of race, social class, and criminality were brought together.[29] He gave scientific legitimacy to concepts that linked the European criminal to the non-European 'savage'. For him, a chain of regression could mean that 'if the criminal sometimes reverted to the savage, the savage also reverted

28 The Lombroso collection, or what survived of it, is housed in the Museum of Anatomy re-opened in Turin in 2007; see www.museounito.it/anatomia/; accessed 11 November 2010.

29 On Social Darwinism and theories of race, see Eric D. Weitz, *A Century of Genocide: Utopias of Race and Nation* (Princeton: Princeton University Press, 2003), 36–7.

to the animal'.[30] Whatever his own politics, Lombroso's criminology fed into ideologies of colonialism and proto-fascism – phenomena explored later in a series of films by Gianikian and Ricci Lucchi. Second, Lombroso made the body of the criminal (and the artefacts associated with it) rather than the crime the basis for knowledge and scientific inquiry; in David Horn's words, 'the body was made into an index of the interior states and dispositions of suspected individuals, a sign of evolutionary status of groups, and a more or less reliable indicator of present and future risks to society'.[31] Bodies were accordingly 'measured, manipulated, shocked, sketched, photographed and displayed' in order to treat individual and social deviance.[32] At this time – the late nineteenth century – the body was at the centre of a whole series of scientific investigations in which photography was an important tool, the most celebrated being Etienne-Jules Marey's physiological studies of movement.

   Cesare Lombroso. Sull'odore del garofano can be read very differently, however, if seen as part of experimental cinema and contemporary art practice. It was this context that was uppermost in the minds of Gianikian and Ricci Lucchi in the second half of the 1970s when they made the film. They were excited by the parallels between their collages and the organisation and display of materials in the Lombroso museum. Although the film has been regularly screened in recent years without the olfactory accompaniment, it was conceived as part of the *cinema profumato* project. At the Third International Avantgarde Festival in London in 1979 attention was focused on this aspect. One commentator observed: '[they] use smell as a kind of transducer which, while expanding the descriptive and associative power of the viewer's film experience, also adds another texture to the film's ability to produce its own creative reality'.[33] Gianikian and Ricci Lucchi saw themselves as 'performance artists'. In the 'Artist

30   David G. Horn, *Social Bodies: Science, Reproduction and Italian Modernity* (Princeton: Princeton University Press, 1994), 44.
31   Ibid., 1.
32   Ibid.
33   Janis Crystal Lipzin, 'Engaging the Olfactory: The Films of Yervant Gianikian and Angela Ricci Lucchi' in *Yervant Gianikian, Angela Ricci Lucchi*, ed. Toffetti, 30.

File' in the Library of the Museum of Modern Art in New York, there is a letter in faltering English dated 16 December 1978 in which they write to the museum curators: 'Our work in performance include all the time the sense of smell. We send some material about our "recherché"'. A list of the venues where they carried out their performances gives a clear indication of the scene of which they were participants: Filmstudio (Rome), Cineclub Brera (Milan), Settimana Internazionale della Performance at the Museum of Modern Art (Bologna), Museum of Modern Art – Palazzo Diamanti (Ferrara), Biennale (Venice), Cinématheque Francaise (Paris), and the Centre Georges Pompidou (Paris). The venues are mostly film clubs and institutions specialising in contemporary art. The films were not shown in mainstream or even art house cinemas.[34]

Films of this kind were known in the 1970s under a variety of labels: 'avant-garde' (usually in the French, though with a range of spellings); 'underground', 'experimental'.[35] The first term refers to a longer history within the visual arts going back to Futurism, Cubism and, later, Surrealism, and the return to these experiences by artists after the Second World War. 'Underground film' has a more distinctly North American origin and is connected to the counter cultures and radical politics of the 1960s. All the designations point to the roots of 'independent film' (a more neutral term) outside the cinema industry. This film was at home in a fine art or art school rather than a commercial environment. Although artists making

34   In 1980, 'various perfumed films' and their makers, Yervant Gianikian and Angela Ricci Lucchi, were part of the 'South West Film Tour' organised by Rod Stoneman. The programme notes were scented and could be smelt as well as read. Other films toured included Peter Greenaway's *A Walk through H* and *Vertical Features Remake*, Film and History Project's *Song of a Shirt*, Sally Potter's *Thriller*, and Yvonne Rainer's *Journeys from Berlin/1971*. A bold statement summarised the ambition 'of breaking down the relationship of producer-consumer, opening up the possibility of a common investigation between film-maker and film-watcher'; *South West Film Directory*, ed. Rod Stoneman (Torquay: South West Arts, 1980).

35   For an account written at the time, see David Curtis, *Experimental Cinema: A Fifty-Year Evolution* (New York: Delta Book, 1971); for a retrospective survey, see Scott Macdonald, *A Critical Cinema: Book 1: Interviews with Independent Film-makers* (1988; Berkeley, Los Angeles and London: University of California Press, 1992).

films had established filmmaking as their primary practice in the 1940s and 1950s, they still tended to be trained in other media before turning to film. The route taken by Gianikian and Ricci Lucchi was fairly typical in this respect, and while considering themselves 'artists', their practice was entirely dedicated to filmmaking even at the time of *cinema profumato*. Each of the designations – avant-garde, underground, and independent – has pertinence for their work, which increasingly brought together artistic and political concerns.[36]

Typically such filmmakers are authors of their films – the term 'film-maker' being used in preference to 'film director' – in a sense more akin to that of the novel writer than of someone working in Hollywood or Cinecittà. They use the portable, lightweight and relatively inexpensive equipment designed for the amateur market, notably the 8mm and then Super 8, and 16mm.[37] The films themselves often appropriate genres from painting: still life, landscape, and portrait. In response to the dominance of narrative and realism in 'classic cinema', they tend to avoid storytelling and plot, the use of professional actors, studios, and high production values. The films are distributed and screened through an alternative circuit constituted by film clubs, co-ops, educational institutions, and, latterly, museums.[38] This filmmaking has affinities with that of amateur practitioners, on the one hand, and with that of 'early cinema', on the other. Writing in 1967 Sheldon Renan noted that the remarkable continuity over time between the first filmmakers and their end-of-century followers: 'Avant-garde/experimental/underground films have been produced primarily in the way all films have been produced (in the way that even the films of Lumière and Méliès were produced). They are (1) conceived, (2) directed and photographed, (3) edited into more or less permanent form, and (4)

36 For a celebrated discussion of the historic divide, see Peter Wollen, 'The Two Avant-Gardes' in *Readings and Writings: Semiotic Counter-Strategies* (London and New York: Verso, 1982), 92–104.

37 Lenny Lipton, *Independent Filmmaking* (London: Studio Vista, 1974).

38 A.L. Rees, *A History of Experimental Film and Video* (London: British Film Institute, 1999).

projected for an audience from one projector onto one screen'.[39] It is easy to see the similarities between scenes of picnics, watering the garden, and train arrivals in Lumière films, and equivalent scenes shot by amateur or experimental filmmakers decades later. However, the language of film – the conventions governing the type and use of technology, the shooting and the editing – that had taken hold over the century and that had come to be taken for granted by audiences became an arena for rule-breaking and invention. In the 1960s there was a return to an earlier history that is motivated by the search for new ways of seeing and filming. When Gianikian and Ricci Lucchi began to make their 8mm films, they were participants in a history that was already well developed.

Found Footage Films: *Karagoez – Catalogo 9.5* (Karagoez – Catalogue 9.5mm, 1979–81)

In 1979 the discovery of a collection of old films at the premises of a trader in dried flowers in Milan – the filmmakers went there regularly in search of sources for scents –opened up a new area of exploration for Gianikian and Ricci Lucchi. It was a real find that left Gianikian *folgorato* (lightning-struck). The assortment of films was in 9.5mm, known as Pathé Baby, a format launched for the amateur market in 1922, a precursor of the much better known 8mm introduced by Eastman-Kodak in 1932. Gianikian was enchanted by the technology, with the cameras that fitted into the pocket, the projectors in their compact cases, and the films that could easily be mailed, the equivalent of postcards. The scale suggested toys for adults, an idea appealing to filmmakers fascinated by the miniature. Equally appealing was the relationship of the technology to the process of preserving and transmitting memories. The find itself consisted of fictional, burlesque, and

---

39   Sheldon Renan, *The Underground Film: An Introduction to its Development in America* (London: Studio Vista, 1967), 227.

scientific films as well as documentaries and 'filmed postcards' dating from 1922 to 1928, and belonging therefore to the era of 'silent cinema'.[40] Once again, Gianikian and Ricci Lucchi had happened upon a trove of materials for future projects. But instead of being collectors of three-dimensional objects, they now became collectors of 'found footage', of old films. Sometimes there remained whole reels, and, at other times, only a few frames. This find marked the transformation of Gianikian and Ricci Lucchi into makers of found footage films. It also signalled the ending of the *cinema profumato* experiment.

To what extent Gianikian and Ricci Lucchi were aware of the found footage filmmaking going on at the time is not entirely clear. They tend to speak of the change in their practice as brought about by their chance discovery, and do not elaborate on the influences, direct and indirect, on their practice. Recycling old film footage was not new. In Italy, Gianfranco Baruchello and Alberto Grifi, who were leading figures in experimental cinema based in Rome, made a film that aroused widespread interest. Their *La verifica incerta* (Uncertain Verification, 1965) was perhaps the best-known example of found footage films in Italy. David Curtis describes it using clips from a dozen or more cinemascope movies to 'combine random selection and a conscious attempt to manipulate the language of film'.[41] In the United States, experimentation with found footage by artists went back to *Rose Hobart* (1936). Joseph Cornell made this film by cutting up *East of Borneo* – removing all the action scenes and scenes not containing the actress Hobart in the frame – and manipulated the material to create a 19-minute work in which the characters appear to 'move with a peculiar, lugubrious lassitude, as if mired deep in a dream'.[42] Cornell's Surrealist film became a major point of reference for a younger generation of filmmakers who explored found footage filmmaking in the 1950s and 1960s, artist film-makers such as Bruce Conner, Robert Nelson and Ken Jacobs. As regular participants in festivals and film club events, Gianikian and Ricci Lucchi would have known about, if not seen, many of these films coming from

40   Yervant Gianikian and Angela Ricci Lucchi, '*Das Lied von der Erde*' in *Yervant Gianikian, Angela Ricci Lucchi*, ed. Toffetti, 92–3.
41   Curtis, *Experimental Cinema*, 169.
42   Yeo, 'Cutting through History', 16.

America. In the late 1970s, they knew the work of Mekas and Brakhage.[43] In 1980 and 1981 their tour with *cinema profumato* across America, with stays in California and New York, brought them into direct contact with this film scene.[44]

The found footage that attracted Gianikian and Ricci Lucchi was from the era of silent cinema. In this respect, they shared an interest in early, so called 'primitive' cinema that was current among American filmmakers such as Ken Jacobs. Jacobs, a New York-based filmmaker, was author of *Tom Tom the Piper's Son* (1968–9), a re-working of a ten-minute film of circa 1905 made by Billy Bitzer, later cameraman to D.W. Griffiths. 'Rephotographing each frame separately', writes Jeffrey Skoller, 'Jacobs extends the film over ten times its original length [...] By enlarging aspects of the frame, allowing the film to lose its registration in the gate of the projector, and slowing down its movement, Jacobs turns the re-photographed film into an exercise in the dissolution of narrative emplotment to reveal other possibilities of cine-narrative based on the abstract and purely temporal elements of the cinematic experience'.[45] Filmmakers, moreover, were among the most erudite and inquisitive collectors of pre- and early cinema technologies, as evidenced by the collection of Werner Nekes.[46] Historical inquiry, collecting, archives, and filmmaking were feeding into one another in unexpected ways.

43   In an interview they say to a French critic: 'Bien sur nous connaissons le travail de Mekas, de Brakhage'; Vincent Vatrican, 'In Memory', *Bref* 42 (Autumn 1999), 14.

44   However, *cinema profumato* was not always understood by those outside the independent film scene. At Denver airport, a policeman, who had found a container with alcohol – one of the essences used in the performance work – looked at Yervant Gianikian and said: 'Bad man, bad man'; *Piccino* (8 March 1998).

45   Skoller, *Shadows, Specters, Shards*, 8.

46   'The deceptive art appears to be a school of avant-garde experimentation that has spanned the centuries', writes Laurent Mannoni, 'and that persists in our own time with the same vitality [...] The fact that Werner Nekes should also be a maker of experimental films, confirms the existence and importance of this long genealogy. In this light, the Hamburg scholar Aby Warburg, himself a notable collector, was well and truly right when he wrote: "If art has a history, the images themselves have an afterlife"'; 'The Art of Deception' in *Eyes, Lies and Illusions*, ed. Laurent Mannoni, Werner Nekes, and Marina Warner (London: Hayward Gallery, 2004), 52.

Cinema historians, museum curators and film institutes were busy reviving interest in silent cinema after years of neglect. In Italy, the pioneering Pordenone festival dedicated to silent films was established in 1981–2, as was the specialist journal, *Griffithiana*. Surveying the changes that gave greater visibility to silent films, Thomas Elsaesser noted a new situation in which there was collaboration between scholars and archivists, a growing appetite for authentic archive footage in TV programmes, and alarm that the lifespan of nitrate film was coming to an end.[47] Looking back, Nicole Brenez and Pauline De Raymond write: 'silent cinema appears as a continent whose enormous diversity has been hidden and swallowed up by sound cinema. For about twenty years a movement has gained ground that has exorcised this forgetting to the point that audiences may now have greater opportunities for knowing what composes silent cinema than contemporaries'.[48] Gianikian and Ricci Lucchi have been simultaneously beneficiaries of and contributors to this development. They experienced the early 1980s as 'a tough period' because 'people did not understand how in a single film there could be many films. The only game was to recognise citations'.[49] By doing something very different from the mainstream activity of restoring classic or forgotten films, they were out on a limb. However, the reception given their work by critics and audiences at Pordenone and other festivals provided moments of shared enthusiasm in an often lonely and difficult enterprise.

Significantly, it was *Griffithiana* that published Gianikian's account of the making of *Karagoez – Catalogo 9.5* (Karagoez – Catalogue 9.5mm, 1979–81). An initial film of sixteen minutes entitled *Karagoez et les brûleurs d'herbes parfumés* (Shadow Theatre and the Burners of Scented Grasses, 1979) was shot in 8mm and accompanied by the scents of damask rose and

47   Thomas Elsaesser, 'General Introduction: Early Cinema: From Linear History to Mass Media Archeology' in *Early Cinema: Space, Frame, Narrative* (London: British Film Institute, 1990), 2.

48   Brenez and De Raymond, 'Ritorni di immagini. Il cinema delle origini e la pratica del reimpiego', 108–9.

49   'Cataloghi della memoria: Conversazione con Yervant Gianikian e Angela Ricci Lucchi (Sergio Toffetti e Daniela Giuffrida)', 17.

bitter almonds. The title 'Karagoez' refers to a tradition of 'shadow theatre' in the Ottoman Empire in which a candle threw shadows from behind a screen of puppet figures manipulated by a puppeteer – a distant precursor of the modern moving image.[50] The exotic in the film was evoked through the olfactory 'track' as well as in the images, foregrounding the idea of travel through space in and through the senses. It brings to mind Laura Marks's notion of 'sense envy', meaning 'the desire of one culture for the sensory knowledge of another; sense knowledge undergoes translation in the movement from one culture to another. For example, the use of incense and perfumes [...] have followed a path over the centuries of importation from East to West.'[51] Subsequently, the exotic is explored in images, and the filmmakers abandon their use of scents. However, in interviews they have continued to insist on the continuity between their work in the 1970s and their later work on found footage. This was their first major film made with found footage. The fifty-six-minute film in 16mm keeps 'catalogue' in the title but it is with reference to the film format and the cataloguing of found footage. The exotic is evoked by images alone.

    Karagoez – Catalogo 9.5 took some three years to complete and was shown for the first time in 1981 at the Millenium in New York, while a shorter version with scent accompaniment was shown the previous year at the Anthology Film Archives, also in New York. The filmmakers had met Jonas Mekas in London in 1979 and he had encouraged them in their new project. *Karagoez* was made by intercutting between several fictional films from their collection of 9.5mm footage: *Carmen* (Feyder); *Der Heilige Berg* (Arnold Fanck, 1926); *L'argent* (Marcel L'Herbier, 1926); *Casanova* (Alexandre Volkoff, 1927); *Messalina* (Enrico Guazzoni, 1923); *La proie du vent* (René Clair, 1926); *Il canto dell'amore trionfante* (Albatross, 1925); and *L'assassinat du Duc de Guise* (Pathé, 1908). They also used short documentaries, rarely dated and without details about the filmmakers responsible

50 'Until the rise of radio and film, it [Karagöz-Hacivat shadow theatre] was one of the most popular forms of entertainment in Turkey. It survives today mainly in a toned-down form intended for audiences of children'; 'Karagöz and Hacivat', en.wikipedia. org/wiki/Karagöz_and_Hacivat; accessed 11 November 2010.

51 Marks, *The Skin of the Film*, 239–40.

for them. These show scenes from Japan, including scenes from the 1922 Kyoto earthquake, and from Timbuktu, underwater photography, and science documentaries. Lastly, they drew on narratives of fairy tales and magic. Gianikian, writing in *Griffithiana* in 1981, explains that he examined 'hundreds of films, thousands and thousands of metres of fictional material considered of marginal importance'.[52] He emphasises that he does not select films because they are masterpieces. On the contrary, he is drawn to the second-rate and the unknown. In this orientation he was following in the footsteps of the Surrealists – 'Epicureans of detritus, they uncovered treasures of poetry and subversion in the bargain basement of cinema', as Paul Hammond put it.[53]

In describing his method of working, Gianikian identifies what he sees as a transformation in his way of looking at images. Initially, he tried to insert parts of the 9.5mm footage into his own films by transferring them to the same format, but it was not technically feasible in the laboratory because the relevant technology had long disappeared. It was no longer possible, as it was with the moviola, to see the images 'in movement'. Instead, he constructed his own hand-operated optical printer, which allowed him to re-photograph the material. However, the technical solution stems from a changed awareness that came from working on the footage *manualmente*, 'by hand', by handling it. He writes: 'by dwelling longer on the images "by hand", I memorised details that I would have overlooked during screening. I analysed the film frames as long sequences of continuous photographs pasted in an album, and read captions as if they were written in an illustrated book'. After some initial resistance, Gianikian allows himself to be caught up in the 'flow of this new vision and to work only from within it'.[54]

By using the optical printer, Gianikian is able to 'decompose' the single frame and to multiply the single frame many times. These technical procedures, however, are subordinated to procedures reminiscent of the Surreal-

52   Yervant Gianikian, '*Karagoez – Catalogo 9.5*' in *Yervant Gianikian, Angela Ricci Lucchi*, ed. Toffetti, 83.
53   Hammond, 'Available Light', 29.
54   Gianikian, '*Karagoez – Catalogo 9.5*', 85–6.

ists. In his account, Gianikian cuts between the technical and the oneiric. The camera or 'memory-machine' casts 'long yearning looks at those "partial objects" that exist, for her, within the frame'. The images seem to acquire a life of their own as they 'prolong, extend and are transferred' and come together through 'contact, contiguity, approximation, juxtaposition, conjunction, prolongation, tension, extension, linear and longitudinal fracture'. The filmmaker imagines himself as a miniaturist, an Egyptian copyist or archaeologist. The objectivity of 'History' or events is rejected in favour of 'what interests me most – the face of things, the physiognomy of objects and surroundings and what we normally overlook'.[55]

In *Karagoez*, the viewers are not guided by any narrative or exposition that connects scenes and suggests progression. As in the wanderings in Nantes of André Breton and Jacques Vaché[56] between different cinemas which they deliberately entered mid-film and left the moment they felt slotted into a plot, the spectator is shuttled between genres and countries, periods of history, black and white and tinted images – one minute in the mountains of Austria and the next amidst masked figures at the Carnival in Venice. The editing evokes the illusion of a continuity of space that would 'impossible in nature as well as in the original films'.[57] It was, in the words of Paul Valéry, 'un rêve artificiel, l'ordre des faits peut être renversé'.[58] In describing the making of *Karagoez* at the editing table, Gianikian borrows the language of Dziga Vertov's manifesto 'The Cine-Eyes – A Revolution'. The Russian avant-garde filmmaker writes: 'I draw near, then away from objects. I crawl under. I crawl on top. I move apace a galloping horse. I plunge full speed into a crowd'.[59] Gianikian writes:

55   Ibid.
56   'As there had been nothing deliberated about our actions, qualitative judgments were forbidden', writes Breton; 'As in a Wood', 81.
57   Gianikian, '*Karagoez – Catalogo 9.5*', 87.
58   'It is a made-up dream. The sequence of events can be reversed'; cited in 'Voyages en Russie: Autour des avant-gardes', *Trafic* 33 (Spring 2005), 48.
59   Graham Roberts, *The Man with the Movie Camera* (London: I.B. Tauris, 2000), 20.

I have frozen the movements of a dance [...] The bodies of the ballerinas look like self-propelled statues [...] In an excess of voyeurism I prolong the five frames of a woman uncovering her breast in an alcove that could not be perceived otherwise. I leave those bodies, faces, scenery and the Venetian fires to shoot a didactic film [...] I photograph the slow movements of an underwater swimmer [...] I observe the evolution of different types of jelly-fish that resemble underwater fireworks [...] I return to Casanova and inside the rectangle of 9.5mm film I isolate a detail of two millimetres – the heart painted on the cheek of the ballerina [...] Three years earlier I moved from Paris to the Berlin of 1924. Through the viewfinder my movie camera can see the movements of Karl Freund's camera [...] I too enter the Wintergarten music hall in Berlin through the crack of the 9.5mm frame.[60]

In Vertov's celebrated film, *Man with a Movie Camera* (1928), it is the contemporary movie camera, the cameraman and, to a lesser degree, the editor that are seen to make the film. In Gianikian's account, the narrator selectively re-photographs and edits by using the 'analytical machine' or optical printer. However, the association with Vertov is not fortuitous. The Kino newsreels were shot in 9.5mm during the 1920s and Vertov's editing of the footage shot by, among others, his brother, Mikhail Kaufman, demonstrates the formal possibilities of the documentary. Vertov, moreover, gave primacy to editing; the footage, as with found footage, has not been shot with future editing in mind – in Sam Rohdie's words, 'the shape of the film comes from the editing, but the editing does not predetermine what is shot'.[61]

There are many influences at work in *Karagoez*. Homage is paid to Luis Bunuel, Salvador Dalí, Fernand Léger, and René Clair. A sequence in which there is a cut from the close up of the screaming face of a woman to hands being washed in a bowl of discoloured water (is it blood?) alludes

---

60   Gianikian, '*Karagoez – Catalogo 9.5*', 86–90.
61   Sam Rohdie, *Montage* (Manchester: Manchester University Press, 2006), 82; 'We have close ties with the Russian avant-garde: Esther Schub, Dziga Vertov, Mikhail Kaufman, and Lev Kuleshov, for example, have all been important for us'; Mereghetti and Rossin, 'Il magazzino della Storia', 121.

to Lev Kuleshov's famous experiments with montage.[62] But Gianikian also acknowledges the genius of unknown or little known filmmakers – for instance, the master of the Pathé short, *Attitudes du gladiateur*, in whose film the protagonist fights himself until through superimposition the two bodies become one. Then there is Segundo de Chamon whose *Boîte à cigars* demonstrates the metamorphosis of cigars, which, when lit, turn into dancing girls.[63] Surrealism's influence is especially significant, bearing out A.L. Rees's observation that 'it remains a living cultural force in the sense not true of the other art movements of its time'.[64] Its influence, he argues is especially visible in the use of 'paratactic montage', which 'breaks the flow or continuity between shots and scenes, against the grain of narrative editing'.[65]

The fascination in bodies is that of the voyeur in whose hands the camera enlarges the detail of the breast, the hands, the feet. Eyes and mouths fill the screen – open in horror, repulsion, desire, or longing – depending on the editing. Sequences show dressing, undressing, washing. Figures (almost always of women) appear in and through veils, curtains, doors, and mirrors. There are blond goddesses, Cleopatras, and Japanese *geisha*. Bodies are subjected to ritual violence – a woman tied up and suspended her back criss-crossed with what must be the marks of a whiplash; a *fakir* lying on the bed of nails. The segments of film are two to three seconds long, and sometimes 10 to 15 seconds. Even when slowed down by step printing, they frustrate the gaze.

Karagoez is, among other things, a celebration of cinephilia.[66] The filmmakers are in love with their materials and display the images with a glorious abandon to their sensuous appeal. The rhythm of the editing and

---

62   'Kuleshov's montage experiments demonstrated the fictive nature not of the image but, in any succession of them, the joins. A bowl of soup and the face of man linked together create a scene of hunger. The same face (expressionless) and the image of a revolver became the face of fear'; Rohdie, *Montage*, 27.

63   Gianikian and Ricci Lucchi, 'Voyages en Russie. Autour des avant-gardes', 47.

64   Rees, *A History of Experimental Film and Video*, 44.

65   Ibid., 49.

66   Christian Keathley, *Cinephilia and History, or The Wind in the Trees* (Bloomington: Indiana University Press, 2005).

the luxuriant tinting in crimsons, reds and blues makes watching enthralling and spell binding. It is odd, therefore, that Gianikian and Ricci Lucchi should abandon the use of fictional materials after making *Karagoez*. It is doubly strange because of their evident scepticism about documentary's claims to truthfulness to reality. Writing on what is perceived through the viewfinder in the documentaries of the Middle and Far East in their collection, Gianikian observes: 'The street could be in Damascus, in Tangier or another Middle Eastern city as portrayed in colonial postcards. The cameraman sees through the same eyes as the photographer. Both have *One Thousand and One Nights* in mind'. Nonetheless, they stopped collecting fictional found footage, and their films from the early 1980s are almost entirely made using documentary material. A signal of the next phase in Gianikian and Ricci Lucchi's filmmaking can already be detected, however, in the closing lines of his contribution to *Griffithiana*. It reads: 'There is still much I could describe of my work, both completed and incomplete [...] I would go on lengthening the time of each image in any discussion of German documentaries dedicated to mountains or of how the Nazis saw Nature ...'. The sentence is left hanging. The reference here is to the film *Der Heilige Berg* sequences of which appear in *Karagoez*. The film with its proto-Nazi iconography of mountain heroism becomes an important point of reference for a new project on the composer Gustav Mahler. From this point, memory, for Gianikian and Ricci Lucchi, is inseparable from history.

CHAPTER 2

Found Footage and History: From Mahler's *The Song of the Earth* to *From the Pole to the Equator*

> Objectively Mahler's music knows and expresses the knowledge that unity is attained not in spite of disjunction, but only through it.
>
> — THEODOR ADORNO[1]

> The 19th century, in Western Europe and North America, saw the beginning of the process [...] by which every tradition which previously mediated between man and nature was broken. Before this rupture, animals constituted the first circle of what surrounds man.
>
> — JOHN BERGER[2]

> Precise reiteration, by intercutting reprints, of those spontaneous movements, expressions and exchanges, can change the quality of the scene from one of informality to that of stylisation akin to dance; it confers dance on non-dancers by shifting the emphasis from the purpose of the movement to the movement itself, and an informal social encounter then assumes the solemnity and dimensions of ritual.
>
> — MAYA DEREN[3]

1   Theodor Adorno, *Mahler: A Musical Physiognomy* (Chicago and London: University of Chicago Press, 1991), 32–3.

2   John Berger, 'Why Look at Animals?' in Berger, *About Looking* (London: Writers and Readers, 1980), 1.

3   Maya Deren, 'Cinematography: The Creative Use of Reality', in *Film Theory and Criticism*, ed. Leo Braudy and Marshall Cohen (Oxford: Oxford University Press, 1999), 222.

In the early 1980s, Yervant Gianikian and Angela Ricci Lucchi continued
to make films using their collection of 9.5mm found footage. In the previous decade most of their work was in 8mm and often of not more than ten
minutes duration. After *Karagoez*, they made 16mm films, but continued to
make shorts – a practice they have maintained, alternating larger projects
with more circumscribed ones. In part, this is due to funding constraints
and the economics of independent filmmaking. In part, it is a choice made
by Gianikian and Ricci Lucchi. It has always been possible for them to make
shorts using their own collection of found footage, and they have followed
rhythms that are not dictated by the market. Moreover, the filmmakers have
assembled the shorts into loose groups for programmes, using titles such
as *cataloghi* (catalogues), *archivi* (archives), or *frammenti* (fragments) –
terms that indicate the diversity of the films as well as common elements.
Frames and sequences have migrated across the *oeuvre*, often re-appearing
in negative rather than positive, or in a re-edited version. The recurrence
and re-cycling carries on within the body of work, a process initiated when
the original found footage is used to make a new film. After a short inter-
lude, however, the filmmakers embarked on their largest project to date,
the making of *Dal Polo all'Equatore*. This film stemmed from their growing interest in historical footage and the period leading up the First World
War, as evidenced in *Das Lied von der Erde. Gustav Mahler*.

   Essence d'absinthe (Essence of Absinthe, 1981) is a fifteen-minute film
in 16mm that occupies a space between two more elaborated and complex works, namely *Karagoez* and *Das Lied von der Erde. Gustav Mahler*
(Songs of the Earth. Gustav Mahler, 1982). It is the re-working of a single
film. Even if a minor work, Gianikian and Ricci Lucchi have included it
in major retrospectives, from that of Milan in 2000 to the retrospectives
at the Jeu de Paume in Paris in 2006 and at MoMA in New York in 2009.
The title evokes *cinema profumato* but it is only the idea of a scent, rather
than a scent 'track', that accompanies the images. Absinthe, of course, is
the demon drink associated with decadence and bohemian living in late
nineteenth-century Paris. The film promises romantic allure only to strip
it away. An extract of a pornographic film made shortly after the First
World War shows explicit scenes of sex that originally involved two men
and two women, but one of the men has been removed in the editing.
The women's faces appear, and sometimes they look to camera, but we

scarcely see the faces of the men. The images are tinted red, crimson and blue. For the filmmakers the detailed analysis of forms and close ups in early pornographic cinema represented a continuation of the research in *Karagoez* in which the female body is fragmented and faces, eyes, and lips are isolated. In particular, Gianikian and Ricci Lucchi are interested by the analogy between the consumption of the film by roomfuls of spectators over the years in private viewings and the consumption of the film footage itself. The latter, which was transferred from 16mm to 35mm in the 1930s, is scratched and worn from multiple projections. The women's bodies, it is suggested, are being subjected to the same repeated exploitation as that undergone by the reel of film.

Essence d'absinthe is made to shock. Its elaboration of the pornographic images brings to the fore two features of Gianikian and Ricci Lucchi's practice that had been present from the earliest films: firstly, the documentation of the human body; and secondly, the attention to the materiality of film. In *Essence d'absinthe*, there is also violence in the address of the spectator: the act of viewing is rendered uncomfortable and problematic. The exploitation and brutalisation of the human body is recurrent in the *oeuvre*. Further films specifically on women's bodies and the male gaze include a short based on amateur 8mm footage *Frammenti elettrici n. 3 – Corpi (Electric Fragments No. 3 – Bodies*, 2003), and an installation, *Migrations – Corps Noir* (Migrations – Black Body, 2006) for the Fondation Maeght's *Le noir est une couleur* (2006).[4]

Das Lied von der Erde. Gustav Mahler
(The Song of the Earth. Gustav Mahler, 1982)

In *Karagoez* there are, as has been mentioned, scenes from Arnold Fanck's *Der Heilige Berg* (The Holy Mountain, 1926) that reappear in *Das Lied von der Erde. Gustave Mahler*. In the first film, the tinted fairy-tale mountain

---

4   *Le noir est une couleur: homage vivant à Aimé Maeght* (Paris: Fondation Marguerite et Aimé Maeght, 2006).

scenery with figures is part of a bewildering kaleidoscope of exotic scenarios. In the second, it loses its innocence and acquires sinister connotations. The make-believe world gives way to a time and place that exist in history: the time – the decade before the First World War; the place – the Dolomites then part of the Austro-Hungarian Empire. Gianikian and Ricci Lucchi tell us that the idea for the new project came when they discovered the summer hut in the woods of Alt-Schluderback where Gustav Mahler had spent the summers from 1907 to 1909 composing his symphony-song cycle *Das Lied von der Erde*. The setting was idyllic but the mountains where Mahler loved to walk with his wife Alma were to become a theatre of war within a few years of his stay there. Moreover, the mountains themselves became the backdrop for a new genre of film in which Nature was recruited to serve National-Socialist ideology.[5]

The films of Gianikian and Ricci Lucchi are informed by literary and philosophical writings, from their research for *cinema profumato* onwards. In the case of *Das Lied*, the relationship is especially significant. Theodor Adorno's essay *Mahler: A Musical Physiognomy*, notably the final section entitled 'The Long Gaze', provide an aesthetic and formal as well as political analysis of the composer's work that decisively influenced the making of the film. The essay, whose brilliance remains undimmed, suggests that Mahler intuited with foreboding not only his own coming death but the coming historical cataclysm of war and fascism: 'The ground trembles under the feet of the assimilated Jew – as of the Zionist; by the euphemism of foreignness the outsider seeks to appease the shadow of terror. That, and not merely the expression of a sick man's premonition of individual death endow the last works with their documentary seriousness'.[6] Mahler's music, according to Adorno, attains unity 'not in spite of disjunction, but only

---

5   Susan Sontag describes Fanck's films as 'pop-Wagnerian vehicles for Riefenstal [...] these films seem in retrospect to be an anthology of proto-Nazi sentiments. Mountain climbing in Fanck's films was a visually irresistible metaphor for unlimited aspiration towards the high mystic goal [...] which was later to become concrete in Fuhrer-worship'; in Susan Sontag, 'Fascinating Fascism', in *A Susan Sontag Reader*, ed. Elizabeth Hardwick (London: Penguin, 1982), 307.

6   Adorno, *Mahler: A Musical Physiognomy*, 150; for the translation in Italian, Theodor Adorno, *Mahler: Due Studi* (Turin: Einaudi, 1966).

through it; he creates a 'provocative alliance with vulgar music', a potpourri in which 'Jacobinically the lower music irrupts into the higher'.[7]

Das Lied, against expectations, is a silent film, and the filmmakers seek visual equivalences of Mahler's music as interpreted by Adorno. Mahler's setting of ancient Chinese poetry rendered into German, which serves as a mask for the sense of rootlessness or 'otherness' as a Jew, the idea of the transient world they express, and the mixing of high and low forms – all these had to be translated into film language.[8] Gianikian and Ricci Lucchi's notes for the 50th International Venice Film Biennale of 1982 calls it a 'catalogue of images that ideally might have belonged to Gustav Mahler by analogy of themes, times, dates, places, and moments of inspiration'.[9] Exoticism comes with the allure of the Far East and the images shot by the first travelling cameramen; Nature with the Alpine landscape and scenes of Moravia, Bohemia and Marienbad in Habsburg times; the Jewish aspect with Palestine, the desert; childhood with leaves from a diary; then there are the kitsch and vulgar elements, and, finally, the war in the mountains. In the film, as in Mahler, exoticism 'provides the basis for the thematic construction'. In the eyes of Gianikian and Ricci Lucchi, Mahler 'fragments' the text, 'makes strange' material taken from tradition, and extends compassion (*pietà*) towards everything that is lost in order that it will be remembered'. They, likewise, assemble a pot-pourri of 'inferior' and 'superior' elements, from unknown early cinema travelogues to 'high' genres of fiction. But the fragments are transformed into 'memories and dreams' by the magic of manipulation – the re-photographing within the individual frame and the slowing down of the film speed; the 'timelessness of slow motion' is likened to the 'live immobility of the *haiku*', and the tinted colours to those of 'autumn leaves'. The materials 'conjoin through a web of analogies'.[10]

7   Ibid., 32–3.

8   Theodor Adorno's writing appealed to the filmmakers also in its colour-filled images: '*Das Lied von der Erde* has colonised a white area of the intellectual atlas', writes Adorno, 'where a porcelain China and the artificially red cliffs of the Dolomites border on each other under a mineral sky', *Mahler: A Musical Physiognomy*, 149.

9   Gianikian and Ricci Lucchi, '*Das Lied von der Erde*', 92.

10   Ibid., 92–6.

For Philippe Azoury, *Das Lied* marks a decisive development in the work of Gianikian and Ricci Lucchi because they have 'stopped playing with the "analytic camera"', and begun to come to grips with its capacity to 'dig under the surface of the image so as to reveal its strategies'.[11] The image has become increasingly suspect to the filmmakers. The exotic is constituted by the complicity of the look. It is not an inherent property of the images. An image rendered exotic hides and disguises what can be seen. The other side of the exotic view of the Far East of the early twentieth century is that of the 'great mass of the disinherited poor in the colonies conquered or in the process of being conquered by religious, military and commercial missions'.[12] Footage of this other world, this Other, is only glimpsed in *Das Lied*, while the footage of war at the end of the film bears out the premonitions that Adorno found in Mahler's late work. If with *Das Lied*, empire and war are already present as major themes, it is with their next film, *Dal Polo all'Equatore* (From the Pole to the Equator, 1986) that they become central.

Dal Polo all'Equatore (From the Pole to the Equator, 1986)

In a pattern that runs through their *oeuvre*, a major find provided the materials for the project that opened a new phase in Gianikian and Ricci Lucchi's filmmaking. In the spring of 1982, they heard that an old film laboratory was about to be demolished and its contents destroyed. It was

11   Philippe Azoury, 'Sur "certaines radiations encore loin d'etre claires"', *Trafic* 38 (Summer 2001), 55.
12   Gianikian and Ricci Lucchi, '*Das Lied von der Erde*', 96. The idea of the 'exotic' as a representation of the Other in a discourse of power relates closely to Edward Said's conception of Orientalism: 'the scientist, the scholar, the missionary, the trader, or the soldier was in, or thought about, the Orient because he *could be there*, or could think about it, with very little resistance on the Orient's part'; *Orientalism* (London: Penguin, 1978), 7.

probably not entirely by chance that they got the news. The proprietor had been trying to sell the archive of documentary films housed in the lab to the Cineteca in Milan, which had been unwilling to take them except as a gift. At the time, conservationists were principally interested in fictional films and films by known directors. The collection, however, was not a mishmash of materials similar to the 9.5mm footage discovered earlier by Gianikian and Ricci Lucchi in the dried flower shop. It had belonged to Luca Comerio, a pioneer of documentary films in Italy, who died in 1940 and whose laboratory had been taken over by his first cameraman, Paolo Granata. It was Granata's nephew who had been looking for a buyer when Gianikian and Ricci Lucchi got wind of it. The fact that the collection contained actuality footage made it more, not less, attractive to them, and their prior knowledge helped them appreciate its significance, even if they had previously been unaware of Comerio's work.[13] For Gianikian, documentary filmmaking at the time was 'much more advanced than that of fiction'.[14]

Recent studies have put Comerio into historical context, showing how his career, like that of most contemporaries in cinema, began as a photographer.[15] A portrait of King Umberto I of Italy he took when he was 16 led to rapid recognition and installation as royal photographer. It is possible that he was responsible for rare footage of the king's funeral in 1900 in which orphans, heads shaved, formed part of the cortège. It is likely that Comerio worked for the Lumière Company as a cameraman.[16] According to Luisella Farinotti, 'Films from life and documentaries were his favoured forms and he always chose to film from a point of view inside

13   Scott Macdonald, 'Yervant Gianikian and Angela Ricci Lucchi (On *From the Pole to the Equator*) in Scott Macdonald, *A Critical Cinema Book 3. Interviews with Independent Film-makers*; reprinted in *Cinema Anni Vita*, 26–7.

14   'Cataloghi della memoria: Conversazione con Yervant Gianikian e Angela Ricci Lucchi (Sergio Toffetti e Daniela Giuffrida)', 17.

15   *Moltiplicare l'istante. Beltrami, Comerio e Pacchioni tra fotografia e cinema*, ed. Elena Dagrada, Elena Mosconi and Silvia Paoli (Milan: Il Castoro, 2007).

16   See Sarah Pesenti Campagnoni and Alessandro Oldani's biographical profile in *Moltiplicare l'istante*, 152–62.

events. Traveller, explorer and lover of risks, he climbed Etna during an eruption, raced in Egypt and Uganda, and followed the Libyan campaign, living in Tripoli for three years. In 1911 he tied himself with his movie camera to the aeroplane of Mario Calderara, and shot footage that realised a 'Futurist synthesis'.[17] In Jeffrey Schnapp's words, 'Comerio was perhaps the earliest Italian film journalist; he can be credited with inaugurating the transformation [...] of the camera eye into warfare's most conspicuous weapon.'[18] Although the Comerio production company had limited success, he was celebrated as a cameraman and commissioned to work on different continents, including Africa and India. His archive of films is therefore rich in materials from the early part of the century through to the 1920s. It consists mostly of films shot by himself and his company but it also has films he collected. Comerio had difficulties getting work, and gave up making documentaries. Instead, he was able to make a series of compilation films designed to appeal to the ultra-nationalist mood under Fascism. 'All of them were films about war: *Sulle Alpi riconsacrate* (On the Reconsacrated Alps), *Al rombo del cannon* (To the Roar of Canons), and *Perché il mondo sappia e gli Italiani ricordino* (So that the World Knows and the Italians Remember)', writes Antonio Costa, with the exception of *Dal Polo all'Equatore*, the only one to survive.[19]

Gianikian and Ricci Lucchi vividly recall their visit to the laboratory: the Prévost movie camera Comerio last used, the contact printer that resembled a 'little cupboard with two black fabric curtains' and that had film in the camera drawn by a single wheel with eight sprockets, the wooden editing table with bakelite plates. 'We looked at a few frames', they write, 'we saw them "still", by hand, back lit on the opaque glass of the table. A sailing boat, painted, the sky blue and the sea pink. We didn't need to see

17   Luisella Farinotti, 'Memoria di copertura. Il cinema di Yervant Gianikian e Angela Ricci Lucchi come catalogo dell'orrore della storia', in *Locus Solus. Memoria e Immagini*, ed. Barbara Grespi (Milan: Pearson Paravia Bruno Mondadori, 2009), 60.

18   Jeffrey Schnapp, 'Propeller Talk', *Modernism/Modernity* 1.3 (1994), 168.

19   Antonio Costa, 'Landscape and Archive: Trips around the World as Early Film Topic (1896–1914)' in *Film and Landscape*, ed. Martin Lefebvre (New York and London: Routledge, 2006), 249.

anything else unless we had everything'.[20] Gianikian and Ricci Lucchi did get everything, including a compilation film by Comerio entitled *Dal Polo all'Equatore*. Not only did they find the footage from which to make their next film but the title too was 'found' not invented.

At 101 minutes, *Dal Polo all'Equatore* was Gianikian and Ricci Lucchi's most ambitious film to date, and took about four years to make. The enterprise would not have been possible without the help of Eckart Stein, commissioning editor for the German television channel, ZDF, which already had a reputation for enlightened support of contemporary film-makers.[21] Earlier attempts to gain funding in Italy foundered in a maze of bureaucracy and politics. By contrast, ZDF maintained its promise not to interfere in the filmmaking. Subsequently, *Dal Polo all'Equatore* was broadcast in prime time on German television, whereas in Italy the film was seen by a much smaller audience in the early hours of the morning. However, the critical success of the film did help Gianikian and Ricci Lucchi to secure some backing from RAI Two and RAI Three television channels in Italy in subsequent years. Although television as a medium, because of its low resolution images,[22] is not particularly suitable for showing films, especially of the kind made by Gianikian and Ricci Lucchi, public broadcasting nevertheless provided ongoing support until the 1990s when commercial and public television fell under the influence, if not control, of Silvio Berlusconi.

20   Yervant Gianikian and Angela Ricci Lucchi, 'La nostra camera analitica' in *Cinema Anni Vita*, 38.
21   See Sheila Johnston, 'The Radical Film Funding of ZDF. Interview with Eckart Stein', *Screen* 23.1 (1982), 60–73; 'Between 1974 and 2000, Eckart Stein directed "Das Kleine Fernsehspiel" programme on ZDF, the second channel of German public television. The programme acquired world fame as a television and film laboratory that helped produce the first works of young filmmakers (Jarmusch, Egoyan, Ackerman ...), authors from Latin and North America, as well as the movies by well known authors facing difficulties with financial support (Fassbinder, Godard, Angelopoulus, and Varda, among others)'; http://cineasta.casadelest.org/uk/template/author.asp?id=5; accessed 18 February 2010.
22   According to Laura Marks, VHS has about 350,000 pixels per frame, while 35mm film has twenty times that number. The contrast ratio of video is approximately one-tenth of that of 16mm or 35mm film; *The Skin of the Film*, 175.

Indeed, Gianikian and Ricci Lucchi's method of working has had little to do with television production and scheduling. They work slowly and painstakingly using the optical printer made for the purpose. It was a refinement of the apparatus used for making *Karagoez*, which involved working on 9.5mm film, and designed to operate with 35mm film. This format came as a great discovery for Gianikian. He describes it as the 'father of all the other formats'. He points out some of its features: 'it is a format from which all the others – 9.5mm, 16mm, and 8mm – are derived. It is as if I had seen the origin of it all – the colour, the grain, inflammable [...] the children always lack something ; for example, with 9.5mm the sides narrow and inevitably something is cut out [...] Furthermore it contains history, the movement you can't find in books, it contains all the things we had read. Then there was finding the negatives – negatives that had been present on the battlefield, had actually been there, and are unique witnesses of the war'.[23]

The new 'analytical camera' has features that Gianikian enumerates:

It is a camera with microscope features, more photographic than cinematographic, and reminds me more of Muybridge and Marey's experiences than Lumière's. 347,600 frames were taken by hand for the film *Dal Polo all'Equatore*. The camera is equipped with devices for lateral, longitudinal and angular running. It can respect the frame entirely in the philological sense. Or it can penetrate the depth of the frame for detailed observation of the marginal zones of the image and the uncontrolled parts of the shot. The camera can respect the colour of the original toning or hand colouring of the frame, but it can autonomously paint vast areas of film. The running speed depends on what you want to emphasise [...]. The film is edited in blocks or themes, and their components cyclically recur in different forms and aspects.

The device has to deal with different widths of film and film in varying states of decay. The manual operation of a crank allows control over the speed and minimised the fire hazard posed by highly inflammable stock.

A second part of the apparatus, aligned to the first, is a 16mm camera that re-photographs the image in transparency.[24]

23   'Cataloghi della memoria: Conversazione con Yervant Gianikian e Angela Ricci Lucchi (Sergio Toffetti e Daniela Giuffrida)', 18–19.
24   Gianikian and Ricci Lucchi, 'La nostra camera analitica', 53.

Travel and the journey were present in Gianikian and Ricci Lucchi's reflections with the discovery of the 9.5mm films, a format designed for maximum portability. However, with *Dal Polo all'Equatore*, the metaphor of travel is coupled with that of the catalogue: 'We travel as we catalogue, we catalogue as we travel through the cinema that we are re-filming'.[25] The journeys of the original compilation film are retraced, dissected, and retranscribed by the filmmakers. Luca Comerio's film is thought to have been completed in the mid 1920s. It was fifty-seven minutes long (1,200 metres of footage) and was divided into four parts. The captions, which have a decidedly D'Annunzian tone, once subdivided these parts with rhetorical flourishes. For example, a scene showing Africans traversing a river carrying supplies for the Italian expedition includes a figure holding the national flag is accompanied by the inter-title: 'Everywhere Italy has flown and flies this glorious flag' (*Ovunque l'Italia ha sventolato e sventola questa bandiera gloriosa*). These intertitles took up some ten minutes of the overall running time. It is unlikely that the original, and in all probability unfinished, *Dal Polo all'Equatore* was ever shown in public. By the time of its completion the genre of the travelogue had become hackneyed and the silent film was about to be eclipsed by the arrival of sound.[26] We only know about the original, moreover, because of Gianikian and Ricci Lucchi's commentary. Although they intended to preserve the original by re-photographing it, their objective in buying the archive was not conservation but re-use. They substantially re-organised the material in their selection. For their film, they kept all the footage shot in Uganda in 1910 and much of that shot in the Arctic, and cut out the other two parts. The captions were stripped out. Footage from other documentary films in the Comerio archive was then used for seven new sections. The compilation was effectively recompiled.

The problem faced by Gianikian and Ricci Lucchi was almost the excess of material they had at their disposal. Footage from the First World War, the largest general category, was in reels of twenty or thirty metres, and

25   Ibid., 32.
26   Costa, 'Landscape and Archive: Trips around the World as Early Film Topic (1896–1914)', 249.

sometimes in separate sequences of less than one metre. The films about India had been shot on Gaumont, Pathécolour, and Ferrania stock, some with hand painting and tinting. Comerio's collection included a wide range of genres: documentaries dating back to 1900, travel films, ethnographic and scientific films, not to mention the war documentaries. Moreover, mould and physical deterioration was already visible and would slowly erode the quality of the images. Some of the footage had lost sprocket-holes making it hard to handle. In their accounts of working on the Comerio archive, the filmmakers refer to the difficulties they faced. It was usually not possible to work on more than one or two minutes of film in one day. Gianikian's own predilection for allowing the images to carry him along proved unsustainable. Not least, the sheer violence of the images made the Surrealist manner, 'à la Buñuel' inappropriate. The tendency to go in circles was a problem when 'there are infinite paths in the film, especially if you begin to go into the single frame in depth'.[27] In this respect, the 'analytical camera' solved some problems but created others. After three years spent re-filming material, Gianikian and Ricci Lucchi had accumulated a mountain of film. It was necessary for them to withdraw into another room without the images and, pen in hand, to group them under themes. The editing only began after they had done a great deal of preparatory work with notes covering hundreds of pages.

The strategy developed by Gianikian and Ricci Lucchi involved working *with* and *against* the found footage in the Comerio archive. On the one hand, they reproduced images that Comerio had shot. On the other, they manipulated them to produce a new work of what MacDonald called 'critical cinema' consisting of a systematic critique of the original.

Antonio Costa has written that by re-proposing the title, *Dal Polo all'Equatore*, Gianikian and Ricci Lucchi 'recapture the idea of the journey', delineating a series of different 'geographical-anthropological spaces'. They are listed by the filmmakers:

27   'Cataloghi della memoria: Conversazione con Yervant Gianikian e Angela Ricci Lucchi (Sergio Toffetti e Daniela Giuffrida)', 15.

1 Topography on the borders of the Austro-Hungarian empire: footage shot from a mountain railway shortly before the First World War;

2 'The White Sphinx': hunting scenes from a variety of sources starting with the Duke of Abruzzi's 1899 Arctic expedition;

3 Topography of the border: the Caucasus along the Persian-Russian border in about 1910 – a train enters Tiflis shortly after the Russian re-conquest of the region;

4 'The Black Sphinx': Baron Franchettti's expedition to Uganda, including 'scenes of missionaries hunting for their religious prey';

5 India, around 1911, footage of 'natives' and of military parades;

6 'A mystic postcard from Indo-China': Buddhist monks in early 20th century;

7 'Exotic postcards from France d'Outremer': Tangier, around 1910, with scenes of the exotic reminiscent of Delacroix and Flaubert;

8 Gondar, East Africa, 1910: a re-enactment of an 'African fantasy' of war;

9 'The Black Sphinx of Baron Franchetti: Uganda, 1910; scenes of big game hunting featuring the baron;

10 The First World War seen by Luca Comerio.[28]

From Comerio, the filmmakers learnt to organise their material into blocks and themes on a geographical basis and into scenes depicting hunting, military parades, and other ritualised activities. Gianikian recounts: 'we discovered in the original *Dal Polo all'Equatore* and other material, – a series of recurrent motifs. There are parades and processions (military, religious, hunting); dances (rituals, dances of death); war landscapes; crowds, and other groups; particular types: the priest, the warrior, the "savage", the hunter, the mystic, the traveller, the conqueror.'[29] Comerio, moreover, was a

---

28 Yervant Gianikian and Angela Ricci Lucchi, '*Dal Polo all'Equatore*' in *Yervant Gianikian and Angela Ricci Lucchi*, ed. Toffetti, 99–110.

29 Scott Macdonald, 'Yervant Gianikian and Angela Ricci Lucchi (On *From the Pole to the Equator*)' in Scott Macdonald, *A Critical Cinema Book 3. Interviews with Independent Film-makers*; reprinted in *Cinema Anni Vita*, 28–9.

very capable cameraman, if within a realist rather than experimental tradition. Scott MacDonald comments: 'The audience of *Dal Polo all'Equatore* is able to retrieve some sense of how the original Comerio footage must have looked, and since Comerio was a skilled cinematographer with obvious artistic pretentions and achievements, this alone makes the film of considerable interest: we see well-made images of peoples, places, and experiences which were exotic enough when they were recorded for European audiences.'[30] It could be argued that Gianikian and Ricci Lucchi help to bring out aspects of the camerawork of which Comerio himself was unaware. It is useful here to bear in mind Angela Dalle Vacche's comment about the gap between doing and thinking: 'cinema in 1920 [...] was in the hands of cameramen of all types and all levels of ability, among whom perhaps none knew, then or later, what a revolution in seeing they were working.'[31]

The exotic images, however, troubled Gianikian and Ricci Lucchi, who recall feelings of repugnance when looking at and studying them. While working *with* the found footage, they set out to work *against* what it embodied politically and ideologically. The most obvious sign of Comerio's politics was in the titles and inter-titles, each stamped with the company name and each full of nationalist and colonialist propaganda of the type promoted by Gabriele D'Annunzio and Filippo Marinetti. Their removal meant the elimination of an explicit framework for interpreting the images. In addition, all references to places and people shown on screen disappeared. The flow of images was not to be interrupted. Gianikian and Ricci Lucchi conceived the film as structured by patterns and motifs within the visual without verbal additions. There is a recurrence of parallels and contrasts. The parade of the British cavalry, for example, is echoed by the procession of Buddhist monks in the following section. The mechanical movements of African children under instruction from a nun is in contrast with the carefree gestures of the children seated on the ground in India in a later sequence. The hunting scenes in Africa ('the Black Sphinx') are analogous to those in the Arctic circle ('the White Sphinx').

30   Scott Macdonald, '*From the Pole to the Equator*' in *Yervant Gianikian and Angela Ricci Lucchi*, ed. Toffetti, 34.
31   Angela Dalle Vacche, *The Visual Turn: Classical Film Theory and Art History*, ed. Angela Dalle Vacche (New Brunswick, NJ, and London: Rutgers University Press, 2003), 128.

According to Raymond Bellour, ever since painting abandoned the idea, it is cinema that has assumed the task of relating bodies to the physical and social mass from which they issue. Gianikian and Ricci Lucchi are masters at revealing the ballet of human movement with its 'regulated play of chance' and the 'crossing of lines and overlapping of bodies'.[32] When it is not caged or militarised, human movement in *Dal Polo all'Equatore* is celebrated in moving images that slow the step and turn the most mundane of gestures into dance.

However, before they arrived at their conception of the film as a whole, Gianikian and Ricci Lucchi had to know how it would begin. It was the opening sequence of the railway journey that gave them the implicit structure in which the original is reconfigured as a journey through time as well as through space – a journey through history that is also a journey through cinema. The two are conjoined in the figure of Luca Comerio to whom there is a dedication after the credit sequence that reads: 'To Luca Comerio, pioneer of documentary cinema, who died in 1940 in a condition of amnesia. Chemical amnesia, mould, physical decay, decay of the image is the condition surrounding film materials'.[33] The screen then fills with the image of a tunnel and railway track, and the journey begins.[34]

As part of the Comerio collection, the footage would have been a standard of the travelogue genre popular in the first decade of cinema of which Alpine panoramas would have been a favourite. The original reel would have been about two or three minutes long and have been tinted – tinting that had largely faded by the time of the re-making. Projected at a normal speed of sixteen frames a second, the film would have given the sensation of speed with the rush through tunnels and the rapid disappearance of vistas. And while the excitement of rail travel might have moderated by 1909 when it was shot, there was still a climate in which the inauguration

32   Raymond Bellour, 'Des instants choisis de l'espèce humaine', *Trafic* 38 (Summer 2001), 80–1.

33   'A Luca Comerio, pioniere del cinema di documentazione morto nel 1940, in stato di amnesia. L'amnesia chimica, la muffa, il decadimento fisico dell'immagine, è lo stato che circonda i materiali filmici'.

34   For a fuller account of the credit and opening sequence, see Robert Lumley, Amnesia and Remembering: *Dal Polo all'Equatore*, A Film by Yervant Gianikian and Angela Ricci Lucchi', *Italian Studies* 64.1 (Spring 2009), 134–43.

of a tunnel through the Alps was headline news. New technology, especially in transport, excited contemporaries. Cinema and the railway had a special relationship to one another that helped shape the perceptions of the world. Cinema historians have variously referred to the development of a 'panoramic perception' in which travellers 'see the landscape/objects through the apparatus that moves them through the world', and to the shrinkage of space and time.[35] When Gianikian and Ricci Lucchi decided to initiate their film with this sequence, they were handling material rich in such associations; they note the parallels at work: 'the perforation missing on one side of the film, like the tracks on which the train runs, have been repaired one by one'.[36] However, it is the transformation of the original film that has made it into one of the most haunting and memorable opening sequences of cinema. The filmmakers cut out footage shot from outside the train – shots from the platform, for example – so that all the footage is shot from the train in movement. When re-photographing the original with the 'analytical camera', they multiplied the number of frames by about three times so that the sequence was extended to last for some eight minutes. They inserted filters with the result that whole blocks of images are saturated in monochrome colours, predominantly reds and blues. The imperfections and corruption of the original were kept in the new version, which showed the fading, scratches and fogging that in places threaten to obscure the entire image – the 'visual manifestation of the word amnesia'.[37] Finally, Gianikian and Ricci Lucchi added a soundtrack commissioned from two composers, Keith Ullrich and Charles Anderson.

Although in a residual sense, we are still looking at films that Comerio made, the new work has been marked, literally, by the passage of time, and time has become its subject. There is no departure or arrival, no acceleration or deceleration. The speed varies almost imperceptibly but remains in slow motion. There are virtually no people to be seen. Sometimes there

---

35   Lynne Kirby, *Parallel Tracks: The Railroad and Silent Cinema* (Exeter: Exeter University Press, 1997), 45.
36   Gianikian and Ricci Lucchi, '*Dal Polo all'Equatore*', 110.
37   Ibid.

are pans across the valley, and sometimes the train itself is visible as it winds into view but mostly the camera mounted at the front directs our look onwards. The slowing of the speed of the film heightens awareness of the act of looking – we have time to observe what would otherwise have flashed by. We are made conscious that we are watching a film. The 'reality' in Comerio's original film was 'out there' – the landscape, the train, movement. In Gianikian and Ricci Lucchi's film reality is a 're-recorded reality'. The tinting adds another layer, further distance from what we see.[38] The experience of 'being transported' approximates more to dreaming or hallucination.

The minimalist soundscape of echoes and repetition, strangely undefined and fluctuating contributes significantly to a mood of disquiet. Changes mark transitions but, as Azoury comments, the music seems to emanate from the image or rather from its duration.[39] Macdonald writes that the 'subtle analysis provided by Gianikian and Ricci Lucchi's precise modulation of the speed with which we see individual frames of Comerio's imagery (and by the more conventional gestures of their editing) is confirmed and extended by the sound track and their use of colour'. The Anderson/Ullrich score, which he associates with the serial music of Philip Glass, Terry Riley and Steve Reich, is 'eerie, haunting; it tends to emphasise the grimness of the events we are watching [...] It helps to convey a sense of the overwhelming sadness about the events Comerio documents, about what was lost through the colonisation and domination of people and animals'.[40]

In the final section of *Dal Polo all'Equatore* elements of the soundtrack from the opening sequence recur. It begins with soldiers entering a tunnel dug in the 'white war' in the mountains in 1916–18, paralleling a shot of some thirty seconds of a similar scene inserted, with the function of a mnemonic device, between the second and third sections, between the scenes of the Arctic and those of the Caucasus. The film has taken

38 I owe this observation to Matilde Nardelli.
39 Azoury, 'Sur "certaines radiations encore loin d'etre claires"', 59.
40 Macdonald, '*From the Pole to the Equator*', 42.

spectators from the Pole to the Equator. Now it brings them back to the landscape that is being transformed from a place of tourism into a theatre of war. The tunnel, in Gianikian's words, is where the soldiers spent long years in darkness. It is primary structure, an elementary form of architecture that humans have in common with animals. The tunnel, in the film, is one of the frames that directs and controls the look of the spectator, another proscenium arch, the place where the dissolve is invented, another passageway between light and darkness.[41]

For Gianikian and Ricci Lucchi, ways of looking and, more specifically, ways of looking through the camera lens are not neutral or innocent. Their re-working of Comerio's footage analyses how the movie camera functioned as a weapon in the hands of European colonialists before it became a weapon in the war between Europeans. This analysis is particularly evident in the sections that deal with hunting in the Arctic and in Uganda – sections two, four and nine. It is not by chance that the first human figure that the spectator sees at the centre of the image is raising his rifle and that the subsequent 'shot' shows a polar bear reeling after the impact of the bullet. In another sequence, a hunter on board a ship lines up his telescopic sights to take aim at a bear swimming and diving in a vain attempt to escape. The point of view of the hunter, which is also that of the cameraman in the original film, is one of calculated detachment and sovereign power. In Geoffrey Skoller's words, the film emphasises the gaze of the hunter in relation to the uninhibited display of power and brutality. The use of shot-reverse shot in these cases becomes part of a circle of gazes in relation to the domination of the animals and the indigenous people as well, who are often seen looking on while assisting the hunters. The circle of looks implicates the camera, the filmmaker, and viewer in a web of cruelty that goes beyond the killing to the act of seeing. The slowing down of the images forces the viewer to contemplate the act of looking as an integral part – both literally and metaphorically – of the act of killing.[42]

41   Gianikian and Ricci Lucchi, 'Dal Polo all'Equatore', 110.
42   Skoller, Shadows, Specters, Shards, 19.

In Comerio's film, there would have been no time for 'contemplation' – only thirty-six frames were devoted to the hunter studying his prey. Gianikian and Ricci Lucchi prolong the action by slowing the sequence so that it is twelve times longer. Christa Bluminger has shown in a detailed study how the filmmakers used the optical printer to work on the individual frame rather than on the shot.[43] Virtually all of Comerio's footage has been re-framed as well as re-photographed. Using his mattes – for instance, the circular matte for the telescopic sights – they reconstructed the point of view shot, heightening the sense of the 'object observed'. But the re-shooting resulted also in drawing out the death of the bears in a slow dance of death in which the empathy of the spectator is engaged, thereby reversing the point of view established in the original film.

Further hunting scenes take place in Uganda when Comerio accompanies Baron Franchetti on his expedition.[44] The hunter looks with hands shading his eyes and the camera follows his gaze. He surveys the landscape as a master of all he beholds. Mattes in the shape of binoculars or a shallow arch frame the animals sighted in the distance.[45] The baron acts out significant moments in the hunt – the moment the rhinoceros appears on the horizon, the finding of the lion's tracks, the advance into range. The accentuated gestures draw attention to themselves as if to say 'look, I am looking', a reminder of the staged nature of much documentary film from its earliest days. However, the animals themselves do not act. The camera, moreover, is pitiless in recording their movements as they stumble and fall, as wounded animals are goaded and forced to look to camera as if already

43   Christa Blümlinger, 'Cinéastes en archives', *Trafic* 38 (Summer 2001), 68–78.

44   Baron Franchetti is figure shrouded in mystery, not least because of the circumstances of his death – the aeroplane on which he was travelling exploded in a flight to Asmara in 1935. A big game hunter in the period 1910–14, and one of the first to have his exploits filmed, he was subsequently active in military intelligence; see 'Raimondo Franchetti Junior: Da cacciatore a esploratore ad agente segreto' www.comune.re.it/museo/museire.nsf/e9c715c6691a6e19c1256e1b00; accessed 22 October 2009.

45   See Gianikian and Ricci Lucchi, 'Dal Polo all'Equatore', 109.

trophies on the wall.[46] Comerio documented an orgy of killing – zebras, gazelles, a lion, a hippopotamus, and a rhino are slaughtered. Some of the most graphic and disturbing images show the dismemberment of the dead rhino whose horn and feet are hacked from the body to become prized souvenirs housed in a collection.

In Luca Comerio's original film, as re-worked by Gianikian and Ricci Lucchi, the depiction of animals and the natural world serves to demonstrate conquest and domination. Animals are shown being objectified and turned into trophies for display. Film, unlike photography, has the power to register the imperceptible passage from life to death, and a fascination with dying and death was a major preoccupation from the earliest days of cinema. André Bazin writes not only of the 'mummy complex' – man's psychological need to conquer death through the survival of his own bodily appearance – but also about the 'Nero complex' – his pleasure in destruction, disaster and horror.[47] The Nero complex, however, was subjected in film to the taboo against actually showing the moment of a human's death. The killing of animals acts as a kind of surrogate in which death and dying are filmed without inhibitions.

Christa Bluminger suggests that in *Dal Polo all'Equatore* the massacre of animals 'appears as the symbolic prefiguring of the violence of the First World War'. An extraordinary sequence of sheep on a hillside filmed from the air towards the end of the film brings to mind the imagery of lambs waiting to be slaughtered – the flocks are penned into formations that spell out the words 'VIVA IL RE' (Long live the King). Then the very final images, which Ricci Lucchi has called the 'key to our film', show a scene in which hunting dogs are provoked to attack a rabbit. It is not violence as

46   The hunting scenes bring to mind Peter Kubelka's *Unsere Afrikareise* (1961–6) in which a lion's death prompted Jonas Mekas to comment: 'the dying lion lifts his eye and looks directly into the camera accusingly and forgivingly and then dies. If there is a great moment of cinema, this is one'; Jonas Mekas, 'Interview with Peter Kubelka' in *Film Culture: An Anthology*, ed. P. Adams Sitney (London: Secker and Warburg, 1971), 287.

47   See Elena Dagrada, 'La seduzione del vero' in *Moltiplicare l'istante. Beltrami, Comerio e Pacchioni tra fotografia e cinema*: 9–22.

such that is the theme but gratuitous violence and cruelty to animals. An impeccably dressed man dangles a terrified rabbit above the dogs to the intense amusement of the women at hand.[48] They are the audience within the film while we are the audience that is also being entertained, whether we like it or not, – a situation rendered even more uncomfortable when the frames appear to slip and to repeat. In Skoller's words, 'the shot is re-photographed so that the film strip is sliding through the gate of the optical printer, showing the repetition of each frame rather than continuous motion, creating a sense of endless repetition of violence, aggression and domination'.[49] The home movie too is shorn of its innocence. The private and domestic spheres were not immune to the 'process of brutalization, the progressive erosion of the limits of cruelty and violence' which was to explode in the First World War, but the precedents for which could already be found in the genocides and oppression that came with colonialism.[50]

48 The man in question is the composer Giacomo Puccini.
49 Skoller, *Shadows, Specters, Shards*, 21.
50 Jay Winter, *Remembering War: The Great War between Memory and History in the Twentieth Century* (New Haven and London: Yale University Press, 2006), 80.

CHAPTER 3

Armenia

People have a greater understanding nowadays than was earlier the case that a violent traumatic experience in an individual person's life causes severe damage if it is not raised to the level of consciousness [...] I have been convinced for a long time that in the lives of nations too, there are collective traumatic experiences which sink deep down into the psychic economy of the members of these nations and cause severe damage if one denies them the possibility of a cathartic cleansing.

— NORBERT ELIAS[1]

There was some beautiful boiling water in a pewter teapot and suddenly, a pinch of wonderful black tea was thrown into it. That's how I felt about the Armenian language.

— OSIP MANDELSTAM[2]

Edited from material shot several years previously, *Io ricordo* (I remember) was made in 1997, shortly after the death of Raphael Gianikian, father of Yervant. This eleven-minute video is divided into two parts: the first shows Raphael Gianikian in an armchair reading aloud from his memoirs; the second part cuts to a ruined chapel at Gegard in the Republic of Armenia in which Walter Chiari, close friend and travelling companion of the film-

1   Norbert Elias, *The Germans: Power Struggles and the Development of Habitus in the 19th and 20th Centuries*, trans. Eric Dunning and Stephen Mennell (Cambridge: Polity Press, 1996), 430–1.
2   Osip Mandelstam, *A Journey to Armenia*, trans. Clarence Brown (London: Redstone Press, 1989), 57.

makers, places a candle in the earth and bursts into song.[3] Chiari died in 1991 after a long illness. While Raphael Gianikian reads his account of the massacre of Armenians – he was one of seven to survive in a small town of 10,000 inhabitants – his son, facing the camera and in the background, listens. The video camera, towards which the reader occasionally glances, is operated by Angela Ricci Lucchi. The title of the film, *Io ricordo*, can therefore be understood as more complex that might first have seemed the case. There is the first person narrator, the father who is handing down his memories to his eldest son and the next generation; there is the son who is remembering his father and what he is being told; finally, there is the camera that is recording the testimony and turning a private and family act of remembrance into a public event. In addition, Walter Chiari is both enacting a moment of remembering and is himself being remembered in *Io ricordo*.[4]

3   The importance of churches for Armenian identity can be seen in Atom Egoyan's film *Calendar* (1993); 'Armenians take pride in having been the first nation to accept Christianity'; Donald E. Miller and Lorna Touryan Miller, *Survivors: An Oral History of the Armenian Genocide* (Berkeley, Los Angeles and London: University of California Press, 1993), 33.

4   Gianikian and Ricci Lucchi have spoken about the possibility of making a film using the extensive material they have shot with Walter Chiari, including footage shot with him in Armenia. The short film *Ti regalo il mio ultimo respiro* (2009) shows Chiari, a brilliant comic, raconteur and actor, talking about what he has left for expressing himself when his voice has gone after an operation on his throat. He manages 'hate' but has difficulty with 'Io ti amo'; conversation with the filmmakers, 8 December 2009; 'a handful of minutes that immortalize a Walter Chiari at the end of his life [...] one of the most intense moments of this Festival', according to the programme of the Festival, 'Vento del cinema', held on Procida in 2009.

Ritorno a Khodorciur. Diario Armeno
(Return to Khodorciur. Armenian Diary, 1986)

The 'video reading' in *Io ricordo* recapitulates a reading of a similar kind in *Ritorno a Khodorciur. Diario Armeno* (Return to Khodorciur. Armenian Diary, 1986). This eighty-minute video consists almost entirely of a single shot, hand-held sequence of a reading by Raphael Gianikian from his written account of a journey back to his homeland undertaken in 1976. Only the seated reader, in semi-profile, is in shot. He reads without modifying his tone of voice or the expression on his face and without gesture or sign of emotion. He describes and narrates with a minimal use of adjectives firstly his 'pilgrimage' and encounters on the way, and, secondly, the terrible events of the massacres and forced marches to which he bore witness once more, this time in the presence of the Turkish people inhabiting his people's lands.[5]

Raphael Gianikian travels by car to Istanbul, Ankara, Sivas, Erzindjian, Erzerum, Ispir, and then completes the last mountainous stretch of the journey in Anatolia on foot. It is the first time he had been back since 1915. At Hanud, he remembers his brother had a friend called Mahmud, and, asking after him, he quickly finds himself surrounded by old men who recall his family. As he journeys on, news of the fellow-countryman of Khodorciur travels before him. His story is full of incidents of hospitality – he is greeted as '*Amidjia*' (uncle). He is invited to stay overnight by a shepherd and describes his home and how he makes yoghurt and cheese. The landscape is full of memories of uncles and cousins. But amidst the beauty of the place, he hears the voices that warned against the Turks – the priest

---

5 The following summary is drawn from the text in French translation from Italian, Raphael Gianikian, 'Retour à Khodorciur: Voyage d'un pèlerin à la recherche de sa patrie perdue' in *Raphael Gianikian Yervant Gianikian Retour à Khodorciur* (Paris: editions du Jeu de Paume, 2000), 7–22. A fuller and different version was published in Italian with photographs of the family and villages from early years of the century: Raffaele Gianighian, *Khodorciur. Viaggio di un pelligrino alla ricerca della sua Patria* (Venice: Casa Editrice Armena, 1992).

of Hunud who in 1828 led his people in exile; an aunt who said the Turks made her more afraid than the wild bears. On his journey he encounters familiar prejudices, such as the idea that he was returning to find hidden Armenian treasure. At Kisak, his birthplace, he bears his father's greetings to his mother, who is buried there, and tells her she had the good fortune to die in her land and not suffer the 'torture and humiliation of a tragic exile'. He sits among the ruins of the family home with a photograph of Kisak on his knees. He shows the old photographs to some Turkish men who remark on how fine and wealthy the town was. One of them then asks him to what country the inhabitants had emigrated. Here Raphael Gianikian begins his account of 'how the Armenian Catholics died'.

In June 1915 a government official arrived with ten gendarmes and within days the inhabitants were forced to leave their homes with only the possessions they could carry. Raphael Gianikian, who was nine years old at the time, was among the young, the old, and pregnant women, who followed in a second group. The reading recounts the horrors without elaboration – the invalids unable to move who are burnt alive, the men hung in front of the church, and the relatives not allowed to bury their dead (Djiobergantz); the women raped and thrown into the river (Axunm), the refusal to allow Armenians to drink from fountains, the stench of corpses floating down the Euphrates, the headless bodies (Kergoes). In front of the church of Saint Gregory the Enlightened, Raphael Gianikian says that he cried out in Armenian: 'Christ is dead in Khodorciur'. When his friend Mustapha asks whether he wants to visit the picturesque village of Hunud, he replies: 'No, I want to follow the route of the deportation of 1915. I want to take this route a second time'. The reading concludes with the words: 'I am the wandering pilgrim who carries on his shoulder the Cross of Jesus Christ. Mustapha follows me as if he were the apostle Joseph'.

In notes which accompany the presentation of *Ritorno a Khodorciur. Diario Armeno* at the Pesaro and Venice film festivals in 1986, Yervant Gianikian writes of the genesis of the film and its significance. [6] He calls

---

6   Yervant Gianikian, '*Ritorno a Khodorciur. Diario Armeno*' in *Yervant Gianikian, Angela Ricci Lucchi*, ed. Toffetti, 112–14.

it an exceptional document because 'one of the few direct testimonies by a survivor of the 1915 massacre in Eastern Turkey'.[7] It is the 'spoken work of eradicated culture' (*opera parlata di una cultura cancellata*) and important in ethnographic terms for Armenians. Raphael was the only Armenian to go back to his place of origin.[8] It was the first time that he had spoken of the events – neither his wife nor his children had ever heard him mention them before. Ever since his return from his pilgrimage of 1976, Yervant's father had been writing and tape-recording himself reading from the 'diary'. One day, without notice, he decided to read the text, roughly translated into Italian from Armenian. The tale of the journey has some of the qualities of fable: an old man, alone, goes back to his home to find himself a guest in a land once his carrying with him a promise he made his father, a message from his brother, and seven photographs of the village as it had been. He completes the last part of the journey in the mountain region on foot revisiting the places he had known as a child. He finds he can speak the Turkish he had long forgotten.

Gianikian draws attention to the method and philosophy within his father's account. He points out the attention to the geography of the places,

7   The genocidal nature of the massacres is concisely described by Charles Maier: 'The Turkish slaughter of perhaps a million and a half Armenians presents a closer parallel to the National Socialist targeting of Jewish victims. Here after all was a deliberate massacre of an ethnic minority, ordered by the Ottoman minister of the interior in 1915, organised under government supervision, and carried out by frequent pogrom-like slaughters in local communities, followed by mass deportations to concentration camps in the Syrian desert, where the victims were left to weaken and die of exposure and starvation'; Charles S. Maier, *The Unmasterable Past: History, Holocaust and German National Identity* (Cambridge, MA: Harvard University Press, 1987), 72. There is an extensive literature on the history of the genocide and eyewitness accounts; see Richard G. Hovannisian, *The Armenian Genocide* (London: Macmillan, 1992); Vahakn Dadrian, *The History of the Armenian Genocide: Ethnic Conflict from the Balkans to Anatolia to the Caucasus* (Oxford: Berghahn Books, 1995); Taner Akcam, *From Empire to Republic: Turkish Nationalism and the Armenian Genocide* (London and New York: Zed Books, 2004).

8   Told that he must be a 'lion' not to be afraid of being killed, Raphael Gianikian replies: 'I am a lion but an old one without teeth and claws'; 'Retour à Khodorciur: Voyage d'un pèlerin à la recherché de sa patrie perdue', 13.

the names of the trees, the recognition of ancient stones, the rediscovery of
the taste of certain foods – all this is a way of giving order to the traces left
of his long-lost childhood. The story told is an 'uninterrupted interweaving
of past and present'. The mode of narration and transmission – the writing,
translation, tape-recording, reading and re-reading – has a strategic value.
'My father', says Yervant Gianikian, 'holds history and his emotions at a
distance'. It is a history summed up by the son with brutal concision: 'a
village Khodorciur (destroyed), the inhabitants (disappeared), the family
(dispersed)'. The emotions of the son are hard to contain when faced with
the burden of the memory borne by the father: 'And that is how I learnt of
the tragedy of my father's family, dragged from the mountains of the far
North East to the Syrian deserts to die. How he survived all alone then,
alone now to tell the story'.[9]

Ritorno a Khodorciur is rarely shown and is relatively little known but
it is arguably a key work in Gianikian and Ricci Lucchi's *oeuvre*. Danièle
Hibon had this insight when she included it in the season entitled 'L'autre
moitié de l'Europe' in Paris in 2000 with a translation of Raphael Gianikian's text. She refers to a 'kind of equivalence between the text and the
"analytic montage" of the two filmmakers' and found herself thinking of the
unpunctuated juxtapositions of images in *Dal Polo all'Equatore* when listen-
ing to Raphael Gianikian's reading.[10] Hibon suggests that an understanding of their 'creative method' might be derived more from seeing *Ritorno a
Khodorciur* than from critical accounts of their work. Above all, she refers
to the 'essential message of Raphael's words: the infinite, paradoxical, and
enduring capacity of humans to pass from horror to beauty'.[11]

It is difficult to assess the degree of influence Raphael Gianikian had
on his son's filmmaking, not least because he was a man of words, whereas
Yervant has devoted his energies to the moving image. However, Yervant
Gianikian's interpretation of the text of *Ritorno a Khodorciur* provides some

9   Ibid.
10   Danièle Hibon, 'Retour sur un exil' in *Raphael Gianikian Yervant Gianikian Retour
     à Khodorciur*, 3–4.
11   Ibid.

clues with its emphasis on the 'work of memory', the ethical imperative to bear witness, the love of precise description and classification, the journey as (re)search, the Armenian cultural identification. It is clear that *Ritorno a Khodorciur* and *Io ricordo* record the handing on and the handing down of a cultural legacy. Studies of trauma within families who suffered from the Holocaust suggest that silences and the unspoken communicate, not only what is said. Not speaking about the experience of loss and suffering may be a way of wanting to protect the children from what the survivors have gone through, but it is likely to be felt and pieced together by the children nonetheless. Trauma is carried across generations and can haunt the children of survivors.[12] The work of memory in such circumstances can become a life's work. In an interview in 2009, Yervant Gianikian reflected on how his father's words had kept him company ever since the making of *Ritorno a Khodorciur*:

> Alongside our work on the archival images on the violence of the last century stands this archive of words, which I now connect to my memories – memories of my relationship to my father over the years [...] He loved to go walking in the company of other people. When an old man, he enrolled in a marathon with thousands of participants. Only subsequently have I linked this passion of his with the memories he had of the deportation, the forced marches, the physical elimination of partici-pants, massacred by fatigue, hunger, thirst, and by bloodthirsty mobs that the 10,000 Armenian inhabitants of his town faced [...] during a walk lasting over six months in the year 1915. By walking he was celebrating his survival in the past, paying silent homage to those who did not make it, that is, to almost all of them.[13]

In 1987 the filmmakers began a new project – a search for images in the archives that would provide visual evidence for the genocide. The project resulted in the making of *Uomini anni vita* (Men Years Life, 1990), a film described by Yervant Gianikian as 'autobiographical'. It continued with the archive-based filmmaking associated with *Dal Polo all'Equatore*, which had

12 See Dina Wardi, *Memorial Candles: Children of the Holocaust* (London: Routledge, 1992).

13 Mereghetti and Rossin, 'Il magazzino della Storia', 123.

proved a major critical success in Italy and internationally. Again financial backing came from Eckart Stein of ZDF. Gianikian and Ricci Lucchi went to the Caucasus and to the Republic of Armenia,[14] and to Leningrad in the period 1987–8, spending months at a time travelling and researching. These coincided with a period of intense upheaval and crisis that shook the Caucasus region. In February 1988 there were massacres of Armenians in Sumgait in Soviet Azerbaijan. In December a major earthquake struck the Republic of Armenia, killing about 100,000 people. The scenario of buildings burnt down, shops looted and extensive ruins seemed to replay older patterns of conflict in which geological and metaphorical tectonic plates shifted in this border region with catastrophic consequences. Once more the collapse of empire – this time the disintegration of the USSR – unleashed nationalist movements. Gianikian and Ricci Lucchi, inveterate video diarists, filmed the places and people they visited. *Terremoto* (1989–2006), for example, shows grief-stricken survivors holding photographs of those they have lost, scarcely able to speak.

The filmmakers, however, focused on their archival searches, which, with the fall of Communism, offered new opportunities because of the loosened grip of censorship and control. This temporary opening of a window onto the past did not last long but for a brief period archives previously so highly policed were made accessible. Nonetheless, the task brought a good deal of frustration and difficulty. Gianikian recounts the 'endless waiting' and the 'often useless trips'. The aim was to find materials relating to the events in Armenia after 1915 and to combine them with family histories and diaries of exile, to 'bring together the materials dispersed and scattered like their people, ever on the move'. They did come across lost film that gave greater historical breadth to their project and 'long buried events' came to light.[15] However, they found little of the visual evidence they were searching for in order the document the Armenian history.

---

14   The filmmakers were officially invited by the government film agency of the Soviet Republic of Armenia thanks to the film director Bakrad Oganesyan; Yervant Gianikian, '*Uomini anni vita*' in *Yervant Gianikian, Angela Ricci Lucchi*, ed. Toffetti, 119.

15   Ibid., 119–22.

If one of the original aims to find film that would help to substantiate the case that there had been a genocide of Armenians in 1915 – something that the Turkish state has continued to deny – the project subsequently evolved into one that revolved around the relationship of Armenians to Russia and the USSR. In *Uomini anni vita*, Armenia appears as part first of a Christian empire and then of a Communist one. The imagery of the former is condensed in the *tableau vivant* that opens the film in which we see the figure of Holy Mother Russia. She protects and stands above the people of the Caucasus. Christians and Moslems are kneeling at her feet, kept in place by her sword. The imagery of the second, the USSR, is represented by the happy, smiling and hardworking fishermen who harvest the rich waters of Lake Sevan, embodying harmony between popular tradition and the technology promoted by the new state. The footage discovered by Gianikian and Ricci Lucchi is mostly designed to promote the dominant ideology. There are, on the one hand, the parades and ceremonies that marked the 600th anniversary of the Romanov dynasty in 1906, and, on the other, the choreography of happy workers typical of Socialist Realism. Although the filmmakers found material that spoke of a different history – rare scenes of workers and soldiers demonstrating on the street in 1917 – Armenian history, in the imperial perspective, becomes a site for the projection of an idea of a people that is cruelly remote from their real situation.

Rare footage from the Russian archives discovered by Gianikian and Ricci Lucchi show scenes shot after the massacres of 1915 – a woman sitting on a heap of stones once her home weeps, villages and towns lie empty. It was shot in order to show the Czar the victorious progress of his army against the Ottomans. In a letter to his wife, Nicholas II, after seeing films remarks on the 'mountain peaks of incomparable beauty and the snow glinting in the sunlight'. Footage from 1918 filmed by a British expeditionary force sent to secure oil-fields, which comes at the end of *Uomini anni vita*, shows columns of Armenian deportees on the road leading away from the killing grounds of Karabagh: 'It is painful progress for the old men, women and children. On the dust roads they cross mountains and deserts. A faceless people head into exile, dispersal. Metaphorical images of all the exoduses of history'.[16]

16   Ibid.

Uomini anni vita scarcely contains any text. There are no inter-titles. The viewer cannot know from the film where or when the events are taking place. The footage is grouped into episodes within a loose structure. But the disparate materials have been subjected to the same procedures, slowed down, re-framed and edited to create rhythms undreamt of by the original cameramen. A unifying element is provided by the music of Giovanni Pergolesi's *Stabat Mater* (1736), which starts to play from the shots of the woman weeping in the ruins and finishes with the final shots of the road to exile. For Michel Hommel, Gianikian and Ricci Lucchi 'always bring us to the tragic character of the images by appealing not to the intellect, but to the heart. Why should history', he asks, 'always be explained rationally [...] The image tell us all we need to know. To watch is sufficient.'[17] For Ugo Casiraghi the film is the 'sweetest and most unbearable song of farewell'.[18] In Alberto Farassino's words, it is a 'requiem for the death of a people. The film risks being admired only for reasons of avant-garde aestheticism, but is in fact overflowing with emotion and historical breadth reaching at points a perfect equilibrium of diverse elements – technique, passion, art. Work, research, denunciation, tears.'[19]

It has often been said that the Armenian genocide is remembered because of its denial. The consistent refusal of the Turkish state to recognise the state-organised and systematic nature of the massacres has meant for Armenians that the repeated narration of the history is an obligation towards future generations.[20] The denial has been countered by acts of remembrance, such as the 24 April day of memory. For their part, filmmakers have been especially concerned with the visual evidence of the genocide and the transmission of cultural memory through its inscription

---

17 Michel Hommel, 'A History Beyond the Facts' in *Yervant Gianikian, Angela Ricci Lucchi*, ed. Toffetti, 48.
18 Ugo Casiraghi, '*Inventario balcanico* e la guerra', in *Cinema Anni Vita*, 163.
19 Alberto Farassino, *La Repubblica* (5 February 1991).
20 Leshu Torchin, 'Since We Forgot: Remembrance and Recognition of the Armenian Genocide in Virtual Archives', in *The Image and the Witness: Trauma, Memory and Visual Culture*, ed. Frances Guerin and Roger Hallas (London and New York: Wallflower Press, 2007), 82–97.

in images.[21] According to Gianikian the problem remains: 'The power of words is greater than that of the images of the genocide which has not been documented in film (or rather the images have been carefully hidden or destroyed, but I for one will go on looking for them)'.[22]

21 The work of Atom Egoyan, for example, continually returns to the genocide and is driven by anxiety about the diasporans' loss of cultural identity; see the films: *Early Development* (1990), *Calendar* (1993), *Ararat* (2002); and installations '*America, America*' (1997), and *Diaspora* (2001). His work combines a formal inquiry into the means of reproduction that are, at the same time, increasingly, the means of the cultural transmission.
22 Mereghetti and Rossin, 'Il magazzino della Storia', 123.

CHAPTER 4

The War Trilogy:
Prisoners, War in the Mountains, the Aftermath

Along with the growth of the big cities there developed the means of razing them to the ground. What visions of the future are evoked by this.

—WALTER BENJAMIN[1]

From the original watch-tower through the anchored balloon to the reconnaissance aircraft and remote sensing satellites, one and the same function has been indefinitely repeated, the eye's function being the function of the weapon.

—PAUL VIRILIO[2]

The order of general mobilisation issued on 31 July 1914 opened for the Trentino, in the Southern part of the Austro-Hungarian Empire, the bloodiest chapter of its entire existence, representing a 'veritable martyrdom'.[3] Most of 55,000 men were sent to the Eastern front: 10,000 died on the battlefields of Galicia; the remainder became prisoners-of-war of the Rus-

---

1   Walter Benjamin, 'Über einige Motive bei Baudelaire', cited in Susan Buck-Morss, *The Dialectics of Seeing. Walter Benjamin and the Arcades Project* (Cambridge, MA. and London: MIT Press, 1993), 317.

2   Paul Virilio, *War and Cinema. The Logistics of Perception* (London and New York: Verso, 1989), 4.

3   Diego Leoni, 'Quei luoghi, quei volti' in *Cinema Anni Vita*, 173; for a lucid account in English of the Italian Front during the First War, see Mark Thompson, *The White War. Life and Death on the Italian Front 1915–1919* (London: Faber and Faber, 2008); for a wider survey of research in Italian, see Antonio Gibelli, *La grande guerra degli italiani, 1915–1918* (Milan: Rizzoli, 2007).

sians, 2,500 of whom returned in 1920 after an odyssey of deportation and internment. During and after the war, the whole region was a battle zone occupied at different stages by the Austrian and German armies, and then by Italian and Allied armies. Each side deported civilian populations suspected of treason or unreliability – sending 30,000 to the South in the Italian case, and 70,000 to *lagers*, the so called 'timber-towns' of Mitterndorf, Braunau, Oberhollabrunn and Wagna in that of the Austrians. The war was not between two distinct camps but divided neighbourhoods and families with some of the 360,000 Italian-speakers following Cesare Battisti's nationalist call, and others staying loyal to the Emperor. Even when the hostilities ceased and the treaties were signed, this border region remained a microcosm of ethnic, linguistic and cultural diversity on which the national state sought to impose homogeneity in the place of plurality of identity. It was a kind of laboratory for the regime of 'total war' characterised by the targeting of civilians, deportations, and internment that prevailed in the Second World War.[4]

The terrible ordeal of the people of the Trentino became central to three films made by Gianikian and Ricci Lucchi over a ten-year period from the early 1990s to 2004, films that have retrospectively been presented as a trilogy: *Prigionieri della guerra* (Prisoners of the War, 1995), *Su tutte le vette è pace* (Uber allen Gipfeln ist Ruh; On the Heights All is Peace, 1998), and *Oh! Uomo* (Oh! Man, 2004). There were good reasons why the filmmakers were drawn to the project. The First World War was the cataclysm that led to a century of war and genocide, starting with the genocide of the Armenians in 1915.[5] Gianikian and Ricci Lucchi's films, from *Das Lied von der Erde. Gustav Mahler* and *Dal Polo all'Equatore* to *Uomini anni vita*, already contained scenes if not of the war, then scenes that anticipated its coming. They had already begun to do research in public archives across Europe as if historians themselves. The mountains of the

4   Ibid., 173–82.
5   An important figure for the filmmakers that links these events is the writer Franz Werfel. Werfel served in the Austro-Hungarian army on the Russian front in the First War. Later he published *The Forty Days of Musa Dagh* (1933), a novel about the Armenian genocide written after hearing stories from survivors on a journey to the Middle East in 1929; see en.wikipedia.org/wiki/Franz_Werfel; accessed 25 August 2010.

Trentino and Alto Adige were a familiar landscape to Yervant Gianikian whose father and mother lived in Merano where he had been brought up. Walking in the Dolomites where the battles had once raged meant often coming across ruined military outposts and remnants of weaponry.

However, the project was first conceived by historians based in Trento and Rovereto, who were exploring the war through sources and methods of research that dealt principally with the experience of the ordinary soldier or family in the words of that soldier or family.[6] Working on letters, memoirs and 'popular writing', and collecting oral testimonies along with private collections of photograph albums and souvenirs, they were linking individual life-stories to the wider narrative of the conflict.[7] Memory and history were brought together. Furthermore, they were looking for ways of communicating the findings in what would now be called 'public history'. This meant not only publishing materials, organising conferences, and overhauling the presentation of exhibits in museums, but finding a 'cinematic equivalent' of the history they were writing. In Diego Leoni's words, 'it would be at once an act of memory and a reflection on history, an attempt to establish a visual anthropology of the war documentary, and a micro-physiology of its participants'.[8] In Gianikian and Ricci Lucchi, Leoni and his fellow historians discovered filmmakers with whom they established a long and remarkably productive collaboration.

6　Historians associated with the journal *Materiali di lavoro. Rivista di studi storici*, and with the Museo Storico Italiano della Guerra in Rovereto, directed by Camillo Zadra, and the Museo Storico in Trento. Interestingly, the initiative began as part of the 150 Ore radical education programme in the late 1970s, and the main protagonists have been teachers in high schools, not university lecturers; Camillo Zadra and Diego Leoni, interview with the author, 18 September 2008.

7　A book series entitled 'Scritture di guerra' has made available material gathered in the 'Archivio di scrittura popolare'. Number 10 in the series includes the autobiographical memoir of Giovanni Pederzolli, a carpenter and polisher, one of whose poems is incorporated in the soundtrack of *Oh! Uomo*; *Scritture di guerra 10: Rodolfo Bolner, Giovanni Pederzolli, Francesco Laich*, ed., Gianluigi Fait (Rovereto: Museo Storico di Trento and Museo Storico Italiano della Guerra, 2002); for a compendium of visual sources, see Laboratorio di storia di Rovereto, *Il popolo scomparso. Il Trentino, i trentini nella prima Guerra mondiale* (Rovereto: Nicolodi Editore, 2003).

8　Ibid., 176–7.

Prigionieri della guerra (Prisoners of the War, 1995)

The title *Prigionieri della guerra* (Prisoners of the War, 1995), the next
feature length film after *Uomini anni vita*, was chosen not just with reference to the soldiers taken captive in the First World War but to refer to
all those who were made into prisoners by the war.[9] The film is divided
into parts that correspond to the different stages of the war and different
groups of prisoners. We see footage from 1914–15 from the Russian archives
of Austrian prisoners who are taken to Siberia. Scenes in camps are pictured in such a way that the harsh conditions are hidden behind images
of cheerful wood-cutting, log-cabin-building, meals and relaxation. Subsequently, *Prigionieri della guerra* has footage from 1915 from the Vienna
film archives that show the 'timber-towns' in which the deported civilians
from the Trentino lived out the war.[10] Much of the material deals with
orphans and the children of prisoners-of-war.

The prisoners in Russia are exhibited as trophies of war, a spectacle
for the people of Moscow and other towns. The filming itself replicates
the event as part of the propaganda campaign, using a variety of devices
to exaggerate the numbers, such as having the men pass the camera more
than once. Gianikian and Ricci Lucchi, in turn, vary the speed of the film,
slowing down, and sometimes speeding up the endless flow of humanity.
The *défilement*, the act of walking past a fixed camera, is a trope of early
cinema – in Laura Mulvey's words, 'a distilled movement in which the
succession of people almost seems to merge from a succession of frames,
echoing the projector's movement'.[11] There is, however, a cruel paradox at

9   One title proposed for the film was *I nostri generali vittoriosi*. It is worth noting,
     however, that Gianikian and Ricci Lucchi tend to avoid polemical connotations.
     The title *Prigionieri della Guerra* was taken, according to the filmmakers, from Elias
     Canetti, who, after seeing Karl Kraus's *The Last Days of Humanity*, declared that
     everyone was a prisoner of the war and no one was free of it.
10   Subject of the major study by Diego Leoni and Camillo Zadra – *La città di legno.
     Profughi trentini in Austria, 1915–1918* (Trento: Editrice Temi, 1995).
11   Laura Mulvey, *Death 24x a Second. Stillness and the Moving Image* (London: Reaktion
     Books, 2006), 68.

work. The cameramen might well have intended to give a picture of the humanitarian treatment of prisoners, and the prisoners themselves take the opportunity offered to wave and smile as if they were greeting their loved-ones, perhaps hoping that the film might even be seen by them. A great humanity suffuses the scenes. And yet this mass of men is also subject to the machinery of war and the machinery of the film camera that directs their movements and their lives, enslaving them to powers beyond their control. In the words of Marcello Flores, 'the prison camps that Gianikian and Ricci Lucchi show us have this common feature – in their structure, even in the physical forms of the watch-towers, showers, roll-calls and forced marches, they already fully anticipate the tragic examples to come in the shape of Stalin's gulag and Hitler's concentration camps [...] the impression remains in this wonderful film that, despite the signs of humanity, it is the structure, the institution, once created, that drives ever onwards towards greater and greater inhumanity and cruelty in its use'.[12]

Inter-titles give the essential information of place and date without adjectives or elaboration. There are only seven of them. Nothing offers a narrative or history of the war. The last inter-title 'Attack, Retreat, Defeat' serves only to sow confusion in the minds of viewers already at a loss to distinguish between one army and another. According to Raymond Bellour, 'One becomes indifferent to the national identities that are discreetly recalled as if to reassure us about the truthfulness of this tangled conflict of which we are children'.[13] The final scene of *Prigionieri della guerra* shows rare footage of a mass grave. Corpses are taken from a cart, dragged to the edge of a deep trench, and tipped unceremoniously onto a pile of bodies below. At this point, it is entirely unclear and clearly irrelevant as to which army is victorious and which defeated. The soldiers have metamorphosed into rigid and awkward bundles to be manhandled like any other cargo. The slowing down of the film turns the movements of the living into an ungainly *danse macabre*.

12   Marcello Flores, 'La grande guerra dei contadini', *L'Unità* (4 December 1995).
13   Bellour, 'Des instants choisis de l'espèce humaine', 82.

In a film constructed out of the mirroring of apparent opposites – the victors and the vanquished, the guards and the prisoners, the living and the dead – the final scene, like the opening shots, show burial grounds after the battle is over. The battle – scenes of combat – meanwhile is never seen, except in the very last sequence in which shells explode in the distance in a snow-covered landscape. The beauty of the explosion stands in stark contrast to the human cost it exacts.[14] It also anticipates Gianikian and Ricci Lucchi's next project – a film on the 'white war' in the Dolomites.

Prigionieri della guerra had its world première at the Pordenone Festival of Silent Cinema in October 1995 where it was accompanied by a live performance by Giovanna Marini. Marini, who composed the music for the soundtrack, went on to collaborate with the filmmakers with their next two films.[15] She recalls her astonishment at seeing *Prigionieri della guerra*, and comments on the difficulty of putting music to the images: 'When I saw those images for the first time, I realised that I had never thought films like that could be made [...] Everything appeared transformed and seen by another eye, rarefied and even dream-like images, yet there was always the harsh reality, utter truth [...] And the silence, this extraordinary silence of the film in which the explosions of the bombs are explosions of light alone [...] How was it possible to cover such expressive silence with music? [...] The great temptation later on was to get rid of it'.[16] The music, however,

---

14 Robert Musil was one of many writers and artists fascinated by the sensations induced by war and by the act of observing oneself react to sights and sounds. Serving in the Austrian army in the Tyrol, he noted in his diary the 'impression one has of an uncanny turmoil in nature' in response to the sounds of shells in the air and exploding; *Robert Musil Diaries, 1899–1941*, ed. Mark Mirsky, trans. Mark Mirsky and Philip Payne (New York: Basic Books, 1999), 185.

15 Giovanna Marini is a composer and singer who has dedicated great energy to the study and revival of popular musical forms. She was a leading light of Nuovo Canzoniere Italiano, which involved *cantautori*, such as Ivan Della Mea, and she sees herself principally as a composer and performer for whom such music is a means to rethink musical codes in contemporary idioms; see 'Musica popolare e "modernità". Incontro con Giovanna Marini' www.culturaspettacolovenezia.it/index.php?iddoc=9607; accessed 2 October 2009.

16 Marini, 'La musica', *Cinema Anni Vita*, 115.

works *with* the film. It gives voice to suffering and endurance but follows the images without imposing on the audience a sense of how they should respond. Two songs are sung – Ivan Della Mea's and a song by Mordechai Gebirtig about the Warsaw ghetto[17] – suggesting that it is all wars and not just the First World War that is depicted.[18]

The reception of *Prigionieri della guerra* in Italy and beyond has varied according to region and nationality, sometimes in unexpected ways. Two cases provide an insight into this reception: firstly, the response in the Trentino, an area with which the film is directly concerned; and, secondly, that in the Balkans, the part of the world in which the conflict ignited and spread in 1914 and in which new wars broke out in 1992.

Diego Leoni, the historical consultant, gives us a vivid account of his and the audience's responses when he presented the film in different venues, from cinemas in Rovereto and Trento to schools and village meeting-places: 'From 1995, when *Prigionieri della guerra* came out, I accompanied the film on numerous occasions to public screenings and I can say from personal experience that each time there was added to the emotion I felt as I watched those events, those places, those faces of fathers, and of fathers of our fathers, the emotion of the *trentini* in the audience who saw and understood more than anyone else could have. One could, for instance, see the solemn procession of prisoners in Russia with a neutral eye. Or, alternatively, think of them as men who, before the war might have travelled the East selling prints and images, preparing the way for the arrival of cinema only to become its involuntary actors. It is different again to watch the arrival of the prisoners in the camp in that endless river of humanity as if it were live on television'. Audience response can, Leoni says, be informed by historical knowledge about how the film was shot

17 Marini sings lines from Gebirtig's *Yankele*; Mordecai Gebirtig was born in Kraków (Cracow), Poland where he was killed in June 1942. He became famous as the poet and composer of a wide array of Yiddish folksongs; findingaids.cjh.org/index2. php?fnm=MorGebirtig&pnm=YIVO; accessed 24 August 2010.

18 *Kaim* was composed in 1973. It is also known as *Lettera a Chaim*; lines from *Kaim* that are sung by Marini include: 'se il cielo fosse bianco di carta, se qualcuno ti fa morto' (If the sky were paper white, if someone makes you die).

and in what circumstances. However, he finds himself responding as part of audiences for whom the history is also collective memory, a memory driven underground that is now rising to the surface.[19]

On 4 May 1996 *Prigionieri della guerra* was shown at the Teatro Miela in Trieste as the first stage in a series of presentations in what has become known as the 'former Yugoslavia' with screenings in Sarajevo, Zagbria/ Zagbreb, Lubiana/Ljubljiana, and Belgrado/Beograd. The initiative was symbolic: the filmmakers were not going only to Sarajevo, destination of choice of committed artists and intellectuals in North America and Europe, but to all the capital cities in the Balkans. Moreover, their film was about a war which had, in a sense, only just been re-fought and whose wounds were still open. If the reaction to it in the Trentino was framed in terms of a healing-process, that was not to be the case here. In interviews ten years later, Gianikian and Ricci Lucchi have spoken of the difficulties and hostilities they encountered: in Zagreb the police entered the auditorium and it was claimed that the film was anti-Croat; in Belgrade there was great suspicion and students were not allowed to attend; in Ljubljana the audience wanted only to talk about the landmines sold by the West. 'Everyone saw the film from the point of view they wanted. I asked myself whether we were still prisoners of the war', commented Gianikian.

The combustible nature of the images was highlighted by a particular error of nomenclature. In *Prigionieri della guerra* there is an inter-title with the words 'Gypsies accused of spying' that anticipates a scene in which men are led away to be shot, accompanied by an Orthodox priest. Members of an audience in Cambridge (England) shouted that they were Serbs not Gypsies. In fact, the filmmakers had made the mistake of relying on the original inter-title of the Austrian army film unit. In the climate of the time, such mis-identification could only be seen as a partisan act on the part of Gianikian and Ricci Lucchi.[20]

---

19   Diego Leoni uses the metaphor of the 'catacomb' as the underground hiding-place of the memories of the trentini; Diego Leoni, 'Quei luoghi, quei volti' in *Cinema Anni Vita*, 176. Leoni has also reflected on how memory of the war played out between the 'generation of 1968' and their fathers, see Diego Leoni, 'Testimonianza semiseria sul '68 a Trento', *Rivista di storia contemporanea* 2 (1989), 293–306.

20   Conversation with the author, December 2009.

Su tutte le vette è pace (Uber allen Gipfeln ist Ruh; On the Heights All is Peace, 1998)

Su tutte le vette è pace takes its title from Goethe's second *Wayfarer's Night Song* of 1780, words subsequently put to music by Schubert.[21] The poem evokes the stillness of peace that takes the place of grief and pain. In the film, peace has been driven out of the mountains by a war in which the Austrian and Italian armies struggled to control the peaks that dominated the valleys below. The images show the topography overlaid by the machinery of war. The soundtrack, again composed by Giovanna Marini, puts music to words from the diaries and letters of soldiers caught up in the conflict and their longing for an end to it all. The words are fragments assembled and transformed through methods analogous to those applied to the frames of film.

In notes on *Su tutte le vette è pace*, Gianikian and Ricci Lucchi cite a passage from Robert Musil's Diaries in which his eye moves from the mountain panorama to the mute objects that survive the fallen: 'Mobility of the eye, immobility of the vast mountains. The shrapnel – it is heard long in advance, a sound like the whistling of the wind. Time to you seems to go on and on. Wrapped in a piece of newspaper the few things of the dead man lie on the table: a wallet, the rosette from a beret, a short pipe ... The list of the fallen: dead ... dead ... dead ... dead ... written thus, one after the other' (Unnumbered notebook, not later than 1916–18, in the Alps).[22] The men who in *Prigionieri della guerra* disappear into the mass are given visibility as distinct and different from one another. Gianikian and Ricci Lucchi write of their 'search for the individual, the "soldier as human" (*soldato uomo*) in film archives that assemble the anonymous masses. In the details, in particular features, expressions, micro-physiognomy, individual forms of behaviour'. They were also looking to construct a 'social portrait' found in war situations: 'panic, fear of not surviving, the urge to flee, the

21 See *Goethe: Selected Verses*, trans. David Luke (London: Penguin, 1964), 49–50.

22 Gianikian and Ricci Lucchi, '*Su tutte le vette è pace*', in *Cinema Anni Vita*, 215–16.

intoxication of killing; war and beauty of panorama – elements in stark contrast; prisoners and deserters separated into "ethnic groups".[23]

The discovery of 'popular writing' (*scrittura popolare*), thanks to the collaboration with the historians based in Rovereto and Trento had a major impact on the filmmakers. If, as Leoni claimed, the images gave faces back to the soldiers, words, in turn, gave voices to the soldiers portrayed. As in the earlier film, footage is organised according to source, usually propaganda for one side or the other, but in such a way that the opposition is subverted and common ground is found in the experience of the ordinary soldier. The soundtrack, moreover, is arranged so that the same words are sung – what Gianikian refers to as *'recitar cantando'* – in Italian, German and English. The repetition also serves as incantation as in a Gregorian chant. The music – and this recurs in their films – works to 'orient the reading of the image'; 'the music implies a feeling, rather than a thought, and helps to hypnotise the spectator by playing on duration and repetition'.[24]

When *Su tutte le vette è pace* was shown at MoMA in New York in February 2009, it was accompanied by a six minute short, *Trasparenze*, which was made in the same period as the feature-length film. *Trasparenze* (Transparences, 1998) throws light both on the working practices and philosophy of Gianikian and Ricci Lucchi. Luisella Farinotti writes:

> The film is an 'essay' on film materials that lasts a few minutes [...] Yellowed frames of an old Kodak film reduced to tatters are shown as precious archeological finds, they are carefully moved with pincers and scoured by the eye of the camera that searches obsessively for traces in what has been largely erased by the chemicals of time [...] Some frames, subjected to a chaos of sepia stains, seem part of an abstract film by Brakhage; others, less damaged but of which only fragments survive, reveal figures in transparency [*in trasparenza*] – parts of bodies, profiles of mountains, unrecognisable shapes. A voice-over registers each new discovery – 'a missing splice' ... 'here the image has dissolved' ... 'they seem to be soldiers'.[25]

---

23   Ibid.
24   *Cahiers du cinema* 547 (1999).
25   Farinotti, 'Memoria di copertura', 49–50.

Farinotti notes the intensely tactile and material quality of the film as it is unwound and the rustling noise it makes as it passes through the hands of the filmmaker, who could also be a healer or diviner of images. This brings to mind Hibon and Païni's observations about the 'sculptor's hands' at work in modelling and manipulating the material.[26] Gianikian has spoken of the experience of working with old footage in terms of liminality, of standing at the threshold between the world of the living and the world of the dead. He has also likened the smell of decaying nitrate stock to 'the stench of a corpse'.[27]

In *Su tutte le vette è pace* Gianikian and Ricci Lucchi use the materiality of the film with greater freedom and expression than in *Prigionieri della guerra*. In part, this may be due to the use of Comerio's footage in the former – the filmmakers had much more control over this material as it belonged to them. But it also marks a readiness to exploit the very properties that derived from the deterioration and sickness of the film examined in *Trasparenze* that embodies the physical dismemberment and destruction inflicted on the soldiers. References to the 'wounded body' of the nitrate material speak of the damaged sprockets, mould, discolouration, and of traces of blood and fingerprints. As in the epigraph of *Dal Polo all'Equatore*, human and historical memory and the 'memory' of the film material itself is treated as consubstantial.

Christa Blümlinger's analysis of a sequence of *Su tutte le vette è pace* in which Italian soldiers are engaged in operations on Monte Adamello shows how Gianikian and Ricci Lucchi use enlargement, slowing down of the film, and repetition of images to make visible what would otherwise pass unnoticed – movements and gestures can now be observed, and faces are in close-up.[28] Both time and space are stretched. Blümlinger identifies three shots from the opening sequence in which soldiers are filmed in close-up: First, as they leave a village – a soldier with a moustache advances slowly towards the camera and exits to the right; in the next shot he reappears

26   Danièle Hibon and Dominique Païni, 'Del documentario fatto a mano. Note coniugali sul cinema di Yervant Gianikian e Angela Ricci Lucchi' in *Cinema Anni Vita*, 98–9.
27   Conversation with the author, 9 December 2009.
28   Christa Blumlinger, 'Cinéastes en archives', *Trafic* 38 (Summer 2001), 68–78.

in close-up and the movement is repeated. The original shot is doubled and edited as if sequential. Second, a shot isolates faces in an advancing column of soldiers making its way past rocks in a snow-covered landscape; 'the images are slowed down to the point that it ends by pausing briefly on the face of a young soldier; then the scene is repeated. Third, under the eye of an officer soldiers leave a remise and run in Indian-file – young men in helmets smile as they pass the camera. There is no repetition of the scene that has something direct and irrevocable about it. These shots are in close proximity to one another but alternate with scenes in which men are shown *en masse*. According to the film historian, the enlargement, repetition, and slowing down of images, but also the new order and rhythms to which they have been subordinated, establishes a 'discursivity as different levels'.[29]

The first level has to do with the film's appeal to a historical referent: 'it has taken place and must never be forgotten'. The use of footage from the period and its careful documentation provides the basis for this documentary aspect of the film. Indeed, this understanding underpins many of the statements by the filmmakers, their collaborators, and commentators more generally. However, Blümlinger argues that the work of Gianikian and Ricci Lucchi as a whole and *Su tutte le vette è pace* in particular goes beyond this conception of the documentary that she calls 'historicist'. It offers an artistic truth that is achieved through manipulation and 'fiction' and that is grounded in the present. Furthermore, the filmmakers' 'aesthetic classification of images' brings into the open the 'rules of the operation of the discourse' that determine what survives and what is eradicated – what in the culture decides which *énoncés* appear and which disappear.[30] The question of history in the *oeuvre* will be discussed more fully in the final chapter. However, it might be useful here to underline, following Blumlinger, the importance of aesthetic choices in *Su tutte le vette è pace*.

The use of colour is a case in point. It has as little to do with naturalism as the soundtrack. There is an extraordinary use of yellows and reds. The diary entry by an Austrian officer at the front inspired the filmmakers to explore colours more freely. The officer, who spent four years in the

29   Ibid., 76–7.
30   Ibid., 78.

glaciers, noted that his 'eyes had changed' – 'the snow that he saw was red and the sky yellow'.[31] To achieve these effects, Gianikian and Ricci Lucchi used filters, mixing the colours themselves and experimenting as they went along. The effect is to abandon a referential code for an expressive code. The colours help to flatten the images so that landscapes lose their depth and details are eliminated. The variegated tints of pinks and yellows bear the marks of dabs and touches. Objects, people and surroundings are 're-centred against a white background'. There are scenes in which soldiers leaving tunnels seem to be swallowed up by the light. If the instability of the film itself helps to create strange smudges and blots that in one sequence literally 'wipes out' a column of soldiers, colour adds to the aesthetic strategy of destabilisation and de-familiarisation.

Oh! Uomo (Oh! Man, 2004)

Oh! Uomo was made with the same producers, historical consultants and modus operandi as the preceding two films about the First World War, completing what was now a trilogy. This time the subject is the aftermath of war. According to the original proposal for a new film presented by the filmmakers in September 2000, the focus would have been on the Alpine areas and would have dealt with the complex outcomes of the conflict, from the imposition of a nationalist agenda to the commemoration of the dead and the establishment of 'winter sports' out of the machinery of war.[32] However, the primacy given to wide-ranging historical survey and to the border region was revised once the work on the film got underway.

---

31   'Nous utilisons le archives du passé pour parler du future. Propos de Yervant Gianikian et Angela Ricci Lucchi', Interview with Vincent Vatrican in *Bref* 42 (Autumn 1999), 15.

32   'Appunti per terzo film trilogia Gianikian-Ricci Lucchi: Il dopoguerra'; Private archive of Diego Leoni.

A series of faxes to Diego Leoni report on Gianikian and Ricci Lucchi's findings in the Vienna film archives: 'Hunger – adults rifle through
bins in search of food; children search the ground for things to eat after
the market; people eat sitting on the ground or walking. In a square women
distribute food from large pots to children'. 'Sickness: children in hospital
ill with tuberculosis, rickets, scrofula, malnutrition, bellies and necks swollen, they can't stand upright ... A procession passes of little cripples, lame
and mutilated children' (12 November 2001).[33] These discoveries – the
above descriptions almost exactly match footage used in *Oh! Uomo* – may
well have led Gianikian and Ricci Lucchi to concentrate their research on
the effects of the war on the bodies of survivors. Evidence of the terrible
famine in the Volga region of the Ukraine in 1921 shows children in the
last stages of the struggle for life. Skeletal figures crawl on the ground to
find grains of corn or curl up in a foetus-position in readiness for death.
Restored medical documentaries from archives in Bologna provide rare
Italian footage of the treatment of war wounds. The original project for
Oh! Uomo was redefined to enable a closer examination of the human
body, which, in turn, became a metaphor for the human condition in the
wake of the war.

The text at the beginning of *Oh! Uomo*, after the credit sequence, is
explicit: 'From the emblems of totalitarianism to the individual physical
reality of human suffering. Representation of man violated, brimming with
anger, on coming out of the war. An anatomical catalogue of the decon-
struction and artificial re-composition of the human body'. The inter-titles
follow suit while remaining characteristically laconic, dividing the film into
sections with reference first to the bodies of children and then to those
of veterans. The booklet that accompanies the DVD contains a series of
quotations under the heading '*Oh! Uomo*: Work Diary'[34]. There is Ludwig
Wittgenstein's diary entry for 24 October 1914 in which he writes of his
brother, Paul, who has lost his arm at the front. Paul, a concert pianist,
subsequently commissioned several compositions for music for the left

33   Private archive of Diego Leoni.
34   *Oh! Uomo* DVD (2004), unnumbered booklet.

hand from Ravel, Richard Strauss and Prokofiev, among others. An extract dealing with the experience of being in a military hospital from Robert Musil's diary for 1916 pulls no punches in its descriptions of closeness of bodies in this confined space. The filmmakers also refer to the drawings of Georg Grosz and August Sander's photographs of war veterans and other people on the margins of society as further sources of inspiration. There is also a passage of 'popular writing' – a poem by Giovanni Pederzolli from his memoir of life at the front in which he describes the 'before' and 'after' of war through the picture of young men returning home:

> Carefree and strong they left,
> Now back, half dead;
> No arms, no legs,
> Some faces half gone.[35]

The quotations themselves function as analogues for the frames of film in the work of Gianikian and Ricci Lucchi – they are fragments from a shattered world, parts of a dismembered body. They also help to situate *Oh! Uomo* in a web of intertextuality. Attention is drawn to the sources from which Giovanna Marini's songs derive their words – Pederzolli's memoir, Musil's Diary. On the other hand, they reference literary and artistic figures who were not only victims of the war but who documented its consequences for individual lives. In response to a question about cinematic influences, Ricci Lucchi replied: 'We like to think that our films refer back more to painting and literature than to the history of cinema'. She went on to mention Goya's *Disasters of War*, Pieter Bruegel's *The Parable of the Blind Leading the Blind*, and Bosch's work as key points of reference for

---

35   Eran partiti, giullivi, e forti,
      Ora ritornano, sono quasi morti;
      Chi senza gambe, chi senza braccia,
      Chi fracassata, l'intera faccia.
      Ibid.

them.[36] She adds that the title of *Oh! Uomo* was taken from a poem by Georg Trakl.[37]

The structure of *Oh! Uomo*, as in their other films, is not given by a narrative or chronology. The first part opens with the inter-title 'VICTORY! From the pilgrimages and celebrations on the battlefields in the 1920s and 30s to the "humanitarian" colonial war in Ethiopia'. Using footage mainly shot or collected by Luca Comerio, scenes include an open air mass and parades in Trento – scenes that are subsequently repeated in negative, transforming the already slow motion film into a ghostly return. Footage in negative of skiers burst onto the screen – white phantoms against the dark snowscape. The shadows of the skiers – white forms that double those on the crest above – create a world of spectres. The easily recognisable profile of Mussolini on horseback hand raised in a Roman salute serves to remind us that Fascism arose from the ashes of war. War is everywhere – the skies are filled with planes, aerial bombardment is unleashed on North Africa.

The virtuoso collage of this first part contrasts with the footage that follows in which signs of manipulation and editing are minimised. There are then two main parts: one dedicated to children with the inter-titles 'The body of the child: Austria 1917', and 'The body of the child: Russia 1921', and the subsequent one dedicated to former soldiers with the inter-title 'The body of the soldier'. The footage of the Russian famine was shot by cameramen working with Dziga Vertov's Kino-Pravda organisation. The images – corpses in heaps, a child seeking to feed from the breast of a dead mother, a horse too weak to stand up, and children reduced to skin

---

36 Paolo Mereghetti, '*Oh! Uomo*', *Corriere della Sera* (20 May 2004). The persistence of certain images over the centuries is noted by Geoff Dyer. He sees 'visible through the palimpsest' of the painting *Gassed* (1919) by John Singer Sargent and Sean Smith's photograph for the Guardian of blind-folded Iraqi prisoners being led by an American soldier, the figures of Pieter Bruegel's *The Parable of the Blind Leading the Blind*; see www.guardian.co.uk/artanddesign/2010/nov/13/geoff-dyer-photograph-decade; accessed 22 November 2010.

37 'The formal beauty of his poetry is often in conflict with the violence and ugliness of many of its images. This gives it a tension and a modernity which has ensured its survival and resonance'; *Georg Trakl Poems and Prose*, trans. Alexander Stillmark (London: Libris, 2001).

and bone waiting for death – are very hard to watch. The original Soviet film unit conceived the footage as propaganda in which shots of the plight of the children are inter-cut with scenes of Orthodox Church rituals.[38] Re-edited by Gianikian and Ricci Lucchi, the children stare at the audience, leaving no place to hide. A similar operation is carried out on the medical documentaries with children filmed for the Austrian authorities and those of veterans undergoing plastic surgery and rehabilitation in the Italian hospital.

The genre of the medical documentary at this time was largely informed by a Positivist outlook – an outlook that saw the body principally as a machine. Photography, and subsequently film, were given the role of aiding in the work of measuring and classifying bodies for institutional and scientific purposes, as seen earlier in the work of Cesare Lombroso. For the medical film, the individual was of interest as a specimen or type that presented a particular condition. The intervention of Gianikian and Ricci Lucchi, however, transformed the shot of a 'type' or 'specimen' into a kind of moving-image portrait. This process can be seen in the part dedicated to the body of the soldier. Footage showing men suffering from shellshock and then of men who have undergone facial surgery has been re-filmed. In the original films, only the surgeons and doctors would have been named and the inter-titles would have outlined their achievements. The soldiers, who featured in the film, went unidentified, unless by military insignia. In *Oh! Uomo*, the medical professionals and inter-titles are cut out, and the images are re-framed. The speed of the film is slowed down through step printing.[39] Spectators find themselves, as a result, faced with men who look out from the screen at them for a length of time that requires us to acknowledge their presence and remember their faces. The gallery of figures maintains the sequence of 'one man after another' but invests each image with a presence that is disturbing and immediate. Roland Barthes

---

38   The images appear in Cine-Pravda no. 1 (June 1922); see Jeremy Hicks, *Dziga Vertov: Defining Documentary Film* (London: I.B. Tauris, 2007), 6–7.

39   This account of the making of *Oh! Uomo* is based on the Q&A session with the filmmakers following a screening at Harvard Film Archive, 17.04.09.

wrote that the problem with film, as opposed to photography, was that the
'pose is swept away and denied by the continuous series of images'.[40] But
here it seems that Gianikian and Ricci Lucchi have managed to reinvest the
moving images with some of the qualities of the still. At the same time, the
film shows only what it, the moving image, can show, or rather what only
the slowly moving image can show – the involuntary twitches and tics of
the men in front of the camera, and the pauses between those movements.
The very attempts by the ex-combatants to quell the spasms show bodies at
war with themselves – veritable embodiments of the memory of the war.[41]
The film gives back time to the images.

The second sequence demonstrates the results of a plastic surgery still
in its infancy. Here subjects turn their heads to left and right as well as
looking directly to camera. Some men insert a prosthetic device that sub-
stitutes a missing part, such as a lower jaw or cheek, and others have artificial ears and noses moulded into shape. They struggle to follow off-screen
directions. One after another the horrific disfigurements are recorded on
film. The images recall the gallery of the war wounded in Ernst Friedrich's
War against War, a book that denounced war by showing images that had
been censored by the press and government after 1918.[42] But whereas Friedrich juxtaposed images to create montages in which the stunted arm of
the worker at his machine was placed next to a photograph of the Kaiser
stretching his arm to play a tennis shot, Gianikian and Ricci Lucchi avoid
explicit political messages. The relationship of inter-title to image is never
didactic, and the soundtrack is never mimetic of the image track.

40   Roland Barthes, *Camera Lucida: Reflections on Photography*, trans. Richard Howard
      (New York: Hill and Wang, 1981), 78.
41   'What was it that these physicians saw?' asks Jay Winter, 'we know something from
      the training films. The disturbing character of these images lay in the body of the
      sufferer and in the gaze of the onlooker. Together they (we) share embodied memory
      [...] There are war stories too in the tremors of a man whose walking is not under
      control'; Winter, *Remembering War*, 55–6.
42   First published in 1924 with texts in three languages as *Krieg dem Kriege* in Germany
      with a dedication to 'To those who plan battles – to those who lead battles – to war
      enthusiasts of all countries'; Ernst Friedrich, *War against War* (Seattle: Real Comet
      Press, 1987).

The sequence of *Oh! Uomo* that uses footage of an eye operation and of blind veterans in an institution shows the uncompromising nature of Gianikian and Ricci Lucchi as filmmakers. Spectators are confronted with the close-up of an eyelid that is opened with tweezers by a disembodied hand before the remaining tissue is extracted from the empty socket. A trickle of blood is wiped away. As if it were the same patient (a trick of montage), a glass eye is inserted and 'looks' to left and right as directed. The original training film has been transformed using the optical printer. The eye has now been placed at the centre of the screen in close-up. A film about surgery has become a defining scene in a film about looking (and not looking), a film that pivots around the relationship of the eye and the body. The sequence clearly alludes to the opening shots of *Un Chien Andalou* (1928) in which a razor blade cuts through an eyeball and a cloud cuts across the moon.[43] There is an element of homage here to Surrealist film's assault on the rationalist all-seeing eye. However, the filmmakers are making nothing up; 'we are not interested in fiction', they say, 'but in the complexity of reality, even when it comes in the form of propaganda that we seek to take apart'.[44] For them, the material has potential unimagined by the original cameramen and commissioning bodies: 'they are really upsetting images that have reached us without passing through the filter of censorship. They were useful to the doctors as documentation. The films were not meant to be shown in public'.[45] The difficulty of looking at an eye operation is matched throughout *Oh! Uomo* by other scenes observed by the mechanical eye of the camera that are similarly unwatchable, such as those of children starving or in pain. There is the look to camera that is directly aligned to the look of the audience, a haunting example of which is reproduced on the cover of the booklet and DVD of *Oh! Uomo* – a child looks down and looks up, looks down and looks up, a child near death's door.

43　See Rees, *A History of Experimental Film and Video*, 48–9; Curtis, *Experimental Cinema*, 30–1; Steven Shaviro, *The Cinematic Body* (Minneapolis and London: Minnesota University Press, 2006), 54.

44　Ilario Belloni, 'Memorie d'archivio contro la guerra. Intevista a Yervant Gianikian e Angela Ricci Lucchi', http://www.jgcinema.org/pages/view.php?cat=articoli_dossier&id=90&id_film=40&id_dossier=16; accessed 6 March 2009.

45　Mereghetti, '*Oh! Uomo*', *Corriere della Sera*.

The condition of blindness has historically raised questions about what it means to see in ways that go beyond the physiological. There is something particularly disturbing about looking at footage of the blind that triggers an equivalent unease to that felt when watching a blind person walking along the street. We can see them but they cannot see us. Sensory awareness is heightened in *Oh! Uomo* by the slow motion that accentuates the deliberate movements and gestures of the blind. A scene of men following one another under the guidance of nurses towards a door – they enter and leave the frame from right to left – resembles a slightly awkward dance in which the figures struggle to keep up with the flow. The minimal and irregular percussive sounds of Luis Agudo's composition contributes to this effect of fragility and vulnerability.[46] Yet when there is footage of blind veterans playing mandolins seated on benches in a garden, there is no musical accompaniment. We hear the silence. We listen with our bodies.[47]

In 2003, one year before the release of *Oh! Uomo*, Susan Sontag published *Regarding the Pain of Others*, a book whose arguments appeared to the filmmakers to be questioning their approach to making films about war and violence. For Sontag, images documenting atrocity and suffering had become another consumer product not unlike pornography. She wrote: 'Perhaps the only people with the right to look at images of suffering of this extreme order are those who could do something to alleviate it – say, surgeons at the military hospital, or those who could learn from it. The rest of us are voyeurs, whether or not we mean to be [...] In each instance, the gruesome invites us to be either spectators or cowards unable to look'.[48] Sontag's text is uneven and sometimes contradictory. She makes a case for the photography of war as well as arguing that photographs often serve to substitute rather than enhance memory. She attributes to painting a power to move and communicate that is denied to photography-based media, but she also maintains that it is through written language, notably literature, that explanation and critical understanding are really made possible.

---

46   Luis Agudo, composer and musician, whose *Cicatrice* is used for the soundtrack of *Oh! Uomo*; see www.redrec.net/agudo.html; accessed 17 December 2009.

47   There are other moments of silence in *Oh! Uomo* in which the image suggests sound while there is none on the soundtrack: when the bell tolls in the opening section; when children in pain cry in the hospital.

48   Susan Sontag, *Regarding the Pain of Others* (London: Penguin, 2003), 38.

The importance of looking at images of war and confronting how violence was (and is) used lies at the heart of Gianikian and Ricci Lucchi's work. On the many occasions on which they have presented their films, they have told audiences of the moral obligation to look horror in the face. Before showing a clip of *Oh! Uomo* at a conference at Tate Modern on the archive and film, the filmmakers asked for the audience to 'have the same courage in watching as we had in the four years making this film'.[49] Reviews of *Oh! Uomo* frequently highlight audience reactions: 'While the images came up on the screen only the breathing, and sometimes the gasps, of the spectators could be heard, occasionally interrupted by Giovanna Marini's music – a sort of submerged wail' (*La Stampa*);[50] 'The first rows of the public at the Quinzaine emptied, cut down by the lethal cannon-shot of an eye surgically removed' (*L'Unità*);[51] 'Take a Festival-goer. Exploit him to the utmost. Allow him to marinate for ten days in a mixture of sun, screen, spicy sauce and gin fizz. Stop him sleeping. Break him down. Drive him mad, blind, impotent, and insane. Demolish his nerves. Scalp him, tear his nails out. Wait for the dawn of the 11th day, when his eyelids are finally burnt, his brain melted down [...] He is ready. Now the latest Gianikian film can start' (*Libération*).[52] For Gianikian and Ricci Lucchi the film is not about a war remote in time but about the wars being waged in the world today. Just as yesterday the dead were remembered and celebrated while the mutilated and seriously wounded were forgotten or hidden away, so it is now, they say. In the words of *Il Manifesto*: '*Oh! Uomo* is the children of Rafah or of Bagdad, the violence of the army of occupation in Palestine, in Iraq, and it is Rwanda, Sarajevo'.[53]

The injunction to the artist from Leonardo da Vinci to be 'literally pitiless' in painting battle scenes and to be ready to appal onlookers with the *terribilità* of the images is cited with approval by Sontag. Leonardo da

49   Angela Ricci Lucchi speaking, with Yervant Gianikian, at the conference 'Anticipating the Past: Artists: Archive: Film' at Tate Modern, 12–13 May 2006; audio-tapes in Tate Research Library.

50   Marco Belpoliti, 'La Storia cancellata', *La Stampa* (13 February 2006).

51   Enrico Ghezzi, *L'Unità* (22 May 2004).

52   Philippe Azoury, '*Oh! Uomo* – L'oeil scalpel. Le documentaire hypnotique des Gianikian', *Libération* (22 May 2004).

53   *Il Manifesto* (22 May 2004).

Vinci is also quoted by Gianikian and Ricci Lucchi in the opening texts after the credits in *Oh! Uomo*: 'Are you as wise as you think you are? Are these things that should be done to men?'[54] The reference deliberately places their own work in the context of the history of art and the history of human inquiry and self-examination. The horror and the *terribilità* are to be thought through, but the thinking cannot be indifferent. Ricci Lucchi, speaking of wars, observed: 'artists have only their work with which to protest and show these things.'[55]

Two Installations: *Topografia aerea* (Aerial Topography, 2007) and *Trittico del novecento* (Triptych of the Twentieth Century, 2006)

When *Oh! Uomo* was nearing completion, Gianikian and Ricci Lucchi received two commissions for installations in Rovereto – one from the National War Museum, which had co-produced the war trilogy, and one from the Museum of Modern and Contemporary Art (MART). For the first, they made a short film, *Topografia aerea* (Aerial Topography), which is based on Italian aerial reconnaissance footage shot in the First World War, for a new exhibition area in the museum dedicated to the war in the air.[56] For MART, the filmmakers reworked archival footage of the kind that they had been working on for at least a decade. The resulting installation consisted of video images on tall panels located in the newly refurbished galleries devoted to the permanent collection of twentieth-century art.

54   'Chi ti pare, omo, qui della tua specie? Se tu così savio, come tu ti tieni? Sono queste cose da esser fatte a omini?'
55   Angela Ricci Luchi at the conference 'Anticipating the Past: Artists: Archive: Film'.
56   The new commission was preceded by a major research project on aerial reconnaissance photography in the Trentino; see *La macchina di sorveglianza: La ricognizione aerofotografica italiana e austriaca sul Trentino, 1915–1918* (Rovereto: Nicoledi Editore, 2001) with preface by Diego Leoni.

Trittico del novecento (Triptych of the Twentieth Century) was meant to provide a history in images.[57] The installations mark, on the one hand, the completion of a cycle of films concerned primarily with the First World War, and, on the other, a new direction in the work of Gianikian and Ricci Lucchi that grew out of work for the Venice Biennale of 2000 in which they exhibited *La marcia dell'uomo* (see Chapter 5). The installations, moreover, throw into relief the different and sometimes contradictory expectations of them on the part of institutions and spectators. Whereas the National War Museum gives priority to historical documentation, conservation, and education, the Museum of Modern and Contemporary Art is concerned principally with the presentation of its collection and exhibitions with an emphasis on aesthetics.[58]

Topografia aerea is projected onto a wall of the museum next to the newly restored Nieuport 10, a two-seater bi-plane armed with a Lewis gun that entered service in 1915. The Nieuport is suspended from the ceiling and the visitor can watch the black and white images of the aerial film through its wings. The footage, shot by a cameraman taking the place of the machine-gunner or by a camera fixed to the wing, shows the Alpine topography of mountains and valleys over which the opposing armies were fighting for control. The images are not always clear, the filmmakers explain.[59] Flying at an attitude of about 5,000 metres for safety, clouds occasionally blot out shots, and sometimes the lens fogs over. It is possible to recognise torrents, valleys, and high plateaus without habitation or roads. The shadow of the pines suggests it is late afternoon. Lower down, on a promontory there is a road, a fortification, a defensive line with its distinct geometry. This fort is probably the reason for the reconnaissance flight.[60]

57   Gabriella Belli, director of MART; interview with the author, 18 September 2008.
58   Francesco Bonami included *Cesare Lombroso. Sull'odore del garofano* in the exhibition, */Italics/ Arte italiana fra tradizione e rivoluzione, 1968–2008* held at Palazzo Grassi in Venice, 27 September 2008 to 22 March 2009. It was projected so that principal staircase formed an auditorium for the often ghoulish images whose spectators also numbered the eighteenth-century ladies and gentlemen of leisure pictured on the wall frescoes.
59   Yervant Gianikian and Angela Ricci Lucchi, *Topografia aerea* (Rovereto: Edizioni Osiride, 2008).
60   Ibid.

The images give a vivid impression of war as seen 'from above'. The 'high verticals' give a point of view in which the landscape is flattened out and starts to resemble a map.[61] There is no soundtrack, no engine-noise or the sound. To get some idea of how to interpret the images historically it is important to read the text in which Gianikian and Ricci Lucchi use diaries and letters to reconstruct the thinking and outlook of the airmen as well as their missions. Descriptions of aerial combat and reconnaissance work are juxtaposed to passages full of calculations of flight-times, altitudes, distances, and descriptions of enemy aircraft. Images of men jumping to avoid being burnt alive and accounts of expeditions to collect trophies amid charred human remains sit next to accumulations of technical information. There is little explicit analysis as such. The analysis is in the montage. Death is presented with indifference. Technology creates a visual spectacle and a distance from what is seen. Yet the modern aviator does not hesitate to race by car to the downed enemy plane to extract souvenirs as his warrior ancestors had done before him.

In trench-warfare, the eye struggles to see. Experience is overwhelmingly tactile. It is the world of the tunnel and the trench. This 'Landscape of the First World War' is traversed in the film trilogy, say Gianikian and Ricci Lucchi, 'by land', at ground level.[62] With the war in the air, the eye is sovereign and enjoys a panoptic vision.[63] This different view of the landscape of war is what the filmmakers discovered in making *Topografia aerea*. The full implications of this discovery are only touched on at this stage. It is as if Gianikian and Ricci Lucchi are themselves engaged in reconnaissance,

---

61   The appreciation of military photographs as works of art revealed an 'unqualified beautification of warfare'. According to Sekula, the responses elicited by aerial views varied considerably according to their vantage point. While "high verticals" reduced the field of vision to the abstract patterns of a planar image, "low obliques" reproduced the customary space of perspectival vision'; Davide Deriu, 'Picturing Ruinscapes: The Aerial Photograph as Image of Historical Trauma' in *The Image and the Witness*, ed. Guerin and Hallas, 191–2.

62   Gianikian and Ricci Lucchi, *Topografia aerea*, 8.

63   I owe this counter-position of the tactile and the optical to Emily Braun's observations in her paper 'Shock and Awe: The Futurist Vision of the Air' at the conference 'Shock and Awe: The Troubling Legacy of the Futurist Cult of War', Hunter College, CUNY, 11 November 2009.

making a sortie into territory yet to be mapped. The scope of the project, however, has a significant bearing on how warfare, politics and the technology of visualisation developed at this time.[64] It relates, moreover, to Gianikian and Ricci Lucchi's ongoing critique of the mythologies surrounding Futurism.[65] For them, Futurism under the leadership of F.T. Marinetti is inextricably connected to war. The idea that war brings regeneration – 'the only hygiene' – is not seen as an aberration but as part and parcel of Marinetti's ideas about art and politics. The aestheticisation of war is a mode of waging war.[66] Aerial warfare, furthermore, offers enormous possibilities for developing this 'vision' in which the spectacle was an aspect of battle and in which aerial warfare had primacy – a vision of which Italians were among the principal artificers.[67]

Trittico del novecento began as a single-screen work in 2002. Gianikian describes the work in which a passage from Erasmus – 'May it be that war is the arena and mainspring of every glorious action? Of the fallen none count' – precedes 'images of a surgical operation to a woman's brain, the only record of its kind found in the archives. It is the broken and disfigured human body that emerges from the suffering of the First World War. For us it is this image of the still open "wound" that opens the new century'.[68] A further work was added two year later headed by a citation from Baudelaire, namely 'Ai vinti' (To the Vanquished)[69] in which

---

64   The classic text is still Paul Virilio, *War and Cinema: The Logistics of Perception* (London and New York: Verso, 1989). For a brilliant cinematic inquiry, see Harun Farocki, *Images of the World, and the Inscription of the War* (1988).

65   Yervant Gianikian and Angela Ricci Lucchi speaking at the conference 'Futurism at 100: The Measure of the Century', 17–18 April 2009, Center for European Studies, Harvard University.

66   See Deriu, 'Picturing Ruinscapes: The Aerial Photograph as Image of Historical Trauma', 190–1.

67   For Giulio Douhet, author of *The Command of the Air* (1921), and the influence of Marinetti's ideas on his thinking, see David Lewis, 'On the Military History of Art: Douhet, Marinetti, and "The Command of the Air"' at the conference 'Shock and Awe: The Troubling Legacy of the Futurist Cult of War'.

68   Mereghetti and Rossin, 'Il magazzino della Storia', 24–5.

69   By chance, Susan Sontag includes '... Aux vaincus!' (Baudelaire) as an epigraph in *Regarding the Pain of Others*.

two panels around the symbolism of food and famine are counter-posed – one
cataloguing buried memories – the exodus of Armenians from Turkey during the
genocide, burials, death from exhaustion and malnutrition [...] scenes of collective
hunger in post-war Europe and shots from the 1960s in which an African child
scrabbles for sweets thrown on the ground by tourists. U.S.A. a woman operates the
latest cooker in a modern kitchen – the model of the victors.

Finally, the triptych was finished in 2008 with the addition of two further
screens under the theme 'Terrorism' with a passage taken from Montaigne:
'Every man carries within him the entire form of the human condition'.
Gianikian describes the figures in the sequences of images as figures from a
Brueghel painting – 'worn-out, beaten, failed, trodden under foot, all those
whom the hammer of poverty or wars near and far have struck down [...]
The social selection works with terrible inevitability. The fearful invasion
of ragged, starving beggars invokes anxiety. The outsiders are disturbing,
repugnant, menacing [...] People take up arms to drive out the poor from
the states, to send them back to the hell they came from, and so terrorism
is guaranteed'.[70]

At MART, the *Trittico del novecento* forms a 'kind of chapel'. There are
three pairs of screens – panels on walls in a space set slightly apart from the
entrance area of the gallery. Spectators are faced on three sides by sequences
of images on synchronised loops of about seven minutes in length. They
are free to enter and leave at will, to watch one screen and then another,
or to switch between them. The installation does not impose the limits of
duration and viewing position typical of the cinema with its darkened auditorium. Spectators can look at the moving images in much the same way
as they look at a fresco in a church or a painting in a gallery. How exactly
visitors to MART have responded to *Trittico del novecento* is a matter for
speculation. It can be said, however, that the filmmakers have adapted
their work to the new format without compromises. There is no attempt
to engage the spectator in narrative or to edit out disturbing images. Nor
do the filmmakers resort to any of the strategies that characterise historical

70   The text is in the leaflet produced by MART for the inauguration of *Trittico del
      novecento*.

documentaries. There is no soundtrack. If anything the hypnotic effect of slowing down the flow of images is enhanced by the continual repetition of the loop. The hare in *Ai vinti* zigzags across the open field to escape and runs again and again into the waiting net. The installation stands as a reminder not only of a history of cruelty and suffering but of the place of art in describing and reflecting on that experience.

CHAPTER 5

Fascism, Colonialism: Film and Installations

The white man possesses a quality that has enabled him to make his way: disrespect. The white man allows nothing to block his way.

— HENRI MICHAUX[1]

Many Europeans concerned to forget that past [the Holocaust] look to a future which focuses on Europe and discard uncomfortable memories of colonialism. Perhaps before we can embark on the construction of new myths we need to do some 'memory work' on the legacy of Empire.

— CATHERINE HALL[2]

In the poster of the film *Dal Polo all'Equatore* – the artwork is by Angela Ricci Lucchi – words and tiny figures dart from the central nucleus of the globe and carry shots, sequences, and mini-narratives in all directions. Most of the sketches refer to moments in the film but others to footage that would later constitute the basis for new shorts. In them the theme of Fascism was to be especially evident, notably in *Archivi italiani n. 1. Il fiore della razza* (Italian Archives No. 1. The Flower of the Race, 1991), and *Animali criminali* (Criminal Animals, 1994). These films, together with *Lo specchio di Diana* (The Mirror of Diana, 1996), show aspects of Fascism from the 1920s and 1930s. The filmmakers worked both on official

---

1   'L'homme blanc possède une qualité qui lui fait faire du chemin: "l'irrespect". Le Blanc ne se laisse arrêter par rien'; Henri Michaux, *Un barbare en Inde* (1933); *A barbarian in Asia*, trans. Sylvia Beach (New York: New Directions, 1949), 8.
2   Catherine Hall, 'Histories, Empires and the Post-Colonial Moment' in *The Postcolonial Question: Common Skies, Divided Horizons*, ed. Iain Chambers and Lidia Curti (London: Routledge, 1996), 66.

propaganda footage and on amateur films that document private life at the time. It was Fascism, a direct consequence of the First World War, that Gianikian and Ricci Lucchi were hoping to work on after the completion of *Oh! Uomo*. They had expected to do so by extending the collaboration with the historians and museums of Rovereto and Trento into a new phase. Due to various difficulties, such as the withdrawal of financial support by the regional government, the plans did not materialise.

The proposal of Gianikian and Ricci Lucchi for the third film, later to become *Oh! Uomo*, contains a number of pointers to the way the war trilogy might have led into films concerning Fascism and Nazism. On the basis of archival research, the following scenes were envisaged: 'Celebrations of a Mass in memory of the "defeat" at Innsbruck. In the open air ex-soldiers wear the traditional costumes of the Tyrol ... Military elements hidden in folklore'; 'Revisiting the sites of battles, the new frontiers, groups, parties and processions of ex-soldiers in a new uniform, in black shirts, "return"'; 'The remains of the fallen are collected, graves on the edges of the battle grounds. Large cemeteries and ossuaries are built. The architectonic forms as a warning of war and symbols of victory and power of the new regime'; 'Filming of sporting documentaries that inaugurate the new cinematographic style of Alpine heroism of Fanck, Riefensthal, Trenker, as with Fascism and Nazism'; 'Tourism and home movies in the Alps, "reconsacrated conquests".[3] The project brings together the commemoration of war, 'reconsacrated' landmarks, family, political ideology, and cinema.

In 2005, shortly after finishing *Oh! Uomo*, Gianikian and Ricci Lucchi came up with another film proposal with the title *Paese Barbaro* which gives an insight into how the filmmakers carried with them a storehouse of images and ideas waiting to be put to use: 'Unknown found film belonging to an Italian engineer in Ethiopia. Images that have not been touched, there is no editing, they are in the same sequence as in the shooting. Sequences of aerial mapping of the territory, the loading of mustard gas onto bombers, the use of which has always been denied. They show its effects on dead

---

3   'Appunti per terzo film trilogia Gianikian-Ricci Lucchi: Il dopoguerra'.

animals'.[4] The violence of colonialism depicted in *Dal Polo all'Equatore* anticipated not only the brutalisation and inhumanity unleashed by the First World War but the full development of those tendencies in Fascism. In turn, Fascism gave fresh impetus to colonialist activity and propaganda.[5] In their work, Gianikian and Ricci Lucchi continued to pursue their preoccupation with empire and the imperial imaginary.

When large commissions were lacking, Gianikian and Ricci Lucchi continued to make short films. The shorts have been brought together in programmes under headings with titles such as 'archives' or 'fragments'. For the purposes of this study, the films made over two decades when the filmmakers were not fully engaged on feature-length films are organised into two broad thematic groups, 'On Fascism' and 'On Empire'.

A third category concerns films that deal with war in the Balkans – *Nocturne* (1997) and *Inventario balcanico* (Balkan Inventory, 2000). The Balkans is a region where the disintegration of empire and the rise of nationalism have led to recurrent wars. In common with other border regions, the Balkans has seen both peaceful coexistence and endemic conflict. In the films of Gianikian and Ricci Lucchi such areas feature strongly, for example the Trentino and Armenia. The filmmakers are attracted to certain parts of the world, and they, in turn, have accumulated, researched, and recycled a geography of images from the early twentieth century. Theirs is a cinema in which geography and history are endlessly superimposed on one another, creating a dense layering of images. The *oeuvre* as a whole, moreover, is formed of layers with recurrent motifs so that cumulatively it gives the impression of a single unfolding work rather than with a multitude of single films.

4   *Paese Barbaro*; private archive of Diego Leoni.
5   See Ruth Ben-Ghiat, *Fascist Modernities: Italy, 1922–45* (Berkeley: University of California Press, 2001); *A Place in the Sun: Africa in Italian Colonial Culture from Post-Unification to the Present*, ed. Patrizia Palumbo (Los Angeles and London: University of California Press, 2003).

On Fascism

The memory of Fascism is present in Gianikian and Ricci Lucchi's films from an early stage, from the mid-1970s. In a work that belongs to the cycle of *cinema profumato*, *Catalogo n. 3. Odore di tiglio intorno alla casa* (Catalogue No. 3 Smell of Lime Trees Around the House, 1976), the filmmakers assembled a visual catalogue of the contents of a house whose occupants had been militant Fascists. The men were summarily shot in the aftermath of the Second World War.[6] They had been ardent followers of Mussolini, a portrait of whom is in the house – it shows him with plaster on this nose, a photograph taken shortly after an assassination attempt. Objects in the house are filmed as the camera pans slowly across walls and furniture: pictures of the sons in army uniform in Tripoli, bare-breasted African women – the latter photograph is juxtaposed to an image of the Madonna. The camera lingers on the texture of fabrics and embroidery, on stains. This 8mm silent film in colour was shot over successive summer evenings when the light fell on the table in the living room. It recreates an atmosphere of haunting, of *Unheimlichkeit*, in a house in which the objects are the only inhabitants, left undisturbed after the family abandoned it when a suicide compounded its tragic wartime history. The scent of lime (linden) in flower – released during screenings – was the scent from the trees outside the house that filled the air. Gianikian and Ricci Lucchi spent a week in the house in order to shoot the film, which was edited in camera.[7] The whole enterprise gives a vivid picture of their abiding fascination with place, objects, smells, and the cues to memory. There are also already signs of their concern for the dark side of Italian history that is examined in later work, including an interest in Fascism in its domestic manifestations.

---

6   The *resa dei conti* (settling of accounts), which was especially widespread in Emilia Romagna, constituted a particularly dark episode in Italian history in and after 1945, the memory of which was often repressed or suppressed; see John Foot, *Fratture d'Italia: Da Caporetto al G8 di Genova, la memoria divisa del paese* (Milan: Rizzoli, 2009), 353–4.

7   Yervant Gianikian and Angela Ricci Lucchi; conversation with the author, 8 December 2009.

The photograph of Mussolini in *Catalogo n. 3. Odore di tiglio intorno alla casa* brings to mind the way iconic images of the dictator appear in the *oeuvre*: in *Dal Polo all'Equatore* footage of Mussolini in horseback shot in Tripoli in 1926; in the first part *Oh! Uomo* again on horseback at a parade in Rome; in *Ghiro, ghiro tondo* (2007) a figurine from the 1930s giving the Roman salute. Instantly recognisable, the profile of Mussolini functions as a mnemonic that reminds spectators of politics and history.[8]

A more sustained treatment of the cult of Mussolini is found in *Lo specchio di Diana*. This thirty-minute video draws on documentary footage in Comerio's archive, though it is unlikely that Comerio himself was the cameraman responsible. The film recorded the recovery of Roman galleys from the Lake of Nemi – a major archeological project designed to associate the Fascist regime with the power of the Roman Empire.[9] An inter-title of 1928 found with the material declares: 'Unique and solemn monument that records the skill of the Romans in the construction of the warships with which Rome launched its conquest of the empire and with which it maintained its domination for centuries'.[10] Once the water level of the lake was lowered using pumps – a feat of engineering and labour celebrated in the footage – the propaganda opportunities were fully exploited with crowds of young women in local costumes bearing wild strawberries gathered to greet Mussolini on his official visit to the historic site. The documentary film does its work as propaganda by showing the cooperation of workers of hand and brain, the leadership of Fascist officials, and, finally, the charisma of the Duce himself. However, in the hands of Gianikian and Ricci Lucchi, the images acquire altogether more sinister connotations. The narrative of the conquest of Nature and the affirmation of power becomes

8   Luisa Passerini, *Mussolini immaginario* (Laterza: 1991); *Against Mussolini: Art and the Fall of a Dictator*, ed. Christopher Duggan, Stephen Gundle and Giuliana Pieri (London: Estorick Gallery, 2010).

9   See Ann Thomas Wilkins, 'Augustus, Mussolini, and the Parallel Imagery of Empire' in *Donatello among the Blackshirts: History and Modernity in the Visual Culture of Fascist Italy*, ed. Claudia Lazzaro and Roger J. Crum (Ithaca and London: Cornell University Press, 2005): 53–66.

10   Yervant Gianikian and Angela Ricci Lucchi, 'La nostra camera analitica' in *Cinema Anni Vita*, 49.

that of the desecration of a sacred place and the unleashing of destructive forces. The use of slow motion and the soundtrack by Keith Ullrich rends the emptying of the lake strange and disturbing in keeping with the title and captions that refer to the cult of Diana as described in the pages of Frazer's *Golden Bough*.[11] The second part of the film, using footage of the military campaign in Tripoli in 1926, underlines Fascism's readiness to use any means, including chemical weapons banned under the Geneva Convention, against the indigenous population.

The figure of Mussolini, however, is but the most recognisable face of Fascism. For Gianikian and Ricci Lucchi, Fascism is not only manifested in public discourse but in everyday objects and images that penetrate households and homes. Nor is Fascism exclusively identified with a period, a leader, or a particular nation. The phenomena can and do recur over time, and are found in private as well as public spaces.

Archivi italiani n. 1. Il fiore della razza uses footage from the Luca Comerio archive to examine sport in the discourse of Fascism: '"Sport" is the first chapter in the series of Italian Archives, moving between public and private spheres in the Fascist era', write Gianikian and Ricci Lucchi, 'the compilation is a celebration of national character. An ironic montage of the celebration of the "race", the "perfect body", and the "strong heart" in the shots of aviators, racing drivers, motorcyclists, swimmers, boxers, mountain-climbers, cyclists, skiers, and footballers ... on the deep ties between the sport film and military action, and with the religious aspects of the propaganda documentary'.[12] The images are accompanied by inter-titles full of Fascist phrases, such 'the glorious flag', 'the spirit of fire', 'the field of honour', 'the sanctity of the borders', 'eternal youth'. Steel cuts through waves and Man struggles to dominate Nature.

---

11   'In antiquity', writes Fraser, 'this sylvan landscape was the scene of a strange and recurring tragedy [...] Such was the rule of the sanctuary. A candidate for the priesthood could only succeed to office by slaying the priest, and having slain him, he retained office until he himself was slain by a stronger or a craftier'; James Gordon Frazer, *The Golden Bough: A Study in Magic and Religion* (London: Macmillan, 1929), 1–9.

12   Yervant Gianikian and Angela Ricci Lucchi, '*Archivi italiani n. 1. Il fiore della razza*' in *Yervant Gianikian, Angela Ricci Lucchi*, ed. Toffetti, 125.

Animali criminali[13] deals with a similar view of the world. In a series
of *tableaux vivants*, animals are placed one in front of another to illustrate
how in Nature every relationship is essentially between hunter and prey, life
and death, in a ferocious struggle for existence. The camera in Comerio's
footage watches as frog eats worm, as snake swallows frog, as anaconda
swallows a pig. There are scenes of a cockfight and insect combat. Sometimes a hand is shown manipulating the situation. The philosophy at work
is reminiscent of that of Cesare Lombroso for whom human society, like
Nature, is organised on the principle of the survival of the fittest. After the
title sequence there is text taken from Diderot: 'Oh Nature where is your
providence, where is your goodness in having armed animals, species against
species, and man against all'. The filmmakers make the images reveal the
manipulation and the spectacle as a sign of the camera's collusion. *Animali
criminali*, moreover, exemplifies the way that Gianikian and Ricci Lucchi
use human attitudes towards and treatment of animals as a metaphor for
how life and death are understood in society.

Made almost two decades later, *Ghiro ghiro tondo* (Around and Around,
2007) shows Gianikian and Ricci Lucchi returning to practices typical of an
earlier stage in their filmmaking.[14] The film uses objects not found footage
and these are filmed in a way that is very similar to that adopted for *Cesare
Lombroso. Sull'odore del garofano* in which objects are catalogued 'one after
another'. The chosen objects are all toys. At first sight, they appear as just
that, toys. Toys that are presented to camera in different combinations:
singly, in pairs, in groups that are identical, in groups of a type, in *tableaux*,
in piles. Different combinations are shot from different angles, from the
close-up to the high vertical, so that a catalogue of shots is compiled along

---

13   A clip of *Animali criminali* can be seen on the Arte website: www.arte.tv/fr/recher-
      che/925192.html; accessed 30 August 2010.
14   The title *Ghiro, ghiro tondo* might allude to the children's rhyme: 'Giro giro tondo/
      Tutti intorno al mondo/Casca il mondo/Casca la terra/Tutti giù per terra' (Spin,
      spin in a circle, the world falls down, the ground falls down; all down on the ground);
      the equivalent in English is the rhyme 'Ring a Ring O' Roses'.

with catalogue of objects. Sometimes the doll – dolls proliferate[15] – farm animal, or spinning-top have to be taken out of wrapping-paper or a box. A hand sometimes carefully holds, opens, nudges and handles them with the maximum of respect.[16] Mechanisms are activated, birds peck, tops spin, dolls blink their big eyes. The individual item is first shown slightly out of focus, and then sharply defined, as if replicating the process whereby the eye looks. The camera is hand-held. Occasional rustling or the noise of an animal that is squeezed accompanies the images. The video images are in colour and the bright colours of the toys offer a visual feast.[17] There is a simple pleasure in watching the display. Every kind of material is used – a handwritten list accompanies the title sequence: *papier mâché*, wax, rubber, wood, tin, plaster, biscuit, wool, silk, cellulose. The spectator is led to ask: 'is there a secret plan, a web of meaning, that is hidden by apparent obviousness and directness of the film?'

The inclusion of the figurine of Mussolini in the closing sequence of *Ghiro ghiro tondo* might alert spectators to insidious ideologies that have infiltrated the playroom but the watchful will already have noticed disturbing signs earlier on – the number of board-games dedicated to warfare at sea and in the colonies; the toy soldiers; racial types; the yellow Star of David. These items in the collection are mixed up with the mass of seemingly innocent toys. But what is unnerving is the conjunction of the uncanny of Surrealist inspiration with an imagery of catastrophe and massacre. The dolls stare at us, the horses gallop, the man chops wood – the inanimate come alive. Many dolls, animals and other objects are lucky to have survived. Faces are broken, limbs detached, eyes out of their sockets.

15   The filmmakers speak of the fascination in dolls of Bellmer, Victor Hugo, Benjamin, and, Kokoschka, who 'after the First War had a life-size and life-like doll made resembling his beloved. He had been seriously wounded and feared he had lost his virility'; Mereghetti and Rossin, 'Il magazzino della Storia', 119.

16   Jean Louis Schefer, 'Carrousel de jeux' in programme of *Yervant Gianikian et Angela Ricci Lucchi*, Jeu de Paume, 21 February to 19 March 2006.

17   An earlier and shorter version of the film had the title *Carrousel des jeux* (Merry-go-round of Toys, 2006); see film programme, 'Yervant Gianikian et Angela Ricci Lucchi', Jeu de Paume, 21 February to 19 March 2006.

Broken parts are gathered together. But so are whole bodies in heaps. For many spectators this spectacle would not necessarily prove disturbing. However, for anyone familiar with the other films of Gianikian and Ricci Lucchi it is hard to be unaware of dreadful catalogue of images, the murderous metamorphosis of the animate into the inanimate.

Ghiro ghiro tondo is liable to be understood very differently by different audiences. As Gianikian and Ricci Lucchi have insisted, the toys they catalogue do not come with labels and instructions on how they are to be seen. This approach is also consistent with the filmmakers' own relationship to the toys. They originally acquired them as part of the Mühlbach family collection for use in their scented film. At that time, the objects were conceived as part of an inquiry into the sense of smell, memory and the fantasy world of childhood. A historical approach to the material only came later and in the light of their work on twentieth-century film archives dealing with colonialism and war. The childhood world of the early films was never innocent or free from fear but now there was a keen sensitivity to the infiltration of Nazi and Fascist ideas into this private familial realm. In the words of Gianikian: 'the masks and objects of Lombroso and our collection of poor, worn and chipped toys are intimately connected and have something in common – a sort of morbid side that we have leant to identify and read in image only after the many years of working on the war trilogy'.[18]

War in the Balkans

War in the former Yugoslavia from March 1992 to November 1995 saw the return to Europe of ethnic cleansing, genocide, and mass displacements of population. It is estimated that there were around 200,000 deaths, 12,000 rapes, and over a million refugees from Bosnia, a majority of who were

---

18   Mereghetti and Rossin, 'Il magazzino della Storia', 119.

Muslim – the consequences of the attempt by the Yugoslav government and its allies to create an ethnically homogeneous state through violent means.[19] August 1990 also saw the first Gulf war and the inauguration of a period of continuous war involving American and European armies in former colonial territories. It was against this backdrop that Gianikian and Ricci Lucchi made *Inventario balcanico* and *Nocturne*.

The films are both historical and about the present; 'the materials push us to make connections with the present [...] Ours is a cinema of intervention (*cinema di intervento*). We made the war trilogy when there was the war in former-Yugoslavia and *Oh! Uomo* comes out of the state of permanent war in which we find ourselves today', states Gianikian.[20] The Danube, which flows through the region, is at once a fact of geography and a river of time.[21] *Inventario balcanico* opens with the words: 'a river, the people of its banks. The Danube of Mitteleuropa, Slav, Magyr, Latino, Jewish. From the Black Forest to the Black Sea. The Caucasus faces it. Another frightening river sweeps everything away, annihilates and flows onward – war'.[22] The film follows the Danube, going upstream from Zagbreb and arriving in Georgia, but the journey is discontinuous in space as well as time. Scenes from different places on the river are shot by different amateur cameramen whose footage was collected by Gianikian and Ricci Lucchi. Some of the 8mm film was shot in time of peace, in the 1920s and 1930s, and there is film shot by German soldiers engaged in military operations in the early 1940s. Landscapes of war feature in the first episode in which German soldiers are taking a break from duty, laughing and chatting in groups, and sunbathing – 'war as war, and war as a holiday', says Gianikian.[23] The images slowed and tinted a sickly yellow are accompanied by music commissioned

19   Eric D. Weitz, *A Century of Genocide: Utopias of Race and Nation* (Princeton: Princeton University Press, 2003), 234.

20   Mereghetti and Rossin, 'Il magazzino della Storia', 122.

21   The trope of the Danube in literature is clearly seen in Claudio Magris, *Danube* (New York: Farrar, Straus and Giroux, 1989).

22   Yervant Gianikian and Angela Ricci Lucchi, '*Inventario balanico*' in *Cinema Anni Vita*, 215.

23   Yervant Gianikian and Angela Ricci Lucchi; conversation with the author, 8 December 2009.

from Ullrich in which droning and throbbing sounds fluctuate and return insistently. A second episode consists of German aerial footage shot after the bombing of Belgrade, a city reduced to ruins and whose bridges have all collapsed into the river. In the third episode, *Inventario balcanico* travels back in time. Holiday footage show scenes of carnival in an Austrian village on the river with people dressed in costumes and masks. Everything is tinted red and pink. The music too has changed. The melodies and plangent notes of Djivan Gasparyan's composition for the duduk, an instrument popular in the Caucasus, Eastern Europe and the Middle East.[24] The cityscape of Sarajevo shows mosques, minarets and veiled women in the streets. The filmmakers have slowed the speed and re-framed shots in the film to create portraits of bearded Muslim men. The cameraman-cum-holidaymaker has filmed a meal on the pleasure-boat, people tasting wine at a riverside café, boys swimming, men forming a human pyramid. In Belgrade, the film fades in and out between scenes of streets, parks, monuments, historic buildings, and panoramas of the river. The images speak of a happier world. The melancholy notes of the duduk remind us, however, that it belongs to a past that has disappeared. Again footage of German soldiers take over the screen, this time showing a fieldgun in action. It is a matter-of-fact record of gunners going about their business – men load and fire the weapon while others behind them observe the shells exploding on a distant hillside through binoculars in order to better calibrate the range. Ullrich's eerie soundscape returns. Finally, *Inventario balcanico* concludes with the music of Gasparyan, an Armenian composer whose melodies 'return home' with scenes of two men engaged in a mock-battle on horseback.

Inventario balcanico is less a film about warfare than about what war has swept away, a world of which only fragments remain, not least the pictures caught in the cameras of the amateur filmmakers. Gianikian and Ricci Lucchi are not indulging in nostalgia for its own sake. The inventory they have compiled is of a society in which different peoples, religions, and ways of life coexisted along the banks of the Danube. Like the old postcards

---

24   Djivan Gasparian is an Armenian musician known as the 'Master of the duduk', a double reed woodwind instrument related to the oboe; see en.wikipedia.org/wiki/ Djivan_Gasparyan; accessed 17 December 2009.

that they resemble, the tourists' films record panorama of cities razed to the ground. If the buildings survive, then it is the people who have gone. The nostalgia is that of the refugee for 'lands left behind' for 'homelands lost after the massacres'.[25] The inventory in a sense creates memories in images that replace those who have died.

Nocturne is composed of three sections from video shot by Gianikian and Ricci Lucchi in Sarajevo in January 1995 during the siege by Serb forces, in Belgrade in May 1996, and material from Zagreb from the early 1980s where they had found old footage relating to the First World War. All the scenes take place at night. In Sarajevo a Gypsy celebration is taking place in a bar – the lights are on, despite the blackout, and women are dancing while men judge a beauty contest. The risk-taking strikes the filmmakers as an affirmation of life and sexuality in the face of war. They film through the transparent plastic divide that separates the bar from the street. The images are unclear. The video in Belgrade consists of a high-angle zoom taken from a hotel room overlooking the balconies of a distant apartment block. Again, the camera acts as a voyeur of scenes of everyday life in war-time. Men appear to be engaged in trafficking, in exactly what is unclear.[26] The spectator is likely to be confused and disorientated by footage that deliberately avoids conventional images of the Balkan conflict. There is no side to take. *Nocturne*, moreover, amounts to entries in an ongoing video diary, enigmatic and oblique.

On Empire

At the 39th Venice Biennale in 2001, Yervant Gianikian and Angela Ricci Lucchi were invited to make an installation for the section 'Plateau of Humankind' at the Arsenale. The director of the Biennale, Harald

25   Yervant Gianikian and Angela Ricci Lucchi, '*Inventario balanico*' in *Cinema Anni Vita*, 215.
26   Yervant Gianikian and Angela Ricci Lucchi; conversation with the author, 8 December 2009.

Szeemann, had been following their work, and the curators of the installation, Dominique Païni and Danièle Hibon, had just organised a retrospective of their films at the Jeu de Paume in Paris.[27] The installation,
La marcia dell'uomo/The Walk of Man, can be understood as a work that
brings together a number of the filmmakers' interests – early or so called
'primitive' cinema, the first ethnographic moving images, and the construction of a racialised Other. It constituted at the time a significant political
statement within a world of contemporary art that was opening up to
post-colonial thinking. In Stuart Hall's words, the 're-staged narrative of
the post-colonial' entails an outlook in which 'colonisation assumes the
place and significance of a major, extended and ruptural world-historical
event [...] the whole process of expansion, exploration, conquest, colonisation, and imperial hegemonisation which constituted the "outer face", the
constitutive outside of European and then Western capitalist modernity.'[28]
Debates at Documenta 11 addressed questions of imperial legacy, identity,
and art practice.[29] One of the curators, Mark Nash, saw Gianikian and Ricci
Lucchi as important artists in this perspective. They represented pioneers
in the new developments in the documentary cinema that confronted the
ethical and political imperatives of living in a world shaped by a modernity
inextricably linked from its birth to the history of empires.

La marcia dell'uomo, the full title of which includes the words – *La
marcia della conquista* (the walk/march of conquest) – is divided into three

27 'Szeemann also saw his exhibitions as an "archive in transformation". To me this was
just as representative of his approach as the fact that he worked simultaneously as an
independent curator and curator of Kunsthaus Zürich. Another important facet of
his career was the way he oscillated between large and small, private and public. After
the 1972 Documenta in Kassel, for example, there was the exhibition dedicated to
his grandfather, held in a private apartment in Bern, with no hierarchy between the
larger and the smaller show – entirely in keeping with Robert Musil's observation
that art can appear where one is least expecting it'; Hans Ulrich Obrist, www.frieze.
com/issue/article/harald_szeemann_1933_2005/; accessed 16 September 2010.

28 Stuart Hall, 'When was the "post-colonial"? Thinking at the Limit' in *The Postcolonial
Question: Common Skies, Divided Horizons*, 249.

29 See *Documenta 11_Platform 3 'Créolité and Creolization'*, ed. Okwui Enwezor, Carlos
Basualdo, Ute Meta Bauer, Susanne Ghez, Sarat Maharaj, Mark Nash and Octavio
Zaya (Ostfildern-Ruit: Hatje Cantz Publishers, 2003).

parts which are sequential both chronologically and spatially.[30] In the first space, the screen – a white dividing-wall – shows footage from 1895; in the second, from around 1910; and in the third, from the 1960s. The room is organised so that it is possible to see one set of images or to see them all simultaneously. Each loop runs for about the same length of time, about four minutes. Spectators enter at the beginning, which is also the beginning of cinema, and leave when amateur filmmaking had become a widespread activity. The installation can be visualised as a kind of 'camera' in the double sense of the word in Italian – camera as photographic device, and camera as room. Visitors who enter the installation are placed in a position analogous to that of the filmmaker who uses the 'analytical camera' to 'enter the image' and to explore the smallest details. They can get close to the images or step back and see the three loops contemporaneously. The installation, moreover, is a container for the work carried out on the archival footage – work that reveals the mechanisms of power whereby the technology serves as an instrument of the colonial gaze.

The tripartite division of *La marcia dell'uomo* is premised on the distinction between the non-racialist idea of mankind embodied in the 1895 footage and its subsequent replacement by evolutionary models. The two seconds (32 frames) of film entitled *Hommes nègres, marche* show three black men walking in profile with a white sheet as backdrop. Equivalent films shot by Regnault at Marey's Station Physiologique near Paris showed white men walking in front of black backdrops. The curators of the Venice installation write: 'Etienne-Jules Marey filmed, or rather chronophotographed, *from a distance* – from a respectful distance – and *in profile*, since man's movements are ideally represented in profile'.[31] Great hope in science and knowledge attended the birth of cinema, together with a 'taste for travel that transcended provincialism and xenophobia'. In the second area, there were projected images of West Africa in the early 20th century that are

---

30   Yervant Gianikian and Angela Ricci Lucchi, *La marcia dell'uomo* (Milan: Edizioni Mazzotta, 2001).

31   Dominique Païni and Danièle Hibon, 'Caminare, montare', ibid. (pages not numbered); in French: 'Marcher, monter', *Trafic* 38 (Summer 2001): 66–7.

described as inaugurating the era of documentary cinema and the spread of 'false' ethnography. The footage shows 'natives' dressed in top hats and bowlers, and eating at a table with knifes and folks imitating Western manners and dress. Meanwhile 'false ethnographers, armed with movie cameras, caricature the local customs of the primitive people'. The filmmakers write of the way the camera 'insinuated itself into the faces, heads, bodies, and even inner organs of those it films'.[32] Whereas in 1900 the 'native' peoples were brought to the metropolitan capitals where they were exhibited in reconstructed versions of their African villages, now the camera did the travelling and brought back the same stereotypes for cinema audiences. The camera takes possession of bodies instead of observing their movements from a respectful distance. An equivalent violation of bodily space by the camera is marked in the concluding shots of the installation *Visions du désert* (Visions of the Desert, 2000). The filmmakers comment: 'The words "Africa, a defenceless continent" appears on screen after the anxious look stolen by an invasive camera of a Algerian woman wearing a veil – the final image of the film.'[33] (See the cover of this book).

In the third part of *La marcia dell'uomo*, which is made using 8mm colour footage shot by European tourists in Africa, the lack of respect is even more manifest. Half-naked African women are filmed posing for the camera. The tourists offer money for the favour – 'the subject is considered as without feelings, something to be studied like an insect, something sexually available'.[34] Moving through the installation, spectators can be visualised as retracing the steps of those who have gone before them – the spectators behind the camera lenses who filmed the exotic Other. The installation also allows the space for those who identify with the objects of the gaze, and who see themselves being seen. The experience is not designed to be reassuring or comfortable for the Western visitor. The proximity of the images in the

---

32   Gianikian and Ricci Lucchi, *La marcia dell'uomo*.
33   Paolo Mereghetti and Federico Rossin, 'Il magazzino della Storia', 126. The Cartier Foundation in Paris held an exhibition of six artists on the theme of 'the desert' – *Visions du desert* – from 21 June to 5 November 2000; http://carreartmusee.centredoc. fr/opac/index.php?lvl=categ_see&id=31352; accessed 20 August 2010.
34   Ibid.

semi-enclosed space reinforces their power to disturb, giving a physical charge to responses. The recovery of cinema history entails the recovery of the original power of images to move, to shock, and to provoke.

The rise of post-colonial thought, the new importance of ethnography for contemporary art practice, the turn towards documentary film, and the re-engagement with political and social realities – all these developments created a receptive environment for the work of Gianikian and Ricci Lucchi at the beginning of 21st century. Film history, furthermore, was extending its reach into the long neglected archives of former colonies. Important studies of ethnographic films were examining the way Western societies had represented so called 'savage' or 'primitive' peoples as belonging to an earlier stage of human evolution, as 'without history, without writing, without technology, and without archives' – what Levi-Strauss referred to as *ethnographiable* as opposed to *historifiable*.[35]

These moving images could not be contained within a single genre, such as documentary, because, from their origins, they were at the intersection between anthropology, popular culture, and the politics of empire building. The fascination for the body of 'the Other' might have sought legitimation in science but the association of polytheism, polygamy and cannibalism with the Primitive fuelled the erotic gaze and the eroticisation of the exotic within the wider culture.[36] A scene described by Fatimah Tobing Rony uncannily resembles one in *La marcia dell'uomo*. She writes of the African villages reconstructed for the Jardin d'Acclimation as being 'encyclopaedic *tableaux vivants*', part zoo, part circus performance, part laboratory in which the visitor was 'in a sense invited to act as a scientist and a colonist, to acquire knowledge by looking at the body and its habitat.'[37] The 'villagers' responded to the attention with requests for money. The body – that is the body as distinct from the face – called for study because of the supposed absence of language. The camera provided the ideal instru-

---

35   Fatimah Tobing Rony, *The Third Eye: Race, Cinema, and the Ethnographic Spectacle* (Durham and London: Duke University Press, 1996), 7.
36   Ibid., 9–10.
37   Ibid., 37.

ment for recording the gestures and movements that constituted its supposed equivalent in bodily form. The cinematic eye was omniscient and the technology promised to deliver an ever-expanding archive with which to rank the species of humankind. If Marey's approach was untainted by racial thinking, his follower, Regnault, made it an organising principle in much of his work.[38] Moreover, species in danger of extinction, whether human or animal, could be preserved for posterity in their authentic state by film acting as taxidermy.

Historical analyses of colonialist films have started to uncover the conditions underpinning the modes of representation of ethnographic cinema. However, this research has, at the same time, called for the theorisation and realisation of a counter-cinema, especially on the part of 'people of colour'. Tobing Rony's suggestive metaphor for this revisualisation is the 'third eye', by which is meant the 're-direction of the sense of always looking at oneself through the eyes of others'. She writes that the 'racially charged glance can also induce one to see the very process which creates the internal splitting, to witness the conditions that gave rise to the double consciousness'.[39] She proposes an idea of counter-cinema that has affinities with 'intercultural cinema' (Laura Marks) and 'critical cinema' (Scott Macdonald) in which film practice is marked by reflexivity associated at a different moment in time with the avant-garde.

Gianikian and Ricci Lucchi's work relates closely to these currents in filmmaking, and they represent a link to the avant-garde. Once again, the surrealist legacy played a vital part. In particular, Michel Leiris, author of *L'Afrique fantôme* and the writer and artist Henri Michaux, were a strong influence from the time the filmmakers were working on *Dal Polo all'Equatore*. These figures of 'dissident surrealism' used cultural alterity as a means for constructing a critique of European culture; in the words of Hal Foster, their works 'frame the framer as he or she frames the other'.[40]

---

38   Ibid., 47–57.
39   Ibid., 4–6.
40   Hal Foster, 'The Artist as Ethnographer' in Hal Foster, *The Return of the Real: The Avant-Garde at the End of the Century* (Cambridge, MA: MIT Press, 1996), 203.

For Mark Nash, this reversal of point of view, which simultaneously draws attention to the act of framing itself, describes the approach of Gianikian and Ricci Lucchi in the documentaries on non-European cultures.[41] Their practice was combining political engagement with formal experimentation at a time when documentary filmmaking had once more become an 'almost privileged form of communication, providing a meta-discourse that guarantees the truth of our political, social and cultural life'.[42]

Thanks to the 'documentary turn', and the shift that signalled artists' re-engagement with political and social realities, Gianikian and Ricci Lucchi began to show their work again in contemporary art venues.[43] In 2004 they contributed installations to the exhibition *Experiments with Truth* in Philadelphia, and in 2005 at *Reprocessing Reality: New Perspectives on Art and Documentary* at Ville de Nyon in Switzerland. In both, they drew on the films grouped under the title *Frammenti elettrici*. *Frammenti elettrici* comprises individual works linked by the common theme of migration, racism, and colonialism. The filmmakers describe themselves as revisiting the continents and populations they first encountered in the archives holding film of the early twentieth century. The term *frammenti* or fragments is used for a series short films made between 2002 and 2005. The majority deal with travel in Asia and Africa: *Frammenti elettrici n. 2* is based on footage shot by a French officer stationed in Viet Nam in the

41   Mark Nash, 'Experiments with Truth', in *Experiments with Truth*, exh. cat., ed. Mark Nash (Philadelphia: Philadelphia Fabric Workshop and Museum, 2004), 27.

42   Ibid., 15; 'I would argue that it is only when an artist comes up against the limits of her or his practice that the work becomes truly interesting. Once involved in the messy business of engagement, activism and social change, matters quite rightly get out of hand and develop a social dimension'; Nash, 'Reality in the Age of Aesthetics', www. frieze.com/issue/article/reality_in_the_age_of_aesthetics/; accessed 23 November 2010.

43   'The new interest shown by film and art in social and political reality has never been as great as it is today [...] the documentary is on the advance [...] there is no possibility of separating the genres from one another. We cannot be concerned with establishing which works should be classified as art and which as cinema'; Claudia Spinelli, 'Reprocessing Reality' in *Reprocessing Reality: New Perspectives on Art and Documentary* (JRP Editions, 2005), 12–13.

1940s; *Frammenti elettrici n. 4* and *n. 5* (2005) assemble amateur tourist films from the early 1970s of Pakistan, Afghanistan, Kashmir, Burma, Indonesia, the Ivory Coast, and Senegal. Labelled the 'folkloristic propaganda of tourist development' made before the onslaught of 'devastation and war', they constitute the raw material for the re-framing of images of the remote and the exotic.[44]

Frammenti elettrici n. 1 – Rom (Uomini) (Electric Fragments N. 1 – Rom (Men), 2002) and *Frammenti elettrici n. 3 – corpi* (Electric Fragments N. 3 – Bodies, 2003)[45] consist of 8mm footage shot in Italy. The first shows a family of Gypsies on the shore of Lake Garda or Lake Como in the late 1940s. It is a spring day. The anonymous cameraman, who is presumably a member of the well-dressed party out for a day's sightseeing, films the Gypsies. The children in bare feet play, a baby wrapped in a blanket is placed under a man's hat to protect it from the sun, a father holds another child, the mother smiles, embarrassed. Gianikian and Ricci Lucchi comment: 'the 8mm camera records exoticism on home ground. Diversity is always exotic. The time is significant – the war has just ended, the Gypsies may have returned to Italy after the Nazi genocide. The place too is significant – a centre of tourism, yes, but also an area in which xenophobia towards immigrants and Gypsies has resurfaced with venom'.[46] This onset of racism and anti-immigrant politics in Italy, associated in particular with the rise of the Northern League, formed the background against which the filmmakers were working.[47] 'The images', they recall, 'made us very nervous'. Here the

---

44 Frammenti elettrici N. 4, and N. 5 Asia-Africa, www.filmitalia.org/film.asp?documentID=45580; accessed 30 September 2009.

45 'Italy of the 1950s, 8mm films by an amateur who filmed women, secretly and always from behind. Voyeurism, sexist images, hallmarks of an outlook of unilateral power that can be likened to the racism and or exoticism recurrent in this series of films'; programme notes of the Retrospective, 'Yervant Gianikian et Angela Ricci Lucchi', Jeu de Paume, 21 February to 19 March 2006.

46 *Reprocessing Reality*, 152.

47 For discrimination against Gypsies in Italy, see Piero Brunello and Claudia Baldoli, *L'urbanistica del disprezzo: Campi Rom e società italiana* (Rome: Manifestolibri, 1996); David Forgacs, *Italy's Margins: Photography, Writing and Social Exclusion since 1861* (Cambridge: Cambridge University Press, forthcoming). In 2008 there

title links the way of looking at 'the foreigner within' with perceptions of the foreigner in foreign lands. The addition of the word '*Uomini*' to the title is also worth noting. After the publication of *Se questo è un uomo*, Primo Levi's book of 1947 on the experience of the *Lager*, the reference sounds a warning bell. Harald Szeemann included *Frammenti elettrici n. 1 – Rom (Uomini)* in the exhibition, *Aubes, rêveries au bord de Victor Hugo*, in the birthplace of Victor Hugo to commemorate the 200th anniversary of the poet's birth.[48] Placed near the four-poster bed, the images of the Gypsy family were said by one commentator in keeping with Hugo's dreams of freedom for the poor and oppressed.[49]

Another work incorporated in the *Frammenti elettrici* series is *Nuova Caledonia* (2004). The work was commissioned by the Fabrics Workshop and Museum of Philadelphia. Detailed notes provided by Gianikian and Ricci Lucchi show their interest in both the longer history of colonialism and the specific history of the footage itself. 'The Kanak have lived in the archipelago for 3500 years', they write. 'In Polynesian, Kanak means "human". Discovered by James Cook in 1774, the French seized control of New Caledonia in 1853, turning it into a penal colony. They forced the Kanak to live in reservations. To the new colonists, the life of the indigenous people seemed like a "simple theatre of shadows [...] that the ruling class (when it rules) can pass over without passion or fear" (Hannah Arendt).'[50] Then in 1946 the Kanak became full French citizens. The 16mm and 8mm black and white film found by the filmmakers in France in 1994 was shot by anonymous cameramen during and after the 1946 celebrations. Gianikian and Ricci Lucchi describe one section of the 8mm footage:

---

were attacks on some 700 camps in Italy and the Berlusconi government proposed fingerprinting all Gypsies; see Louise Doherty, 'The History of Terror', *Amnesty Magazine* (November–December 2010).

48   *Aubes, rêveries au bord de Victor Hugo*, exh. cat., ed. Harald Szeemann (Paris: Maison de Victor Hugo, 2002).

49   Cristina Piccino, 'Sogni clandestini', *Il Manifesto* (11 January 2003).

50   *Experiments with Truth*, ed. Nash, 30.

Men wearing only loincloths walk in single file. The women wear short skirts made of tree bark. The village leader wears a French flag across his chest, symbolising his citizenship [...] The film was a whole is a savage portrait of the Kanak in the style of Lévi-Strauss – candid shots in the forest, men, women, jobs, objects, buildings, and sculptures that represent ancestors; moving figures who then become fixed in the small, impoverished cinematic mold, a candid look from which we have idealistically reviewed their tragic history. These short, unexplained films were tossed away, lost, and, finally, recovered, bringing to life the portrait of a people. A Kanak descendant narrates: 'The foreigners came to rip us apart, disturb, disperse, and exterminate. They killed our leaders and men. They robbed our lands.'[51]

The footage includes scenes of the Kanak engaged in basket weaving. Craft is a favourite subject of ethnographic films. For the Fabrics Workshop it represents a rare record. But as Claudia Spinelli observes, there are also analogies between the activity of the weavers and that of the filmmakers: 'the films are reminiscent of textile fragments. Their micro-structure allows us to visualise individual motifs while the real size of the fabric remains in the realm of supposition. The artists confront the public with a picture sequence without beginning or end. These are open, unfinished narratives and textures whose threads lead right into the here and now'.[52] However, Gianikian and Ricci Lucchi do not seek to embalm or preserve artefacts or materials for posterity but to use fragments to narrate histories whose disappearance threatens to wipe clean the slate of Europe's colonial past. The slow motion and the reframing of the footage create haunting images of a lost world of which the film has become a unique testimony.

Terra Nullius (2002), which consists of found nitrate footage of Australian Aboriginal people, was also exhibited as an installation, this time at the Witte de With Center of Contemporary Art in Rotterdam. As such, the exhibition of the work reveals the overlap and reciprocity between the world of contemporary art and that of experimental film, between the gallery and the annual Rotterdam Film Festival. Here it was part of the group exhibition 'Based on True Stories' jointly curated by Catherine David, the

51   Ibid., 30–1.
52   Claudia Spinelli, in *Reprocessing Reality. New Perspectives on Art and Documentary*, 150.

director, and Jean-Pierre Rehm, curator of the Documentary Film Festival of Marseilles.[53] Again the filmmakers re-use rare found footage so that people on the margins, who appear in amateur films as 'exotica', are shown in their ordinary humanity. Exhibition notes describe the film:

> *Terra Nullius* (Latin for 'no one's land') is a new work. The film is constructed from found footage and archival material. The filmmakers spliced together old nitrate sequences to form a filmic topography. The British declared Australia a 'Terra Nullius' and in the same breath denied the existence of Aboriginal society. Captured in the old archive material, the European suburban landscape in Australia stands in stark contrast to the life of the indigenous population – the elegant clothing and hairstyles of the women in the built-up streets stands alongside the portrait of an Aboriginal in shabby clothing who is playing with a boomerang. There is a small group of Aboriginals dressed in European clothing, who are sitting on the ground and cooking close to a tent.[54]

Images d'Orient, tourisme vandale (Images of the East, Vandal Tourism, 2001) represents a more sustained feature-length examination of European visions of the 'exotic Other'. Commissioned by the television arts channel, Arte, it was first screened at the Venice Film Festival as part of a programme entitled 'New Territories'. The footage is largely drawn from Luca Comerio's archive, though it is unclear how much was shot by Comerio himself nor for whom the film was made. The original film documents the visit to India of Edda Mussolini, daughter of the dictator, in 1928–9. It is likely that a reel covering the Tripoli part of the journey is missing.

53   'The pivotal questions when putting together this exhibition were how filmmakers/artists are engaged in their visual testimony and what rhetorical choices they make. After the debunking of the 'meta-narratives' of the modern age it has become impossible to speak for everyone, and all we can do now is offer a personal testimony. This is no different for filmmakers and artists: every documentary is a personal testimony. What is significant, however, is the standpoint taken: what are the maker's ideas and how are these visualized or portrayed? In this respect the documentary can be regarded as a political statement'; www.wdw.nl/project.php?id=4; accessed 13 September 2010.

54   www.wdw.nl/participant.php?part_id=112&id=4; accessed 20 September 2009.

While not a state visit, the fact that the daughter of the Italian Head of State was part of the Italian party travelling to India explains the number and lavishness of the receptions. However, Gianikian and Ricci Lucchi carefully avoid mentioning Edda Mussolini in the notes and interviews that accompanied the release of the film so as not to distract attention from their principal concern – how the East is seen through Western eyes and how elite tourism prepared the way for mass tourism later in the century. The filmmakers write: 'Iconography of Orientalism in documentary cinema. Europeans enter the "exotic realm". A journey to India [...] The First World War had marked the end of the isolated traveller-explorer. The new "travellers" move in compact groups towards the exotic, towards its ruin. The journey takes place by ship, train, car, rickshaw, boat, elephant. Notes on the visual sensations, the local colour, the habits, the behaviour of the travellers'.[55] Although in *Images d'Orient, tourisme vandale* there is the implication that Italian Fascist and British colonial attitudes converged regarding empire and European superiority, no devices are used – such as images of the Duce – to highlight this notion.[56]

Indeed, Gianikian has called *Images d'Orient, tourisme vandale* a 'very formal film' (*un film molto formale*). In part this is due by the importance of ceremony, from the official welcome on board ship in the port of Colombo in Ceylon (current day Sri Lanka) with the British governor-general and local notables in attendance to taking tea on the lawn of an official residence. The Italian visitors, according to Gianikian, seem to assume British manners and behave with comparable display of superiority towards the servants and native population. This behaviour, as a mode of exercising power, is studied by the filmmakers, who quote Henri Michaux: 'the white man possesses a quality that has enabled him to make his way: disrespect. For

---

55   Information sheet on *Images d'Orient, tourisme vandale* issued by Arte at the Venice Film Festival, 29 August 2001, 4.
56   For the contradictory attitude on the part of Italians towards India and the British Empire, see Charles Burdett, *Journeys through Fascism: Italian Travel Writing between the Wars* (New York and Oxford: Berghahn Books, 2007), 54–66.

the white man allows nothing to block his way'.[57] For Michaux, a traveller in Asia with a very different approach, the role of servants and servility was profoundly demeaning of the humanity of the server and the served: 'Servants have always been terribly painful for me. When I see one I am overwhelmed with despair. It seems to me I am a servant – the more he humbles himself, the more I am humbled. In fact, everyone has noticed that people who have a household of servants, whether they be dukes or maharajahs, end up resembling servants. They never have the look of free men'. [58]

The poor and the downtrodden are pictured by Michaux as lambs at the mercy of the powerful; 'For the majority life is short, they are born to be ignorant, to have hunched shoulders, to die in airless places'. On the soundtrack, his words are sung by Giovanna Marini in an incantatory lament[59], as are those from Mircea Eliade's entries in the diary he kept during prolonged stays in India. Diary entries for April-May 1930 describe the violent punishment meted out to Indian Nationalist protesters by the British authorities. Students finding sanctuary in the library where Eliade, a scholar of world religions, is working have burst eardrums, paralysed arms, and internal bleeding. He is shown a list of the dead.[60] The terrible catalogue forms the soundtrack that accompanies images of the Italian guests relaxing and being served in the garden.

The formal qualities of *Images d'Orient, tourisme vandale* also derive from the strategies used by Gianikian and Ricci Lucchi who dissect the original footage with surgical precision. There is one sequence in which the 'analytical camera' has moved ever closer to the figures sitting at a long banqueting table so that the slightest movements of the face and eyes are scrutinised. At one moment, Edda Mussolini's eyes and forehead occupy

57   For the text used in the soundtrack, see Henri Michaux, *A Barbarian in Asia*, trans. Sylvia Beach (New York: New Directions, 1949), 8. In French, *Un barbare en Inde* (1933).

58   Ibid.

59   Giovanna Marini sings the words taken from the French editions.

60   From Mircea Eliade, *Fragments de la revolution civile, Journal des Indes* (1930) cited in information sheet issued by Arte at the Venice Film Festival, 29.08.01.

the entire screen. Slow motion creates a continuous series of pauses on the verge of stilled frames that reveal movements that usually occur beneath the level of visibility on the part of the observer as well as the observed. Laban, the theorist of dance, called them 'shadow movements' – that is, 'the small involuntary movements [...] we don't mean to make, that can be extraordinarily revealing in a way we might not welcome'.[61] Walter Benjamin wrote of the 'optical unconscious' with reference to movements of all kinds made visible and brought to our attention by the camera: 'Whereas it is a commonplace that, for example, we have some idea what is involved in the act of walking (if only in general terms), we have no idea at all what happens during the fraction of a second when a person actually takes a step. Photography with all its devices of slow motion and enlargement reveals the secret. The camera introduces us to unconscious optics as does psychoanalysis to unconscious impulses'.[62]

In *Images d'Orient, tourisme vandale* variations in slow motion and use of the close up within the film frame of the original footage enables an exploration of the everyday movements and gestures whereby micro-power is exercised. We observe the tourists observe, and, in turn, the camera's own role in framing the world is made apparent. Simultaneously Gianikian and Ricci Lucchi produce a film of extraordinary beauty. The deliberate walk of the elephants as they bear the guests in procession has been transformed into absorbing spectacle as the slow motion images tinted in sepia and pinks are accompanied by the spare percussive music of Luis Agudo. However, beauty and horror, beauty and degradation are never separated out. Juxtaposed to the Delhi of trams, tree-lined boulevards and tall buildings are shots of the other India whose presence is otherwise communicated through the words of Michaux or Eliade. Indians are mostly in the background, part of the exotic *mise-en-scène*. A policeman on a wooden podium directs traffic, cars pass, followed by a camel; a holy man crosses mudflats in the

61   Jean Newlove and John Dalby, *Laban for All* (London: Nick Heron Books, 2003), 159.

62   Walter Benjamin, 'Little History of Photography' in Walter Benjamin, *Selected Writings, Vol 2, part 2, 1931–34* ed. Michael W. Jennings, Howard Eiland and Gary Smith (Cambridge, MA and London: Harvard University Press, 1999), 511–12.

direction of the river; men draw water from a well and carry pails across their shoulders while women walk with baskets balanced on their heads. For the cine-cameras following the tourists, and for the tourists with their cameras, Indians are part of the background.

However, Gianikian and Ricci Lucchi edit the material to give new prominence to the overlooked population and counter-pose the world of the colonised and that of the coloniser. They describe the 'strong contrasts': 'On the one hand, the "man in the street" – the poverty-stricken shacks, the impoverished dancers, the fakir, the mutilated man, the naked children, malnourished and with swollen stomachs [...] On the other, the continuous exhibition of luxury and elegance at official receptions in the rich colonial residences and English-style gardens and parks. Numerous liveried servants.'[63] A tracking shot taken from a slow-moving train shows the hard labour of railway workers on the line. Negative and blue-tinted footage of a goat being butchered is repeated and bring to mind Michaux's words about the slaughter of the lambs. *Images d'Orient, tourisme vandale* concludes with a sequence of images, which are not from Comerio's Indian reels, that show young boys, some not more than six or seven years old, who are working in the fields. The army of underfed skeletal bodies dressed in rags move in line with their hoes under the eye of an overseer. The contrast with the children of the privileged dressed up for the reception in Colombo that opens the film could hardly be greater. The slow motion adds heaviness to the mechanical movements of agricultural work. This is the India the tourists do not see, even when it is before their eyes.

63   Yervant Gianikian and Angela Ricci Lucchi, 'Tourisme vandale. Deux projects', *Trafic* 38 (Summer 2001), 63–4.

CHAPTER 6

History, the Body, and the Death of Cinema

Cinema is the art of destroying images.

— PAOLO CHERCHI USAI[1]

My entire bodily existence is implicated in my vision.

— MAURICE MERLEAU-PONTY[2]

The Christian story in the original film *La vie e la passion de Jésus Christ* (1902–5) by Ferdinand Zecca followed the gospels, beginning with the birth of Christ and concluding with the Resurrection. In the short 16mm re-make *Passion* (1988), Gianikian and Ricci Lucchi turn the story on its head so that it begins with the Resurrection and ends with the Birth; 'Christ looks backwards like the Angel of History of which Walter Benjamin speaks', write the filmmakers.[3] The reference to the image of the *Angelus Novus* by Paul Klee in Benjamin's 'Theses on the Philosophy of History' is one of the rare instances in which the filmmakers cite an influence. In this case, it is a reference to a thinker and writer of central importance to the making and reception of their work as a whole. The films have clear affinities with Benjamin's writings on history. The angel of Klee's painting looks backwards 'where we see a chain of events, he sees a single catastro-

---

1   Paolo Cherchi Usai, *The Death of Cinema: History, Cultural Memory and the Digital Dark Age* (London: Palgrave Macmillan, 2008), 7.

2   Maurice Merleau-Ponty, *The Phenomenogy of Perception*, trans. Colin Smith (London and New York: Routledge, 1962), 235, cited in Nead, *The Haunted Gallery*, 184.

3   Yervant Gianikian and Angela Ricci Lucchi, '*Passion*' in *Yervant Gianikian, Angela Ricci Lucchi*, ed. Toffetti, 118.

phe, which keeps piling wreckage upon wreckage and hurls it at his feet
[...] The storm irresistibly propels him into the future to which his back
is turned while the pile of debris before him grows skyward. This storm is
what we call progress.'[4]

Benjamin's critique of historicism – history as reconstruction of the
past 'as it really was' – is fuelled by a sense of urgency and calls for an awak-
ening of historical consciousness.[5] 'It means', writes Benjamin, 'to seize
hold of a memory as it flashes up at the moment of danger'. It also entails
going against the grain of the dominant narrative, which is recounted by
the victors, and interpreting the documents against the flow of orthodox
readings. The task is to 'brush history against the grain'.[6] The vision is
bleak and unflinching. But Benjamin's influence is felt not only through his
concept of history. The translation of his work in Italy, Europe and North
America in the post-war years encompassed the full range of his essays.
They cover areas of inquiry of great interest to Gianikian and Ricci Lucchi:
history and memory, allegory, surrealism and the (after)life of objects,
wandering and collecting, bodily perception and the shock of modernity,
photography and the 'optical unconscious'. A description of Benjamin's
way of working, moreover, brings to mind that of the filmmakers – his
elaboration of the techniques of archiving, collecting, and constructing;
his use of excerpts, quotations, transpositions, cuttings-out, sticking, cataloguing, and sorting. These activities were not preliminary to writing and
producing work but the writing and work used those forms, learnt from
montage and collage as practiced in contemporary film and the visual arts.
Benjamin's question: 'When shall we write books like catalogues?' might
be asked anew, substituting films for books.[7]

4   Walter Benjamin, 'Theses on the Philosophy of History' in Walter Benjamin,
     Illuminations, ed. Hannah Arendt (London: Fontana, 1973), 259–60.
5   See Michael Löwy, *Fire Alarm: Reading Walter Benjamin's 'On the Concept of History'*
     (London and New York: Verso, 2005).
6   Benjamin, 'Theses on the Philosophy of History', 258–9.
7   See *Walter Benjamin's Archive*, ed. Ursula Marx, Gudrun Schwarz, Michael Schwarz
     and Erdmut Wizisla (London and New York: Verso, 2007).

From the late 1960s and 1970s, Benjamin's writings entered the mainstream of the culture of the European left.[8] From the 1980s and 1990s, they played a key part in the analysis as well as articulation of a growing preoccupation with the past, notably the recent European past, and the felt need to systematically address the historical traumas of genocide and of colonialism. This looking-backwards towards a Europe in the ruins of modernity coincided, towards the end of the twentieth century, with the forward-looking impulse generated by the introduction and dissemination of new digital technologies.

Two anniversaries, which resonate in the work of Gianikian and Ricci Lucchi – the hundredth anniversary of the first public film show of 1895 and the hundredth anniversary of the publication of the Futurist Manifesto in 1909 – throw the spotlight on events that are at once 'near', encapsulating the new (and the future), and 'far', representing a remote past of outdated technologies. This sense of proximity and distance, and the analogies between the impact of modernity in the early twentieth century and the shock of the new in the early twenty-first century, have made Walter Benjamin into a cardinal figure for getting one's bearings in a contemporary world of accelerated change and uncertainty.

Gianikian and Ricci Lucchi's films look back on history, employ outdated technologies, and reflect as well as reflect upon the decline of cinema as a photography-based medium. At the same time, they express an intense engagement with the present and contemporary artistic as well as political realities. This Benjaminian paradox is at the centre of the following sections that address the themes of 'History and Memory', 'Body and Embodiment', and 'Death and Cinema'.

8   John Berger in a prescient essay of 1970 wrote: 'The awakened interest in Benjamin coincides with Marxism's current re-examination of itself; this examination is occurring all over the world'; 'Walter Benjamin' in John Berger, *The Look of Things: Selected Essays and Articles* (London: Penguin, 1972), 91. In Italy Benjamin was first published by Einaudi in 1962 thanks to the translator and editor Renato Solmi, while Giorgio Agamben has played a major part in interpreting his ideas.

History and Memory

Anxiety about forgetting and the imperative to remember are recurrent preoccupations in the work of Gianikian and Ricci Lucchi. History is understood through memory, as in Benjamin's conception of 'seizing hold of a memory as it flashes up'. It is not a matter of narrating events or providing an objective or authoritative account. Words are kept to a minimum in the form of titles and inter-titles or words put to music. There is no voice-over, and narrative is never structured into beginning, middle and end. Nor do the films explicitly present an argument. Yet the overwhelming mass of Gianikian and Ricci Lucchi's films deal with historical documents. The found film footage is contemporary with the events recorded – footage, furthermore, that shows scenes and events that are either directly or indirectly linked to major wars, movements, conflicts, and technological developments in the twentieth century. They are filmmakers who have a passionate interest in the historical reality that is documented by the images. In addition, they have worked closely with historians, museums and film archives, engaging in a continuous dialogue with fellow citizens as well as with specialists in the field.

To understand this dimension of Gianikian and Ricci Lucchi's work, it is necessary to put it in the context of the re-conceptualisation of history that took place from the early 1980s onwards. On the one hand, 'history as a discourse there to guarantee', to cite Andreas Huyssen, 'the relative stability of the past and its past-ness' had lost its moorings, and, on the other, 'memory', formerly a 'topic for poets', had become an obsession in western societies'.[9] The obsession, which reached unprecedented levels in the late 20th century, was manifested in its 'colossal investment in museums, in heritage, in memorials to the dead of its many wars, in informa-

---

9   Andreas Huyssen, *Present Pasts: Urban Palimpsests and the Politics of Memory* (Palo Alto: Stanford University Press, 2003), 2; for the debate in Italy, see John Foot, *Fratture d'Italia: Da Caporetto al G8 di Genova, la memoria divisa del paese.*

tion technology, and its ever-larger and expanding archives'.[10] A defining development was the emergence of the figure of the survivor as historical witness. In the words of Jay Winter, 'Holocaust witnesses took on a liminal, mediating, semi-sacred role since the 1970s.They spoke of the dead, and for the dead'.[11] Genocides and mass killings became defining 'events' through which the history of the twentieth century, including the First World War, came to be re-thought in terms of witness and memory. For Jeffrey Skoller, 'the sign of Auschwitz continues to haunt the intellectual worlds of Europe and America as a post-modern condition in which there is no progressive thread of knowledge, no consensus about the nature of events – what they mean or why they occurred. What remains are fragments, fissures, and gaps that create a field of indeterminate and contested meanings, opacities, and eventually silence'.[12]

It has been argued that subsequent genocides were in part possible because of the suppression of the memory of the century's first genocide, that of the Armenians.[13] It is certainly the case that memorialisation of the Holocaust gave new importance to remembering the Armenian tragedy.

10   Adrian Forty, 'Introduction' in *The Art of Forgetting* (Oxford and New York: Berg, 1999), 7.
11   Winter, *Remembering War*, 30.
12   Skoller, *Shadows, Specters, Shards*, xxxiv; see Theodor Adorno's seminal 1959 lecture, 'What Does Coming to Terms with the Past Mean?' in *Bitburg in Moral and Political Perspective* (Bloomington: Indiana University Press, 1986), 114–29.
13   Historians remind us that the mass slaughters of the twentieth century caught up millions of people, and not only Jewish people, especially in Poland, the Ukraine and Belarus. Richard J. Evans writes: 'who, after all, speaks today of the annihilation of the Armenians? Adolf Hitler asked his generals in 1939, as he told them to "close your hearts to pity," "act brutally" and behave "with the greatest harshness" in the coming war in the East. It's often assumed that in reminding them of the genocide of at least a million Armenians by the Ottoman Turks during the First World War, Hitler was referring to what he intended to do to Europe's Jews. But he was not referring to the Jews: he was referring to the Poles. "I have sent my Death's Head units to the East," he told the generals, "with the order to kill without mercy men, women and children of the Polish race or language. Only in such a way will we win the living space that we need"'; Richard J. Evans, 'Who Remembers the Poles?', *London Review of Books* 32.21 (4 November 2010), 21–2.

Bearing witness acquired an urgency that also had a generational dynamic –
the survivors of the events of 1915–19 were fewer in number every year by the
1980s. Why exactly Raphael Gianikian decided to read his autobiographical
account of his return to Khodorciur to his son in 1986 is unclear. He had
begun writing it a decade earlier. However, he was perhaps encouraged by
a cultural climate in which Jewish survivors, of whom Primo Levi was the
best known, had made bearing witness into a principal means of writing
the history of the *Lager*.[14] Although the videoing of this testimony had
not been planned, video and oral recordings of testimonies became well-
established practice, especially in the United States, in this period. Yervant,
moreover, was responding with his own resources of communication to the
injunction implied in the act of 'moral witness', namely that 'the listener
becomes a witness to the witness, not only facilitating the very possibility
of testimony but also subsequently sharing its burden. That is to say, the
listener assumes the responsibility to perpetuate the imperative to bear
witness to the historical trauma for the sake of collective memory'.[15]

The film *Ritorno a Khodorciur. Diario Armeno* is an act of moral witness to the Armenian genocide in which the son witnesses the father's
testimony. This event not only led onto the making of *Uomini anni vita*, a
film described by Yervant Gianikian as a 'painful experience, a catharsis',[16]
but constituted bearing witness as a filmic act that returns again and again
in the *oeuvre*. The filmmakers have been witnesses in person in certain
circumstances and have filmed what they have seen – when, for example,
they recorded on video people caught up in the war in the Balkans or in
the earthquake in the Armenian Republic. However, the idea needs to be
understood in a metaphorical sense. Their staple material, found footage,
is made to testify to events, though in ways never intended by the original

---

14   Robert Gordon, 'Which Holocaust? Primo Levi and the Field of Holocaust Memory
      in Postwar Italy', *Italian Studies* 16.1 (Spring 2006), 85–113; on historical memory
      and Italy in the twentieth century, see John Foot, *Italy's Divided Memory* (London
      and New York: Palgrave, 2009).
15   'Introduction' in *The Image and the Witness*, ed. Guerin and Hallas, 11.
16   'Cataloghi della memoria: Conversazione con Yervant Gianikian e Angela Ricci
      Lucchi (Sergio Toffetti e Daniela Giuffrida)', 19.

cameramen. A strong consciousness of history is ever-present. Apparently insignificant objects or ordinary scenes in old footage are not what they at first seem to be. They may hold secrets. They will have histories and be invested with memories.

The memories of the filmmakers intertwine with that of the subjects of their films; 'we have always travelled a good deal', says Ricci Lucchi, 'and we have got to know many people who have shown us things that we have then discovered in the History, written and filmed. And our films are also constructed around places visited and people met'.[17] An object lesson in this respect is their unfinished film *Interni a Leningrado* (Interiors in Leningrad, 1990), which they have described in a photo-essay, 'Viaggio in Russia: Materiali non montati per un film da fare: *Interni a Leningrado*'.[18] Memory is evoked at three levels: there is Gianikian and Ricci Lucchi's memory of their meetings with survivors of the Russian avant-garde during their visit to Leningrad in the winter of 1989; secondly, the memory of the protagonists themselves; and, thirdly, the memory that, as the film title suggests, is embodied in the interiors – in the furniture, objects and souvenirs of the apartments. Together the interiors and the historical figures form fragile ensembles on the point of being broken apart by death and dispersal. If any visual trace survives it is now only in the images shot by the filmmakers.

In the photo-essay, each of the survivors of Stalin's purges is photographed sitting at a table in an apartment accompanied by objects and images that evoke the presence of partners, friends and relations who have perished. Valia Kozintsev looks down at a photograph of her first husband, Boris Barnet, one time boxer, director, and actor in Kuleshov's films. Ida Nappelbaum holds up a photograph of herself as a young woman, daughter of Mikhail, the great photographer of Meyerhold, Mayakovsky, Akhmatova, Esenin, Blok, Gorky, and Pasternak. Josif Efimovic Kheifitz, the filmmaker, holds up a small movie camera. The names listed evoke a historic avant-

---

17   Mereghetti and Rossin, 'Il magazzino della Storia', 121.
18   *Cinema Anni Vita*, 193–9.

garde killed, driven to suicide, or deported to the camps.[19] The planned
film is intended to keep alive the memory of the art and pay homage to
the filmmakers of the Russian avant-garde – Dziga Vertov, Esther Schub,
Grigori Kozinstsev, Ilya Trauberg and Lev Kuleshov. The film, *Interni a
Leningrado*, would 'alternate sequences of images lifted from their original
context with new images that would together delineate the essential elements of a fresco of society in the Vertovian manner'.[20] The film was made
'in order to save their memory from destruction', a sentence repeated in
the essay. Gianikian and Ricci Lucchi set out to save traces of memories
that Stalin had tried to systematically obliterate and that were then at risk
after the collapse of communism when Russia hurried to forget everything
to do with the revolutionary past. The photographic portraits of men and
women already in their eighties are now rare documents of a vanished
world. The photographs are mostly of interiors with their inhabitants, but
the photo-essay also includes some that document the outside of buildings in Leningrad where the poet and author of *Journey to Armenia*, Osip
Mandelstam, had lived. Dilapidated or uncared for, the doorways are a
mute reminder of absence.

The traditional history documentary has an easily recognised structure.
There is a voice-over commentary, a linear narrative, a consensus-based
interpretation, and a battery of legitimate authorities accredited. Images
tend to be used to illustrate scripts, and words are privileged over pictures in
determining the meaning of events. While this model is undergoing change
and adaptation, it still characterises the majority of television productions
dedicated to historical questions.[21] The kind of filmmaking pioneered by
Gianikian and Ricci Lucchi offers a very different approach whose origins
are not in documentaries but in experimental film. Elements of 'film essay'

---

19   On the literary circles in exile, see Nina Berberova, *The Italics are Mine: Memoirs of
      the Russian Literary Emigration* (London: Longman, 1969).

20   Gianikian and Ricci Lucchi, 'Voyages en Russie. Autour des avant-gardes', 39.

21   'In the United States, even our best historical documentaries tend to be packaged
      in a standard format that includes narration, documentary images of some sort, and
      talking experts combined in a smooth flow'; Dan Sipe, 'From the Pole to the Equator:
      A Vision of Wordless Past', *American History Review* 95.4 (October 1990), 1138–9.

can be found in their work but unlike with Chris Marker, the 'ideas' emerge through a montage of images without a parallel montage of words. The filmmakers have said that they would like to work more with words, but there is little sign of this happening in their films. The single film frame is the basic cell from which they build. Their films of the 1980s – *Das Lied von der Erde. Gustav Mahler, Dal Polo all'Equatore*, and *Uomini anni vita* – did not include inter-titles.

The increased interest of Gianikian and Ricci Lucchi in film as document is due in no small measure to the interest in their work expressed by historians and critics concerned with the historical aspects of their work.[22] For their part, historians, notably Diego Leoni, recognised the potential for new thinking about images offered by the filmmakers. Leoni recalls contacting them about the possibility of collaborating on a project after he had seen *Uomini anni vita*. He wanted the same rigour in research on moving pictures as applied in the analysis of written sources, such as the letters, memoirs and other forms of 'popular writing' at the time of the First World War – material that they were cataloguing, editing and publishing. For Leoni, it was important to give a face to the common soldiers whose memoirs were being read for the first time. But more than providing a visual analogue for the written sources using the film archives, Leoni felt that a new 'cinematic poetics' was needed that was capable of expressing the 'epic and tragic dimension of the experience in a structured narration'. 'The choice', he writes, 'was of a cinema that was poetic, free of ideology, and non-mainstream. It would reveal through images rather than words. It would be at once an act of memory and a reflection on history, an attempt to establish a visual anthropology of the war documentary, a micro-physiology of its participants'.[23]

The aim of visualising a narrative is perhaps the most obvious reason for turning to filmmakers. The attitude of Diego Leoni and his fellow

---

22   There is a growing interest in the relationship of film and history at the time; see Marc Ferro, *Cinema and History*, trans. Naomi Greene (Detroit: Wayne State University Press, 1988); *Revisioning History: Film and the Construction of a New Past*, ed. Robert A. Rosenstone (Princeton: Princeton University Press, 1995).

23   Leoni, 'Quei luoghi, quei volti', 176–7.

historians is unusual in its recognition of the independent status of the image. The film ceases, in this perspective, to be an illustration. It works on the history of images and the history of cinema, and understands them as active in forming reality, in creating ways of seeing, rather than as simply reflecting reality. Far from ignoring the framing and manipulation of images, the cinema of Gianikian and Ricci Lucchi makes re-framing and other types of intervention into matters of inquiry as well as methods of working. Reflexivity replaces the notion of reflection. It is film that looks at itself looking. History is not a past reconstructed 'as it really was', as in the original footage. That footage was never a transparent window onto the world anyway. Everything, from the mattes that surround the image to the positioning of the camera, help to construct points of view that are far from neutral. History can only be constructed from the documents that survive and the memories of the living.

Archival footage is one form of document – a form that in the work of Gianikian and Ricci Lucchi can be likened to the palimpsest. Just as the palimpsest of parchment, vellum or papyrus used in ancient and medieval times became a symbol of the workings of memory and the unconscious when deciphered with the aid of chemicals in the 19th century, so the found footage films provide fragments whose meanings have to be deciphered. Just as the palimpsest consists of text endlessly written over and re-used, so the footage consists of inscription, erasure, superimposition, reframing, enlargement, and other procedures, which, in turn, are used by the film-makers to make new work in a manner well tried and tested by artists in the second half of the twentieth century.[24]

For Gianikian and Ricci Lucchi the found materials with which they work are not restricted to the frames of film. For them it is important to find out about provenance, ownership, technical aspects, and any other details that reveal the history of the object. Many of the activities associated with the historian or the museum curator have been part of their practice as artists and filmmakers, from collecting and cataloguing to consulting

24   Brian Dillon, 'The Revelation of Erasure', *Tate Etc.* 8 (Autumn 2006), 30–41.

archives and visiting sites.[25] The scrupulous attention to minutiae can be seen in their notes concerning the original films on New Caledonia, which bear out Laura Marks's observations on the identity of objects: 'Objects contain a wealth of knowledge if only we could read them. Objects provide maps of their travels, the people who produced and came into contact with them, and the shift in the values as they move'.[26] The filmmakers describe the packages containing the reels of film – the laboratory in Australia to which they were sent, missing and erased addresses, the expiry date for development, the stamps. The picture on the stamps show a ship in front of an industrial building. Geographies of empire and time-space co-ordinates locate the world of the Kanak within that of the colonisers. For Gianikian and Ricci Lucchi, films do not exist only as images in the abstract but as material objects of history and mystery.[27]

Before they came into the hands of Gianikian and Ricci Lucchi, the objects, whether toys or letters belonging to the family in Mühlbach or reels of 9.5mm film, were on the point of being thrown away or dispersed. Taken out of the context in which they had a use value and a place within a nexus of relationships, the objects had been rendered useless, cut loose from memories and associations, and reduced to mere matter. The proprietors of the Comerio archive, unable to sell its contents to the Cineteca in Milan, would have consigned it to the rubbish dump had not the filmmakers intervened. They had already begun to demolish the laboratory equipment of which only the editing-table was saved. The historic collection in Cesare Lombroso's museum in Turin was in the process of being consigned

25   The open discussion of methods and sources sets the practice of Gianikian and Ricci Lucchi apart from that, for instance, of Péter Forgács, despite superficial resemblances. Whereas Forgács's is a poetics of concealment in which the aura of poetry and magic are deliberately, and problematically, heightened, Gianikian and Ricci Lucchi make viewers aware of looking and making sense of the images. Contrast, for example, Péter Forgács's *Danube Exodus* (1999) with *Inventario balcanico* (2000).

26   Marks, *The Skin of the Film*, 96–7.

27   In some instances, the provenance remains open to conjecture. This is the case with the footage shot by a Jewish photographer between the wars from which Gianikian and Ricci Lucchi made *Luci misteriose* (2005). The film was sent to them anonymously and nothing is known of the fate of the photographer in question; programme notes, Jeu de Paume, 21 February to 19 March 2006.

to storage, perhaps in perpetuity, when Gianikian and Ricci Lucchi filmed it *in situ*. The house of the lime trees abandoned with all its contents by the inhabitants survived as a repository of memory too burdensome to bear when filmed. Again and again, the filmmakers salvage artefacts and save things whose life is about to be cut short by irreversible change. However, the saved objects are of interest to them in so far as they have potential for a new life – for being recycled and returned to cultural circulation.

Ricci Lucchi often refers to the 'ready-made' in relation to the found footage films; 'our cinema is the child of Duchamp's gesture: taking the ready made, in order to talk about the present'.[28] The reference is to Marcel Duchamp, the artist who 'would find his name for his new technique, precisely ready made [...] as a label for clothing bought off the rack, potentially mass produced and consumed'.[29] Perhaps it would be more accurate to speak of 'assisted' or 'rectified' ready-made when the object, in their case frames of old film, was subjected to physical interventions. The important point was that something without recognised aesthetic value was turned into art, even if the intention was to attack the idea of art. Another related object is the *objet trouvé* (found object). Again, the object, usually a fragment, is not made by the artist but is found and incorporated into the artwork, especially in collage. As with the ready-made, the *objet trouvé* of the early avant-garde was re-discovered by artists in America and Europe from the late 1950s. In their searches in flea markets and similar venues Gianikian and Ricci Lucchi are in good company. It is research that goes hand in hand with a strategy in which the old and the discarded has served the task of critiquing modernity in the late twentieth- and early twenty-first-century West. The first films that recycled old 'found' footage were made very much within a framework of avant-garde cinema preoccupied with formal experimentation with the medium and its specific properties. But from *Das Lied von der Erde. Gustave Mahler* onwards, the filmmakers addressed questions about Europe's history in the twentieth century.

28   Mereghetti and Rossin, 'Il magazzino della Storia', 122.
29   Hal Foster, Rosalind Krauss, Yve-Alain Bois and Benjamin H.D. Buchloh, *Art since 1900* (London: Thames and Hudson, 2004), 128–9.

The filmmakers underline that their approach to the original film is simultaneously historical and philological – in other words based on a minute analysis and knowledge of the materials and practice of the time – and transformative in making a contemporary film from the 'found' materials. In interviews, Gianikian and Ricci Lucchi have avoided naming names, but they take their distance from what they see as forms of 'found footage' filmmaking with which they do not want to be identified. Indeed, the very term 'found footage' is discarded in favour of the term 'archival'. 'We are among the first to use the archive', Gianikian states, 'we use the term archive and not "found footage" because we re-elaborate, re-film and bring new meaning to the materials, we do not juxtapose or assemble the materials as they are already. When we took *Karagoez* to America, a whole generation of young experimental filmmakers were influenced by the form and conception of our film. Unfortunately, there was then a lack in most of the sequent compilation films made of a political and formal awareness such as you find in our work. These days there is a crass revisionism in which materials are used without any criteria and with crudely utilitarian ends'.[30] For Gianikian and Ricci Lucchi the studied re-use of the materials is what makes them become contemporary rather than something quaint belonging to the past or something with which filmmakers can 'play' without regard to history and politics.

The collection of found footage and research in the archive opened up a whole new/old world to filmmakers. 'For the first time in the history of the art form', writes Skoller, 'filmmakers have an archive to sift through, analyse, and appropriate, allowing them to create their own metahistories. The history of world film culture has been a short but dense one that has permeated the consciousness of much of the planet, allowing cinema to become – like literature – to a way of apprehending the world itself'.[31]

In the hands of Gianikian and Ricci Lucchi, the found footage assumes the form of allegory both in its materiality as the ruins of the modern and as images of a now historical past. Instead of seeking to restore the film to

30   Mereghetti and Rossin, 'Il magazzino della Storia', 124.
31   Skoller, *Shadows, Specters, Shards*, xxix.

its original condition as new and to reconstruct the past 'as it was', they use its ruined condition and aged images as a means of illuminating the present. In this they follow the example of Walter Benjamin.

Jeffrey Skoller gives us an interpretation of Gianikian and Ricci Lucchi's *Dal Polo all'Equatore* through a reading of Benjamin's conception of allegory that can be extended to the films they made subsequently using found footage. With reference to *The Arcades Project*, Skoller writes:

> Benjamin tries to develop a mode of historiographic imagination in which the archaeological examination of antiquated, discarded, or forgotten objects can become the means for finding historical truth through the process of understanding why and how they lost value through the passage of time. Benjamin suggests that to explore what an object from the past means in the present is to turn that object into a text that has as its centre an imagining subject who finds new possibilities for its meaning [...] For modern artists the use of discarded, mechanically recorded images and sounds has allegorical possibility because they remain unchanged while the original context for their existence passes out of visibility. The temporal untranslatability of the object becomes the embodiment of present meanings and is generative of new possibilities for significance.[32]

For Benjamin, the French surrealists were the 'first to perceive the revolutionary energies that appear in the "outmoded" – in the first iron constructions, the first factory buildings, the earliest photos, objects that have begun to become extinct'.[33] For Skoller, Gianikian and Ricci Lucchi, along with Ernie Gehr and some other contemporary filmmakers, make similarly radical use of found-footage film as allegory – film 'which when projected for those who have no connection to that time, produce new possibilities for a *re-membering* of the past in the present'.[34] These artists 'reinscribe new meanings onto old, once-discarded images by producing two simultaneous images out of one'.

The use of the optical printer is a metaphor for this simultaneity: 'Through the process of reprinting, the image is marked by the present – literally shining the light of the optical printer in the present onto the

32   Ibid., 5.
33   Ibid., 6.
34   Ibid., xxxx.

film strip from the past – to produce an image of both past and present.'[35] It is then step printing, using what Gianikian called his 'analytical camera', that slows down the film so that the images that were 'formerly seen as indexical, as emanations of the real, lose their naturalness and opened to contemplation.'[36] The great achievement of a film like *Dal Polo all'Equatore* is that it holds together past and present and explores the tension of their co-presence through the retardation of the images. History is brought into a relationship with the present by what has been made visible in the old footage, and the present is illuminated by the new vision of the past. The past is not 'dead' but continues to impact on the lives of the living. The history of colonialism, from which Europeans have tried to hide, has shaped perceptions, and identities to an extent that is only now beginning to be addressed. The films of Gianikian and Ricci Lucchi bombard us in the present with a past whose unacknowledged effects continue to be felt. They produce what Susan Buck-Morss calls 'cognitive explosiveness'. She writes: 'cognitive explosiveness in a political sense occurs, not when the present is bombarded with "anarchistically intermittent", utopian "now-times" (Habermas), but when the present as now-time is bombarded with empirical, profane fragments of the recent past.'[37]

The Body and Embodiment

'The cinema of Yervant Gianikian and Angela Ricci Lucchi depends essentially on the principle of sensation', writes Philippe Azoury, 'and sensation is always acknowledged as the point of departure for every revelation.'[38] The early films explicitly set out to explore the sense of smell and created an 'odour-track' in the place of the sound-track. Accounts of performances underline the intensely physical sensations evoked in audiences.

35   Ibid., 18.
36   Ibid., xxxx.
37   Buck-Morss, *The Dialectics of Seeing*, 251.
38   Azoury, 'Sur "certaines radiations encore loin d'etre claires"', 53.

Film, filmmaking, and watching the film are conceived in a strongly expe-
riential way, which, as Azoury suggests, persists through their work. In
the 1970s, there were connections between their projects and developments within independent filmmaking, notably with performance-based
expanded cinema and with structuralist currents which fore-grounded,
albeit in very different ways, the sensations and perceptions of the viewer
and the materiality of the medium. Gianikian and Ricci Lucchi's practice,
however, acquired a historical and political dimension that has distin-
guished it from the more formal, individual, and perception-based preoccupations of North American contemporaries. Their identification with
an avant-garde going back to Esther Schub and Dziga Vertov underscores
their European-ness in this respect.

The centrality of appeals to the bodily and embodiment in the work of
Gianikian and Ricci Lucchi acquired a different valency in the late 1980s
in relation to developments in filmmaking and film criticism and history.
Firstly, there was the 'ethnographic turn'[39] and the questioning of Euro-
centric thinking and practice. Laura Marks coined the term 'intercultural
cinema' to refer to a cinema for which experimentation and appeal to 'haptic
visuality and embodied responses to images' were integral to its reflection
on the 'experience of diaspora, (post- or neo-) colonialism, and cultural
apartheid'.[40] Secondly, film theory itself was undergoing a major revision as
a result of the critique of dominant models constructed in the 1960s and
1970s around semiological and psychoanalytical approaches. In their place
was proposed a phenomenological approach associated with the work of
Merleau-Ponty. Both these developments have involved re-visiting the early
history of cinema and the first film theorists, and rediscovering the central
place of the body in early films.[41] It is easy to see, therefore, how Gianikian

---

39   David MacDougall, *The Corporeal Image: Film, Ethnography, and the Senses*
      (Princeton: Princeton University Press, 2006), 1–9.
40   Marks, *The Skin of the Film*, 1–23.
41   Béla Balázs represents an interesting case with reference to the work of Gianikian
      and Ricci Lucchi; 'a point in time existed for Balázs', writes Rachel Moore, 'in which
      language was unmediated and pure gestures were identical with the thought or,
      better, the feeling conveyed'; Rachel Moore, *Savage Theory: Cinema as Modern Magic*
      (Durham and London: Duke University Press, 2000), 67.

and Ricci Lucchi's work could find itself at a crossroads where different developments in early 21st century film theory and practice meet. This section will examine this new concern with the body in film with reference to their filmmaking practice, the films as whole, and the audience.

Filmmaking for Gianikian and Ricci Lucchi is a way of life. Work is not a separate place or activity undertaken only at prescribed times. They are artisans and masters of a craft. They share their small apartment in Milan with the tools of their trade – the editing-table that once belonged to Luca Comerio is in one room with the 'analytical camera'; a study space has shelves stacked high with box files; the living room doubles up as a viewing room when critics visit. The collections of objects and archival footage are housed elsewhere. However, their relationship to the materials is intimate and physical. Gianikian comments on the special smells of the film stock. When he works at the editing-table, he does not run the film through a moviola – it is too fragile. Instead, it is examined frame by frame. The film is either held in the hand and scrutinised by the naked eye, or turned manually through the optical printer and inspected with the help of the prosthetic eye. The work is slow and labour-intensive. There are no shortcuts. Even short films take months to make, whereas the feature-length ones have taken several years apiece. The smallest details are memorised; 'it is a kind of vivisection. We note what is happening in each frame, how many frames there are for every shot and sequence. We are very precise,'[42] says Gianikian. The film usually needs to be repaired and the rate of deterioration contained, all of which requires extensive knowledge of the different formats, film stock, techniques such as tinting and so on. Knowing about the exercise of the craft at the time the original footage was shot feeds into the re-working of the film. Technical expertise includes knowing how to make and adapt the optical printer. But the secret of the filmmaking lies not in the technology as such but in the know-how that informs the mimetic approach that brings the filmmaker into contact with the methods and thinking of his predecessors. Remarks made by Walter Benjamin about learning by copying are pertinent. 'One never really understands a book,' he

42   Macdonald, 'Yervant Gianikian and Angela Ricci Lucchi (On *From the Pole to the Equator*), 15.

wrote, 'unless one copies it'.[43] Re-photographing plays an analogous role in the filmmakers' practice since an intimate knowledge of the original film is the precondition for its subsequent transformation into new work.

The hands too play their part in the process of interpretation and understanding. Direct contact with objects is not cursory. Commenting on the appearance of the hand of the filmmaker in *Ghiro, ghiro tondo*, Jean Louis Schefer notes: 'But what do they mean – this montage and the mysterious delicacy of the adult hand that opens a box, rubs the paper, and accords a second life to these painted figures in wood, metal or fabric in extravagant colours of green, red and rose? Another life?'[44] The sense of touch is part of the making. Immediate contact functions as a metaphor for the intimacy of 'entering into the image'. It is also associated with moments of revelation, such as the first visit to Comerio's laboratory when Gianikian held up the strip of film and saw the tinted images of a sailing ship at sea. The image, moreover, looks back: 'I remember when we opened the tins for *Oh! Uomo* how we became aware of no longer being ourselves the subjects of the look but of having become the objects of the look of those who suffered, people without rank or name'.[45] A sense of mortality accompanies the filmmakers' relationship to the materials of their work. The dedication to Luca Comerio at the beginning of *Dal Polo all'Equatore* signals an awareness of the ephemerality of filmmakers as well as film. But if in the work of found footage filmmakers such as Bill Morrison the disintegration of the original film is dramatised as a Baroque triumph of death, in that of Gianikian and Ricci Lucchi the corporality of the film is more intimately related to histories as well as History.[46]

43   Susan Sontag relates Walter Benjamin's attitudes to work to Baudelaire and the 'malady of monks'; Susan Sontag, 'Introduction' in Walter Benjamin, *One Way Street and Other Writings* (London and New York: Verso, 1985), 22–3.

44   Jean Louis Schefer, 'Carrousel de jeux', Programme of 'Yervant Gianikian et Angela Ricci Lucchi', Jeu de Paume, 21 February to 19 March, 2006.

45   Mereghetti and Rossin, 'Il magazzino della Storia', 122.

46   J. Hoberman writes about Bill Morrison's *Decasia* (2002): 'the calligraphy of decay grows increasingly hallucinatory and catastrophic. The sea buckles. Flesh melts. The boxer struggles against the disintegration of the image. Wall Street is half consumed

The importance of the body in the films brings to mind the work of Eadweard Muybridge and Etienne-Jules Marey to whom Gianikian refers when discussing his 'analytical camera' with its 'microscope features'. Marey was a physiologist who, according to Marta Braun, 'wanted to arrive at a visual description of all common types of human motion – the walk, the run, the jump, and so on – and the forces at work in their execution [...] If motion is the most apparent characteristic of life, there is no doubt that it is also the most difficult to measure. Most of the movements in and of the body are invisible and have an intricacy – in form, duration, regularity, and amplitude – that defies any attempt to either capture or interpret them. Marey had chosen to explore a domain inhabited by invisible ephemera'.[47] For Marey, the body was an 'animate machine'. By contrast, Muybridge was an entertainer and illusionist, not a scientist. Although he pioneered stop-action photography, he produced spectacles, not analytical works, with his sequences of images. These included not only the canonical naked man walking or running but the woman undressing or, naked, turning and bending. As Linda Williams has argued, 'chrono-photography did more than document previously unobserved facts of movement'; 'this very machinery of observation and measurement turns out to be, even at this early stage, less an impartial instrument than a crucial mechanism in the power established over that body, constituting it as an object and subject of desire, offering up an image of the body as *mechanism* that is in many ways a reflection of the mechanical nature of the medium itself'.[48]

Gianikian and Ricci Lucchi share the interest of Marey and Muybridge in using photography to show the movements that the naked human eye cannot see. They too magnify and multiply the image. They look at film

---

in flames [...] The film is like a fierce dance of destruction'; J. Hoberman, 'The Art of Destruction – Back to Nature', *Village Voice*, 19–25 March 2003. By contrast, Gianikian and Ricci Lucchi seem always to want to hold onto the historical referent, even against the grain of images rendered hard to read.

47   Marta Braun, *Picturing Time: The Work of Etienne-Jules Marey (1830–1904)* (Chicago and London: University of Chicago Press, 1992), xviii.

48   Linda Williams, 'Film Body: An Implantation of Perversions', in *Narrative, Apparatus, Ideology*, ed. Philip Rosen (New York: Columbia University Press, 1986), 508.

frame by frame, treating them as the equivalent of the photographs of the chrono-photographers. According to Bernard Benoliel, 'a documentary scene refilmed by Gianikian seems like a Lumière shot filmed by Étienne-Jules Marey'.[49] Ordinary actions, such as walking, turning, bending, and carrying objects, feature in their films. However, Gianikian and Ricci Lucchi's have an anthropological and historical outlook. For them, the movements and gestures are coded and inscribed within cultures, whereas the chrono-photographers with their grid backdrops and laboratory-like conditions, at least in Marey's case, sought to picture ideal, universally valid examples of human movement with society and culture removed. The filmmakers, furthermore, make moving pictures – a time-based form – not the sequence of photographs of the chrono-photographers. Movements and gestures are recorded in their duration, even if the manipulation of speed entails the abandonment of the search for a film speed that seeks to replicate 'natural' motion and the exploration of a frontier zone between the still and moving image.

Gianikian and Ricci Lucchi give us a catalogue of human movement and gesture. If one simply takes the act of walking and looks at different films, the man or woman or child walking in slowed motion occurs again and again. Precise classification might include the stride of the Cossack cavalryman, the rhythmic step of the Buddhist monk, and so on. The differences that strike the spectator have usually to do with the contrasts produced through editing – the contrast between, say, the easy gait of the tourist in India and the limp of the beggar, or between the aggressive assertiveness of the European hunter in Africa and the immobility of African bye-standers. Anthopologists in the early twentieth century studied the bodies and behaviour of 'native peoples' in order to find clues about the nature of their societies. For Marcel Mauss, it was possible to 'divide humanity into those who squat and those who sit'.[50] In *Dal Polo all'Equatore*, *Frammenti elettrici*, and *Images d'Orient, tourisme vandale*, Gianikian and

---

49   Cited without source in Nicole Brenez and Pauline De Raymond, 'Ritorni di immagini', 110.

50   Marcel Mauss, *Les techniques du corps* (1934), cited in Fatimah Tobing Rony, *The Third Eye*, 21.

Ricci Lucchi help us to 'catalogue' the movements and gestures in parts of the world conquered by European powers.

In the war trilogy, the filmmakers show the massed bodies of the European peasantry. Not only were millions of men to die in the First World War but the peasantry of Europe, after centuries of settlement, was doomed to extinction, along with its distinctive cultures and modes of life. Marcello Flores comments on *Prigionieri della guerra*: 'the differences are noticeable, not only because the dance of the Russian prisoners is different from that of the Italian prisoners – in its rhythm, actions, and choral nature – but noticeable in that the way they wear moustaches or the way clothes corresponds to distinctive regional canons. However, what is even more noticeable is the uniformity – the masses of men who in peacetime would be working the fields [...] a landscape monotonous in the harshness to which the men's labour is subjected'. Flores finds the film remarkable for its close observation of 'faces that are the same and yet different' and the contrast between the signs of individuality and the standardised uniforms of the mass.[51] The approach of Gianikian and Ricci Lucchi is reminiscent of the photographic projects of August Sander, such as *Face of Our Time* (1929). Sander believed that 'the photographer with his camera can grasp the physiognomic image of his time'; 'a typology of the body as a social index', writes Graham Clarke, 'is basic to Sander's complex code of social identity. Posture and stance, for example, reflect part of a larger mapping of the body in relation to public status and self-confidence'.[52] The photographer and the filmmakers share the ambition to catalogue and inventory society at a given moment in time, as well as an awareness of the tensions between social roles and individual identities. Humanity appears in all its physical imperfection, social inequality and cultural diversity. In *Oh! Uomo*, the line of children who walk slowly and laboriously past the camera with their crutches and ill-fitting boots replicate movements first captured by the chrono-photographers but in doing so they show bodies ravaged

51 Marcello Flores, 'La grande guerra dei contadini', *L'Unità* (4 December 1995).
52 Graham Clarke, 'Public Faces, Private Lives: August Sander and the Social Typology of the Portrait Photograph', in *The Portrait in Photography*, ed. Graham Clarke (London: Reaktion Books, 1992), 71.

by malnutrition and disease, not perfect machines in motion. The body is made into a machine when it is broken. The hand that lights and holds the cigarette, the fingers that type, the arm that scythes, and the legs that walk – all are prosthetic devices shown by the documentary film. War not only destroys men's bodies, it inaugurates a new world in which bodies too are reconstructed and re-made.[53]

Historically, fascination with the body has been driven by a range of forces, from developments in science to the growth of pornography, not to mention the new technologies of visualisation themselves. Analyses from a post-colonial perspective have argued convincingly that the history of modernity and its notions of the body cannot be separated from Western conceptions of colonised subjects and non-western peoples as 'Other'. Assenka Oksiloff writes that the non-Western body was conceived in its essence as 'primitive', and that the shift in anthropology to an observational mode gave primacy to 'direct, unmediated visual access to the native body'.[54] In films from *Dal Polo all'Equatore* to *Terra Nullius*, Gianikian and Ricci Lucchi show how the cameramen of the time juxtaposed Europeans with their modern technology to the 'natives' with their primitive tools. An evolutionary schema implicitly frames images of Europeans carrying rifles and natives carrying spears. When Australian Aboriginals wear European clothing, it is tattered, when, in *La marcia dell'uomo*, Africans are shown eating with knives and forks it is to mock them. Such images are consistent with that of ethnographic films analysed by Oksiloff in which the 'first contact' is staged; in Rudolf Poch's *Bushman Speaking into a Phonograph* (1908), 'primitive is not simply at the end of the evolutionary time line; he is figured as "outside" of Time, and as an ahistorical Other in relation to naturalized time'.[55]

---

53   These scenes act as a critical commentary on the Futurist fantasy of the metal-lized body; see Christine Poggi, 'Dreams of Metallized Flesh: Futurism and the Masculine Body', in Christine Poggi, *Inventing Futurism: Art and the Politics of Artificial Optimism* (Princeton: Princeton University Press, 2009).

54   Assenka Oksiloff, *Picturing the Primitive: Visual Culture, Ethnography, and Early German Cinema* (London, Palgrave, 2001), 3–4.

55   Ibid., 60.

Audience responses to the films of Gianikian and Ricci Lucchi suggest that a more phenomenological approach is particularly appropriate in their case. This might be deduced from their working methods with its stress on manual intervention and mimesis, and from the depiction of extreme conditions of starvation, poverty, illness and subjection to violence that recurs in them. The filmmakers set out to elicit strong responses. It is as if they are saying, 'the images you are seeing have themselves seen in reality what is now a projection on the screen'. At the same time, the films of Gianikian and Ricci Lucchi draw attention to themselves as historical footage that has been re-made. The viewer is addressed as someone who is watching a film.

Vivian Sobchack gives a good summary of a phenomenological approach that examines how viewers watch films. She argues that there is a mimetic and physical relationship to images that is not reducible to the cognitive and engagement with narrative. 'Watching a film,' she writes, 'we can see the seeing as well as the seen, hear the hearing as well as the heard, and feel the movement as well as see the moved. As viewers, not only do we spontaneously and invisibly perform these existential acts directly for and as ourselves, in relation *to* the film before us, but these same acts are coterminously given to us as the film, as mediating acts of perception-cum-expression we take up and *invisibly perform* by appropriating and incorporating them into our own existential performance; we watch them as a *visible performance* distinguishable from, yet included in, our own'.[56] Such an embodied viewing experience was initially at the heart of Gianikian and Ricci Lucchi's *cinema profumato*, but the films they made subsequently have equally worked in terms of affects not adequately comprehended through notions of 'reading' and 'decoding'.[57] Critics have, for example, compared

---

56   Vivian Sobchack, *The Address of the Eye: A Phenomenology of Film Experience* (Princeton: Princeton University Press, 1992), 10–11.

57   On the limits of critical viewing that is always searching for 'meanings', David MacDougall writes: 'when they see a film they worry about what they are supposed to think. Their thinking keeps interfering with the process of looking [...] They cannot give themselves to the images of a film, and afterwards all that is left in their minds is a series of judgements, or a set or questions, or a list of items they believe

the experience of watching *Dal Polo all'Equatore* to being in a trance or
under hypnosis, suggesting surrender of control and a haptic response to
the images and sounds. Giovanna Marini, the composer, singer and col-
laborator on the war trilogy, spoke of the experience of watching *Prigionieri della guerra*, as one of being pulled between a state of dreaming and
an awareness of a horrific reality: 'Everything appeared transformed and
seen by another eye, rarefied and even dream-like images, yet there was
always the harsh reality, utter truth'.[58] Often members of audiences react to
images of violence in Gianikian and Ricci Lucchi's films by covering their
eyes and looking down, or by letting out involuntary gasps and sighs. The
filmmakers have not hesitated from confronting spectators, whether with
images of pornographic scenes or surgery in medical documentaries. The
body is shown in its vulnerability. Scenes, such as that of eye surgery in *Oh!
Uomo*, focus on what Susan Stewart has called the boundaries and limits
of the body – the slit formed by the eye-lid is one of those apertures, those
'cuts and gaps in the body's surface', that 'work to constitute the notion
of the subject, of the individual body, and, ultimately, the self'. Instead of
the 'body as a functional tool and a body as a still life, the classical nude,
the body is shown as fragmented and disordered'.[59] The audience's dis-
comfort is intensified by removal of the reassuring frames of the medical
documentary that held the images at arm's length and conferred meaning
on them. Instead, the act of showing disfigured faces and broken bodies is
direct and unmediated, shocking.

When the films had an abundance of inter-titles that indicated appropriate responses on the part of audiences as well as informing them about
exactly what they were seeing, they could be allocated a label and classified. Luca Comerio's documentaries, it seems, were full of inter-titles with
a distinctive rhetoric associated with Fascism. Once taken away, without
being replaced by another set of verbal signposts, the images lost a precise

---

have been left out'; *The Corporeal Image: Film, Ethnography, and the Senses*, ed. David
MacDougall (Princeton: Princeton University Press, 2006), 8.

58   Marini, 'La musica', 115.

59   Susan Stewart, *On Longing: Narratives of the Miniature, the Gigantic, the Souvenir,
the Collection* (Durham and London: Duke University Press, 1993), 104.

identification and acquired new potential for meanings. Audiences were no longer told how they should interpret and react to what they saw. The filmmakers allowed themselves only images to work on and (sometimes) sound, and sought to make films that 'made sense' by working with and on the senses. It is the combination of troubling images in which the body (human and animal) is so present with the lack of words that direct us in how to respond that has provoked the greatest criticism of Gianikian and Ricci Lucchi's work. The major anxiety is that privileging the image opens the way to aestheticisation, whether of the bodies of colonialised people turned into spectacle or the bodies of the dead and wounded in war shown in all their macabre horror.[60]

The problem of this criticism is that, in Skoller's words, it 'tends to perpetuate the old and ultimately moralistic mind/body binary in which the rationalist function of critical analysis can take place only within the logos of language and textuality'.[61] The result is that aesthetic pleasure in the image is treated as suspect and incompatible with critical thought and analysis. Images that trigger emotional responses are likewise regarded as a form of manipulation from which the spectator is unable to escape. However, as Skoller argues in his reply to criticisms levelled by Catherine Russell of *Dal Polo all'Equatore*, such an approach 'ultimately reduces and may even obscure the possibility of multiple strategies for generating critical discourse in a medium like film – in which affect and sensation are central to meaning making'.[62]

60 See Catherine Russell, *Experimental Ethnography: The Work of Film in the Age of Video* (Durham and London: Duke University Press, 1999), 21–2.
61 Skoller, *Shadows, Specters, Shard*, 22.
62 Ibid., 22.

Death and Cinema

In January 1995 Gianikian and Ricci Lucchi travelled to Sarajevo, a city under siege. Before leaving their Milan apartment, they took the last rolls of 8mm film from the fridge and the 8mm camera. 'In January of that year', they write, 'we filmed objects and people destroyed in Sarajevo. The burial places, the graves shot in 8mm – a cinematic format that had also gone. Clear and precise images of the site of the massacres covered by a mass of electronic images destined to be erased'.[63] The connection between death and cinema is ritually enacted in this scene in Sarajevo. Gianikian and Ricci Lucchi lament the loss, forever, of a film stock that stands not only for their youth as filmmakers but as a link to the historic avant-garde that is fading away.[64] At the same time, they are remembering the fate of the inhabitants of the city. There is no nostalgia. If anything there is a note of defiance. The last images shot with the 8mm camera are 'clear and precise'. They will continue to bear witness, it is suggested, when the saturation coverage of the television channels will have left no mark. A kind of redemption may be possible in the after-life of the images, though Gianikian and Ricci Lucchi have no illusions about the mortality of their art or of that of cinema itself.

The theme of death recurs in the work of Gianikian and Ricci Lucchi and this constitutes one area of inquiry. A second area is the link between death and the materials and methods of their found footage filmmaking. And thirdly, there is the question of how their films relate to the demise of analogue cinema and the rise of digital technologies. All three are closely interrelated but I will look initially here at each in turn.

Death is continuously evoked in the cinema of Gianikian and Ricci Lucchi. In Mahler's song cycle, in the ruined villages once home to Armenians, in the hunting scenes in the Arctic and on the Equator, in the killing fields of the First World War, in the eyes of starving children, in the many

63   Gianikian and Ricci Lucchi, 'Voyages en Russie. Autour des avant-gardes', 49.
64   8mm film stock stopped being sold in the early 1990s; the more commonly used (but less flexible) super 8 went out of production in 2008.

scenes in which animals die from hunger, exhaustion or are slaughtered by men. Footage in the final sequence of *Dal Polo all'Equatore* shows a soldier die. The footage is very rare as such scenes were censored and the heavy camera equipment militated against filming near combat. The film shows men running forward as they advance towards enemy positions – scarcely distinguishable dark dots in the middle distance. By slowing the film and re-framing the images, the filmmakers show the moment a body is hit and the halting movement as it falls to the ground. The sequence brings Marey to mind and his attempt to visualise the invisible. Only here the invisible is the passage from life (and motion) to death. The documentation of such scenes is also rare because of taboos about showing the moment of death and showing 'one's own dead' as opposed to the enemy dead.

Photographs have been extensively written about in terms of death. Roland Barthes, in particular, writes about the different aspects of the photograph's relationship to death. He muses about the possibility of 'relocating the advent of Photography' in relation to the 'anthropological place of Death' in society.[65] He meditates on the Photograph as 'the general and somehow natural witness of "what has been"', modern society's substitute for the monument. In historical photographs, there is 'always a defeat of time – *that* is dead and *that* is going to die'.[66] Reflecting on Alexander Gardner's photograph of 1865 of the young Lewis Payne, a prisoner about to be executed, Barthes writes: 'I read at the same time: *This will be* and *this has been*; I observe with horror the anterior future of which death is the stake'.[67]

Comments made by the filmmaker Morgan Fisher echo those of Barthes. For Fisher, documentaries and newsreels are different: 'the people are not characters in a work of fiction; they are as real as we are. We know that they will some day die, just as we know that we will die'. There is irony in that the spectator knows what is not known to the subjects, but also 'pathos, shame at our impotence that our knowledge cannot prevent violence from

65 Roland Barthes, *Camera Lucida. Reflections on Photography*, trans. Richard Howard (New York: Hill and Wang, 1981), 92.

66 Ibid., 96.

67 Ibid.

happening. We are helpless, and one response is fascination [...] If motion picture footage of a person is old enough, the person we see is now almost certainly dead, and this is what I thought when I saw *The Children's Party* – all these kids almost certainly now dead'.[68] Fisher shares the premises that the analogue image of photography – whether still or moving – has an indexical relationship to reality; that is, in Barthes's words, 'every photograph is a certificate of presence'.[69]

Barthes's reflections on photography take as their starting point the death of his mother. While his thoughts have a rare reflexive quality, the contemplation of loved ones in and through photographs is a longstanding practice in many parts of the world and, in some parts, images of the deceased are encased in headstones in cemeteries. However, it could be argued that historical and cultural changes taking place in the second half of the 20th century gave a new prominence to the role of images in thinking about mortality in the way exemplified by Fisher. While this is no doubt linked to the obsession with the past in western societies and the importance attributed to memorialisation, it also had to do with transformations in the technologies of image and sound reproduction. Among filmmakers, there was a new awareness of the perishable nature of the medium and the rapid disappearance of cinema's history. It was not just that the people in the photographs or film frames were no longer alive; it was likely that the visible traces that were left of them would disappear as well. Anxiety about death and preserving their memory was being transferred to the very medium that, in Mary Ann Doane's words, was thought to be able not only, like photography, to 'fix a moment' but that 'made archivable duration itself. In that sense, it was perceived as a prophylactic against death [...] What was registered on film was life itself in all its multiplicity, diversity, and contingency'.[70]

---

68   Morgan Fisher refers here to Joseph Cornell's film *Children's Party* (1940s-1968); Morgan Fisher speaking at the conference 'Anticipating the Past: Artists: Archive: Film', at Tate Modern, 12–13 May 2006; audio tapes in Tate library, www.tate.org. uk/research/researchservices/library/.

69   Barthes, *Camera Lucida*, 87.

70   Mary Ann Doane, *The Emergence of Cinematic Time: Modernity, Contingency and the Archive* (Cambridge, MA: Harvard University Press, 2002), 22.

The nature of all analogue technologies, whether of sound recording (vinyl and electronic tape) or film, is entropic – destined to gradual and unstoppable disintegration. Paolo Cherchi Usai has examined the idea that film can be rescued from this condition and exposed it as an illusion that has blinded people to the true nature of film. From the very beginning of cinema, from the very moment that film is fed into the projector, films have been worn down by use and slowly decomposed chemically over decades. That is when the industry itself has not actively destroyed equipment, film stock, and archives no longer regarded as sufficiently modern and up-to-date. The idea that celluloid would come to the rescue when nitrate films were transferred to the new film failed to take account of the fact that celluloid has a shorter lifespan than the admittedly unstable and inflammable nitrate. Cherchi Usai suggests that moving image preservation will be redefined as 'the science of its gradual loss and the art of coping with the consequences, very much like a physician who has accepted the inevitability of death even while he continues to fight for the patient's life'.[71]

Awareness of this situation has been particularly acute, it seems, among independent filmmakers working with what are redundant technologies. Martine Beugnet has spoken of 'death and decay' as a 'core dimension of materialist filmmaking', along with an aesthetics of erosion, decay and erasure. Methods, such as superimposition, scratching, and writing over the image, associated with the historic avant-garde and revived by Stan Brakhage, Carolee Schneemann and others, have been incorporated, she argues in a filmmaking that has elaborated forms of 'mourning'.[72] In an approach that has affinities with Jeffrey Skoller's analyses based on Benjamin's conception of 'allegory', she writes that old film has been endowed with auratic qualities fore-grounded by rituals of mourning that link the death of the image to the loss of friends, kin and peoples. A case study of Fédérique Devaux shows how the artist in exile remembers the plight of her

71 Cherchi Usai, *The Death of Cinema*, 105.
72 Martine Beugnet, 'Mourning in the Age of the Digital: Memory, Loss, and Materialist Filmmaking', paper given at the Autopsies Research Project Day: 'Yesterday's Objects: The Death and Afterlife of Everyday Things', at University College London, 4 June 2010.

people, the Kabyles, through her films. The 'K', in the *K* films series, refers, says Beugnet, not only to the Kabyles but to the letter K of Kodak, which is printed on each frame, and to the Super 8 film (used by Devaux) – film no longer produced after 2008. Devaux described making films as physical – 'like working dough, shaping and re-shaping' the material. She uses of the music of lament – a recalling of the dead – for the soundtrack.

Luisella Farinotti suggests a connection between the fascination with death in the films of Gianikian and Ricci Lucchi and a preoccupation with worlds in the process of disappearing and with technologies that have been, or are about to go out of general use. She writes: 'There is a crepuscular tone in the filmmakers' idea of cinema, a taste for the transitory and signs of finality –something they themselves are aware of when they say in an interview "we deal with that melancholy character and that vaguely frightening thing there is in every photograph – the return of the dead person".'[73] Recognition of mortality accompanies their art. It underpins a deliberate use of redundant technologies and handicraft methods that incorporate the unpredictable and non-repeatable actions of the human hand and eye. Assumptions about technical progress and linear ideas about history are subjected to critique by the way in which they work as well as by the films they make. Their practice consists of layering and collage that create palimpsests in which different temporalities coexist. As Matilde Nardelli has written with reference to the use of redundancy and obsolescence in contemporary art practice: 'what obsolescence ultimately enacts [...] is not a fossilisation of cinema but its plasticity: not its death but its continuation [...] cinema itself is highlighted as a movement, a moment already passing, rather then a thing'.[74]

The history of cinema is punctuated by periods of rapid change. There was the arrival of 'talkies' and the end of 'silent' films, and the introduction of colour and the decline of black and white, not to mention transformations in camera technology, audiences and the geographies of production,

73   Farinotti, 'Memoria di copertura. Il cinema di Yervant Gianikian e Angela Ricci Lucchi come catalogo dell'orrore della storia', 51.

74   Matilde Nardelli, 'Moving Pictures: Cinema and its Obsolescence in Contemporary Art', *Journal of Visual Culture* 8 (2009), 245.

distribution and exhibition. 'Cinema has been down this road before',
notes D.N. Rodowick. In response, for example, to the explosive growth
of television in the 1950s, 'cinema represented itself as a spectacular artistic
and democratic medium in contradiction to television, whose diminu-
tive image belied its potentially demagogic power [...] As television took
on a mass role, cinema reserved for itself [...] the image of an "aesthetic"
experience'.[75] However, rise of digital technologies represents a faster and
more radical transformation: 'In the course of a single decade, the celluloid
strip with its reassuring physical passage of visible images, the noisy and
cumbersome cranking of the mechanical film projector or the Steenbeck
editing table, the imposing bulk of the film canister are all disappearing
one by one into virtual space, along with the images they so beautifully
recorded and presented'.[76] As David Campany has observed, the cinema
is now only one of the contexts in which films are viewed: 'the large auditorium takes its place alongside television, computer screens, in-flight
entertainment, lobbies, shop windows, galleries, and mobile phones'.[77]
For some commentators, the digital is seen as an extension of analogue
comparable to earlier innovations, and have argued that digital visual culture remains cinematic. Others, Rodowick included, maintain that there
is a radical difference between the technologies and the related properties
of the image – the analogue image is defined by the chemical reaction to
light and the trace it leaves, whereas the digital is the result of an entirely
computational process; 'unlike analogical representations, which have as
their basis a transformation of substance isomorphic with an originat-
ing image, virtual representations derive all their powers from numerical
manipulations [...] The analogical arts are fundamentally arts of intaglio,
or worked matter – a literal sculpting by light of hills and valleys in the raw
film whose variable density produces a visible image. But the transforma-

75   D.N. Rodowick, *The Virtual Life of Film* (Cambridge, MA and London: Harvard
      University Press, 2007), 4.
76   Ibid., 4–5.
77   David Campany, 'Introduction: When to be Fast? When to be Slow' in *The Cinematic*,
      16.

tion of matter in the electronic and digital arts takes place on a different atomic register and in a different conceptual domain'.[78]

The scope and consequences of digitalisation cannot yet be adequately measured. Suffice to say that we are living through a period of intense change within visual culture in which the basic frames of reference are being called into question. The changes also present us with opportunities. According to Laura Mulvey: 'the new technology offers an opportunity to look back to the "before", to the "then" of the indexical image in the changing light of the "after", the "now". The aesthetics of the past meet the aesthetics of the present, bringing, almost incidentally, new life to the cinema and its history'.[79] For anyone familiar with the films of Yervant Gianikian and Angela Ricci Lucchi, reading passages of Mulvey's *Death 24x a Second. Stillness and the Moving Image* can bring about the sensation of *déjà vu*. Mulvey argues that avant-garde film anticipated many of the changes in perception that she identifies, and Gianikian and Ricci Lucchi, as latecomers in that avant-garde, made films that relate to her overall analysis. What is striking, however, is the closeness with which her descriptions of 'delayed cinema' fit their method of working and conception of the spectator: the mixing on equal terms of genres that have historically been separated out – fiction and documentary, different types of fiction and documentary; the association of wonder and marvelling as much with the documentaries of Lumière as with the fictional films of Méliès; the decomposition and re-composition of images in chains of association rather than narrative; the 'delaying' and contemplation of images in which moving images are stilled. Mulvey argues that the spectator, thanks to video and digitial technologies, has acquired the ability and taste for re-constructing films when viewing them, thereby questioning traditional assumptions about how films are seen and understood; 'the "aesthetics of delay"', she writes, 'revolve around the process of stilling the film, but also repetition, the return to certain moments or sequences as well as slowing down the illusion of natural movement. The delayed cinema makes visible its materiality and its

---

78   Ibid., 8–9.
79   Mulvey, *Death 24x a Second. Stillness and the Moving Image*, 21.

aesthetic attributes, but also engages an element of play and of repetition compulsion'.[80] Watching films becomes less about following a plot than about using the re-wind facility to dwell on a detail, review a sequence in slow motion, or freeze a frame. The opposition of film and still photography loses its fixity: 'the pensive spectator rescues those aspects of cinema that Roland Barthes felt were lacking in comparison with the complexity of the photograph'.[81]'The technical slowing down the flow of the film is significant, above all, because it opens up the possibility of finding some details that have 'lain dormant, as it were, waiting to be noticed'. The storage function of film, like that of photography, 'may be compared to the memory left in the unconscious by an incident lost to consciousness [...] both need to be deciphered retrospectively across delayed time'.[82]

In 1994 Gianikian and Ricci Lucchi made a 16mm short called *Aria* (Air) in response to a commission from the TV channel, Arte, to celebrate the 100th anniversary of cinema. This 16-minute film, which includes tinted as well as black and white footage, re-cycles material from scientific documentaries shot around 1900. It is a kind of visual poem. A neatly bearded and moustachioed man in a laboratory breathes in white fumes from a glass beaker and exhales. Bubbles balloon and float. The original film has been re-edited and slowed down. The filmmakers even tried to magnify and re-photograph frames to see whether reflections of the original cameraman were visible in the bubbles. In their notes, they speak of the images of the past enclosing an ensemble of cosmic symbols – images that were 'fixed' at the beginning of the century, 'before the onset of catastrophes and massacres'. *Aria* is light, playful, free as air, utopian. Pure cinephilia.

Now veteran filmmakers, Gianikian and Ricci Lucchi are finding it increasingly difficult to make the found footage films using material from the first decades of cinema – the films for which they best known. The images on nitrate film in their collection are vanishing, leaving transparent frames. The film laboratories in Milan have closed down. The skilled

80   Ibid., 192.
81   Ibid., 195–6.
82   Ibid.. 9.

technicians have retired or died. The film stocks that they have used, such as 8mm, are no longer available. The catalogue of difficulties that they have faced in recent years is intimidating. It is remarkable that they have been able to continue working with their artisanal methods for so long. The work calls for concentration, good eyesight, steady hands, patience, and stamina, not to mention energy and imagination. Nor can digital technologies replicate what the filmmakers do with the tools of a fast-disappearing technology. The film stock itself has qualities that digital is not able to achieve, and can be manipulated by filmmakers in ways not possible using digital means. Indeed, the announcement of the death of analogue film has been premature in that a generation of younger filmmakers has sought to keep it alive, not as an alternative to digital but as another a set of practices and histories open to appropriation and exploration.[83]

At the time of writing, Gianikian and Ricci Lucchi are engaged in completing the unfinished film originally titled *Interni a Leningrado* (Leningrad Interiors). What precise form it will take has yet to be seen, but it is likely to represent a new direction in their work. While the filmmakers have collected film shot by others and have used archival footage in public collections, they have also shot film and video themselves over the decades. This archive of their own must by now consist of kilometres of footage in 8mm, 16mm, and video. Gianikian has habitually carried a small movie camera on journeys. In the pursuit of the images shot by cameramen in the early part of the twentieth century, he himself recorded images documenting the history of the second half of the century of which the filmmakers have been witnesses. Not the history seen on the television news or documentaries but the chronicle of the everyday noted on camera in visits to people and places across the world. Significantly, little of this footage has been seen to date. At the MoMA retrospective in 2009, the only reportage of this kind shown was *Terremoto*, screened in conjunction with *Uomini anni vita*, and *Nocturne*, which was placed in a programme of shorts. Gianikian and Ricci Lucchi have not been interested in one of the

83   See the artist-run project no.w.here; see www.no-w-here.org.uk/; accessed 12 November 2010.

principal functions of the documentary film – reporting on the world in the present tense. Instead, their interest in their own material has grown as it has aged and as the images have begun to lose their reference to the 'real' and the 'immediate'. The footage has become archival. Dated colours, signs of deterioration and other material factors help to augment its strangeness. It has become a record of an event now in the past, a fact attested to by the 'dated' quality of the image. An example that illustrates these aspects of Gianikian and Ricci Lucchi's re-working of their own material is *Diario 1989. Dancing in the Dark* (2009), a video shot shortly after making of *Ghiro, ghiro, tondo*.

The full title – *Frammenti elettrici n. 6. Diario 1989. Dancing in the Dark* – contains clues about the filmmakers' approach. Firstly, the word 'diary' is added. The term 'fragments', which had been used to link the series of short films made from 2001 to 2005, suggests continuity with recent work. 'Diario' has already appeared in a title: *Ritorno a Khodorciur* is also 'Diario Armeno', another video shot by the filmmakers. There is a deliberate choice to connect the new work to its predecessor, and, possibly, to films yet to be made. Diary, moreover, suggests a personal view and the compilation of everyday occurences by the author. The video is an entry in the diary which Gianikian and Ricci Lucchi have been keeping for many years – 'putting together more (electric) fragments from their highly personal and extraordinary catalogue of life'.[84] The date, '1989', resonates in contemporary history as the year in which the Berlin Wall fell and in which Communism came to signify a utopia in the past rather than one projected into the future. The historic events echo in private as well as public life. The video records people dancing late in the evening at a festival in rural Romagna. The event, a Festa dell'Unità, proves to be the last one ever in that the Italian Communist Party for whose newspaper, *L'Unità*, it fundraised was dissolved. Finally, there is a title within the title, namely 'Dancing in the Dark'. This refers to two dances – the dance of the festival-

---

84   Aldo Spinello, 'Diario 1989. Dancing in the Dark', di Yervant Gianikian e Angela Ricci Lucchi', article of 24 November 2009; www.sentieriselvaggi.it/articolo. asp?sezo=1&sez1=256&art=34776; accessed 14 December 2009.

goers in Romagna, and the dance in the Vincente Minnelli film of 1953, *The Band Wagon*, in which Fred Astaire and Cyd Charisse dance to the music of the song by that name. But one is no more real or fictional than the other. The figures who dance *ballo liscio* are dancing the last dance, the last to keep up a tradition of ballroom in the open-air, the last to go to the festival. Nostalgia is cinematic.

The filmmakers give a typically spare yet poetic description of the film:

> 60 days before the Event/the trajectory
> as it take place is already in the past
> – a past that has been betrayed, thrown away –
> unrealized
> In the midst of the Italian countryside
> A surreal vision
> mosquitoes, grasshoppers, sausage smoke
> And smoke on the stage, proletarian food
> Carnality, vitality (or vital), rhythm
> But already a shadow theater, too
> Eclipse – Real and unreal
> A primitive, savage world
> Almost
> In which other
> Cultures
> Insert themselves
> Like a card castle
> It will fall in a complex situation
> In a complex catastrophe
> Imponderable
> The present disorientation
> Of a local culture
> With deep roots.
> Che Guevara – improbable dancers
> Flash dance – counter mazurka and
> Even more improbable dancers
> In an exotic Latin American style,
> suburban American
> Far from the rhythms of tangos, of waltzes
> We are in

An awkward suburban Nashville
Going up in smoke
Imitative fake imposed
Far from the initial genuineness
They're not having any doubts
Unconditional devotion to the Cause
Soon to suffer
a cut a derailing[85]

Gianikian and Ricci Lucchi's video is shot using a hand-held camera. The light is poor and comes and goes. The images are grainy, tactile. It is often hard to make out the figures for the blurring and lack of definition. They get lost in the darkness. As a record it is approximate – more a mood than an event. The editing has slowed the speed of the images to produce a ritualised movement. It reprises the work of the ethnographic film, realising the idea of 'reverse anthropology' whereby the anthropologists make themselves and their own society the object of study. The making of the film becomes part of the study, a piece of participant observation. The camera too dances.

85   The English translation in the Turin Film Festival programme; www.torinofilmfest. org/?action=detail&id=8793; accessed 14 December 2009.

Still Images with Words
by Yervant Gianikian and Angela Ricci Lucchi

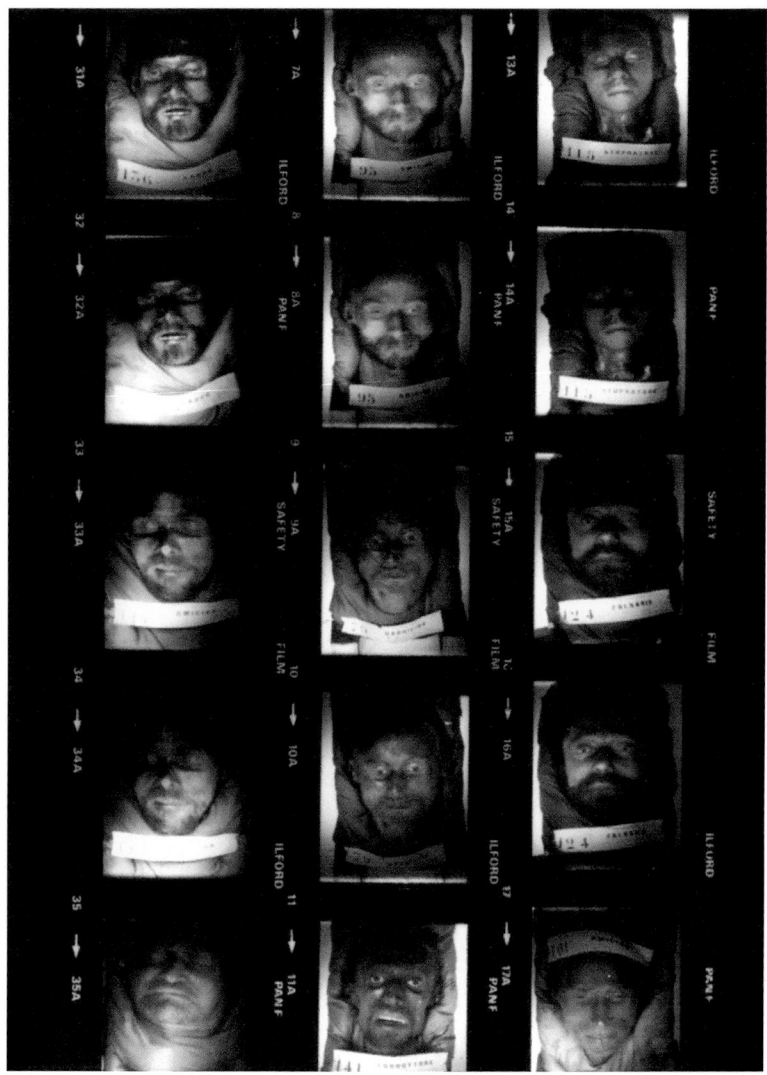

1 'The whole world catalogued in accordance with an obsessive criminological vision'.

2 'I photograph the slow movements of an underwater swimmer – I observe the evolution of different types of jelly-fish that resemble underwater fireworks'.

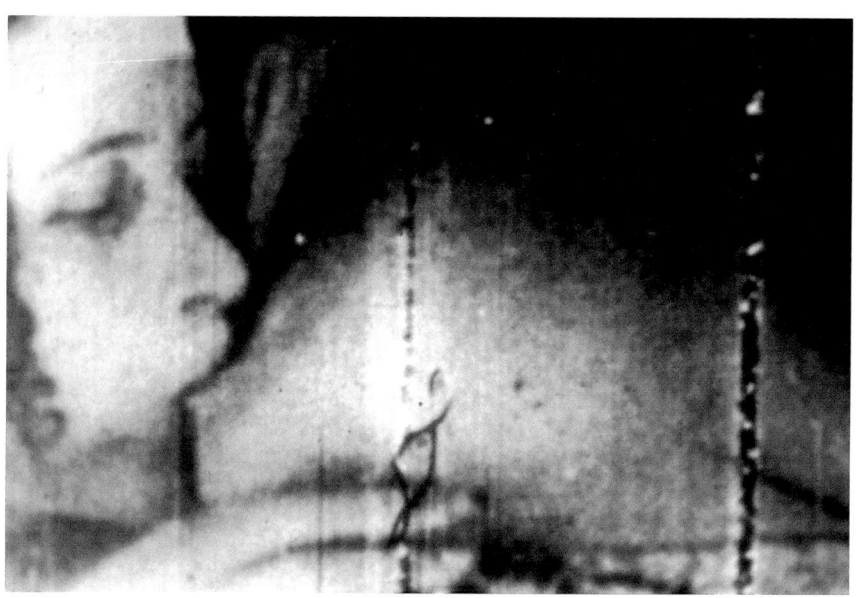

3 'We were very interested in the lines and scratches – it was as if they'd seen the film a thousand times, as if there was a veil, and the image appeared behind it'.

4 'A catalogue of images that ideally might have belonged to Gustav Mahler by analogy of themes, times, dates, places, and moments of inspiration'.

5 'We travel as we catalogue, we catalogue as we travel through the cinema
that we are re-filming'.

6 '"The Black Sphinx": Baron Franchettti's expedition to Uganda, including "scenes of missionaries hunting for their religious prey"'.

7 'I was born in Turkey in 1906, during the reign of the Sultan Abdul Iì Amid, in the mountain village of Khodorciur, amongst the woods, fields and rocks' (Raphael Gianikian).

8 'Everyone saw the film from the point of view they wanted. I asked myself whether
we were not still prisoners of the war'.

9 'War and beauty of the panorama – elements in stark contrast'.

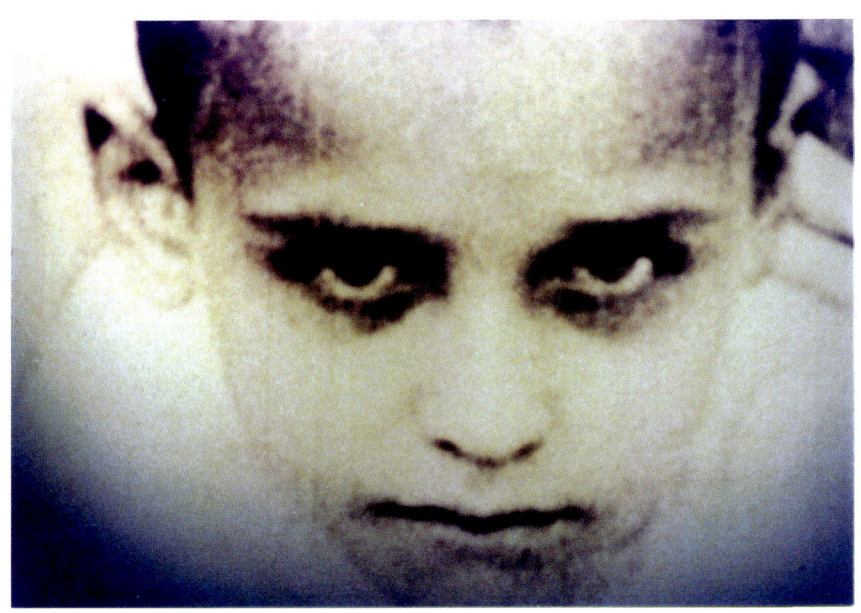

10 'We became aware of no longer being ourselves the subjects of the look but of having become the objects of the look of those who suffered'.

11 'False ethnographers, armed with movie cameras, caricature the local customs of the "primitive" people'.

12 'The First World War had marked the end of the isolated traveller-explorer.
The new "travellers" move in compact groups towards the exotic, towards its ruin'.

13 'We have close ties with the Russian avant-garde: Esther Schub, Dziga Vertov, Mikhail Kaufman, and Lev Kuleshov, for example, have all been important for us'.

14 'Our films are also constructed around places we have visited
and people we have met'.

15 'We have never experienced periods of tranquillity in our work'.

16 'Already a shadow theatre too. Eclipse – real and unreal'

Filmography and Installations

The following titles in Italian and in English have been agreed with Yervant Gianikian and Angela Ricci Lucchi. There has been some variation in titling in both languages over the years. There are also titles in French, and when French has been used as an original title, instead of Italian, this title has been left unchanged with an accompanying title in English in brackets. There is one original title in English. Variation is sometimes due to minor adjustments (use of lower or upper case, word order), and, on other occasions, it marks stages in the making and exhibition of a film (notably, shorter and longer versions), or the reassembly of an installation. I have tried as far as possible to reference these changes in the main text or in footnotes when they are significant.

Erat Sora, 1975, 8mm, colour, silent, scent of rose, 10'.

Wladimir Propp – Profumo di lupo (Vladímir Propp – Scent of Wolf), 1975, 8mm, colour, silent, scent of raspberry, 10'.

Del sonno e dei sogni di rosa limitata al senso dell'odorato (Of Sleep and of Dreams of Rose Limited to the Sense of Smell), 1975, 8mm, silent, scent of lily of the valley and wintergreen, 10'.

Alice profumata di rosa (Alice Scented with Rose), 1975, 8mm, colour, silent, scent of rose, 10'.

Klinger ed il guanto (Klinger and the Glove), 1975, 8mm, colour, silent, disguised scent, 5'.

Catalogo della scomposizione (Catalogue of De-composition), 1975, 8mm, colour, silent, scent of naphthalene, 10'.

Non cercare il profumo di Bunuel (Do not search for the Scent of Bunuel), 1975, 8mm, colour, silent, scent of sweet sultan grains and essence of angelique, 10'.

Catalogo comparativo (Comparative Catalogue), 1975, 8mm, colour, silent, 10'.

Stone Book, 1975, 8mm, colour, silent, 10'.

Dal 2 novembre al giorno di Pasqua (From 2 November to Easter Day), 1975–6, 8mm, colour, silent, 10'.

Cesare Lombroso – Sull'odore del garofano (Cesare Lombroso – On the Scent of Carnation), 1976, 16mm, silent, 12'.

Di alcuni fiori non facilmente catalogabili (Of Some Flowers not Easily Catalogued), 1976, 8mm, colour, silent, 10'.

Cataloghi – Non è altro che gli odori che sente (Catalogues – Nothing but the Scents One Smells), 1976, 16mm, silent, scent of violet and strawberry, 20'.

Catalogo N. 2 (Catalogue N. 2), 1976, 8mm, colour, silent, 20'.

Profumo (Perfume), 1977, 8mm, silent, various scents and odours, 27'.

Catalogo N. 3 – Odore di tiglio intorno alla casa (Catalogue N. 3. – Scent of Lime Trees Around the House), 1977–9, 8mm, colour, silent, scent of lime tree, 12'.

Un prestigiatore/Una miniaturista (A Male Conjurer/A Female Miniaturist), 1978, 8mm, colour, silent, two smells, 10'.

Milleunanotte (A Thousand and One Nights), 1979, 16mm, unfinished.

Karagoez et les brûleurs d'herbes parfumés (Karagoez and the Burners of Scented Grasses), 1979, 8mm, colour, silent, scent of damask-rose and bitter almonds, 16'.

Catalogo N. 4 – Un due tre: immagini. Un due tre: profumi (Catalogue n. 4 – One two three images. One two three scents), 1980, 16mm, colour, silent, 18'.

Karagoez – Catalogo 9.5 (Karagoez – Catalogue 9.5), 1979–81, 16mm, silent, 56'.

Essence d'absinthe (Essence of Absinthe), 1981, 16mm, colour, silent, 15'.

Das Lied von der Erde – Gustav Mahler (The Song of the Earth – Gustav Mahler), 1982, 16mm, colour, silent, 17'.

Dal Polo all'Equatore (From the Pole to the Equator), 1986, 16mm, colour, original soundtrack by Keith Ullrich and Charles Anderson, 101'.

Ritorno a Khodorciur. Diario Armeno (Return to Khodorciur. Armenian Diary), 1986, Betacam SP, colour, sound, 80'.

La più amata dagli italiani (The Most Loved by Italians), 1988, U-matic, colour, sound, 80'.

Frammenti (Fragments), 1987, 16mm, sound, fifty-two three minute programmes for RAI TV.

Passion (Passion 1988), 16mm, colour, sound, 7'.

Terremoto (Earthquake), 1989–2006, 10'.

Uomini anni vita (Men Years Life), 1990, 16mm, colour, sound, 70'.

Interni a Leningrado (Interiors in Leningrad), 1990, 16mm, unfinished.

Archivi italiani n. 1. Il fiore della razza (Italian Archives N.1. The Flower of the Race), 1991, 16mm, colour, sound, 25'.

Archivi italiani n. 2 (Italian Archives N. 2), 1991, 16mm, colour, silent, 20'.

Mario Giacomelli, 1993, 35mm, black and white, 13'.

Animali criminali (Criminal Animals), 1994, 16mm, colour, silent, 7'.

Diario africano (African Diary), 1994, 16mm, colour, 8'.

Aria (Air), 1994, 16mm, colour, silent, 7'.

Lo specchio di Diana (The Looking Glass of Diana), 1996, video, colour, soundtrack by Keith Ullrich, 31ʹ.

Prigionieri della guerra (Prisoners of the War), 1995, 16mm and 35mm, colour, soundtrack with Giovanna Marini, 67ʹ.

Nocturne, 1997, video, colour, silent, 18ʹ.

Io ricordo (I Remember), 1997, video, colour, sound, 11ʹ.

Trasparenze (Transparencies), 1998, 16mm and 35mm, colour, sound, 6ʹ.

Su tutte le vette è pace (On the Heights All is Peace), 1998, 16mm and 35mm, colour, soundtrack with Giovanna Marini, 72ʹ.

Inventario balcanico (Balkan Inventory), 2000, 16mm, colour, soundtrack with Charles Ullrich and Djivan Gasparyan, 62ʹ.

Images d'Orient – Tourisme vandale (Images of the East – Vandal Tourism), 2001, Digital Betacam, colour, soundtrack with Giovanna Marini and Luis Agudo, 67ʹ.

Frammenti elettrici n. 1 – Rom (Uomini) (Electric Fragments N. 1 – Roma (Man)), 2002, Betacam SP, colour, 13ʹ.

Frammenti elettrici n. 2 – Viet-Nam (Electric Fragments N. 2 – Vietnam), 2002, Betacam SP, colour, 9ʹ.

Frammenti elettrici n. 3 – Corpi (Electric Fragments N. 3 – Bodies), 2002, Betacam SP, colour, 9ʹ.

Frammenti elettrici n. 4, 5 – Asia, Africa (Electric Fragments N. 4, 5 – Asia-Africa), 63ʹ.

Nuova Caledonia (New Caledonia), 2004, Digital Betacam, colour, 9ʹ.

Oh! Uomo (Oh! Mankind), 2004, 35mm, colour, soundtrack with Marina Marini and Luis Agudo, 72ʹ.

Luci misteriose (Mysterious Lights), 2005, video, black and white, 12ʹ.

Ghiro Ghiro Tondo (Around and Around), 2007, Digital Betacam, colour, sound, 60ʹ.

Frammenti elettrici n. 6. Diario 1989. Dancing in the Dark (Diary. 1989. Dancing in the Dark), 2009, Digi Beta Pal, colour, sound, 60ʹ.

Ti regalerò il mio ultimo respiro (I make a present to you of my last breath), 2009, video, colour, 5ʹ.

Installations

Visions du désert (Visions of the Desert), Fondation Cartier pour l'art contemporain, Paris, 21 June to 5 November 2000.

El Desert (The Desert) Fundació 'la Caixa', Barcelona, 26 January to 15 April 2000.

El Desert, Fundació 'la Caixa', Seville, 10 May to 22 July 2000.

La marcia dell'uomo (The Walk of Man) in section 'Plateau of Humankind', Biennale Arte, Venice, 2001.

Rom (Uomini) (Rom (Men)) in the exhibition 'Aubes, rêveries au bord de Victor Hugo', Paris, Maison de Victor Hugo, 11 October 2001 to 19 January 2002.

Corpo ferito (Wounded Body), commission for the inauguration of the Museum of Contemporary Art of Rovereto and Trento, 2002.

Terra Nullius in exhibition 'Based on True Stories' at the Witte De With Center for Contemporary Art, Rotterdam, 23 January to 30 March 2003.

Inventario balanico (Balkan Inventory) in the exhibition 'Blut & Honig/Blood & Honey' at Sammlung Essl Kunst der Gegerwart, Vienna, 16 May to 26 September 2003.

Aux vainçus (To the Defeated), commission for the permanent collection from MART (the Museum of Contemporary Art of Rovereto and Trento), 2004.

Electric Fragments in the exhibition 'Experiments with Truth' at the Fabric Workshop and Museum, Philadelphia, 3 December 2004 to 12 March 2005.

Lumières mysterieuses (Mysterious Lights) in 'Belgique visionnaire' at Palais des Beaux-Arts in Brussels, April to May 2005.

La marcia dell'uomo (The Walk of Man) in the Biennial of Lisboa Photo, Centro Cultural de Belém, Lisbon, May to August 2005.

Electric Fragments in the exhibition 'Reprocessing Reality' at P.S. 1 Contemporary Arts Center, New York, 6 April to 29 May 2006.

Train, in the exhibition 'Le noir est une couleur', Fondation Maeght, 30 June–5 November, 2006.

Trittico del novecento (Triptych of the Nineteenth Century), combining two new panels entitled *Terrorismo* (Terrorism) with *Il Corpo ferito* (Wounded Body) and *Aux vainçus* (To the Defeated), commission for the permanent collection from MART (the Museum of Contemporary Art of Rovereto and Trento), 2008.

Topografia aerea (Aerial Topography) in permanent collection of Museo Storico Italiano della Guerra, Rovereto, 2008.

Cesare Lombroso at the exhibition 'Italics – Arte italiana fra tradizione e rivoluzione, 1968–2008', Palazzo Grassi, 27 September 2008 to 22 March 2009.

Cesare Lombroso at the exhibition 'Italics – Italian Art between Tradition and Revolution, 1968–2008', Museum of Contemporary Art, Chicago, 18 July to 25 October 2009.

The films are distributed by:

Museum of Modern Art, New York, USA.
British Film Institute, London, UK.
Film Museum, Amsterdam, Holland.
Museum of Modern Art, Yokohama, Japan.
Cinematheque of Canberra, Australia.
Cinematheque Française, Paris, France.

Lab 80 Film, Bergamo, Italy.

Films available on VHS and DVD:

Prigionieri della guerra (VHS), Museo Storico Italiano della Guerra, Rovereto.
Su tutte le vette è pace (VHS), Museo Storico Italiano della Guerra, Rovereto.
Oh! Uomo (DVD), Museo Storico Italiano della Guerra, Rovereto.

Select Bibliography

Adams, Sitney, P., ed., *Film Culture: An Anthology* (London: Secker and Warburg, 1971).

Adorno, Theodor, *Mahler: A Musical Physiognomy* (Chicago, IL, and London: University of Chicago Press, 1991).

Azoury, Philippe, 'Sur "certaines radiations encore loin d'être claires"', *Trafic* 38 (Summer 2001): 50–62.

Barthes, Roland, *Camera Lucida. Reflections on Photography*, trans. Richard Howard (New York: Hill and Wang, 1981).

Bellour, Raymond, 'Il retromondo' in *Cinema Anni Vita. Yervant Gianikian e Angela Ricci Lucchi*, ed. Paolo Mereghetti and Enrico Nosei (Milan: Il Castoro, 2000).

——, 'Des instants choisis de l'espèce humaine', *Trafic* 38 (Summer 2001), 79–85.

Ben-Ghiat, Ruth, *Fascist Modernities: Italy, 1922–45* (Berkeley: University of California Press, 2001).

Benjamin, Walter, 'Little History of Photography' in *Walter Benjamin: Selected Writings, Volume 2: Part 2, 1931–1934*, ed. Michael W. Jennings, Howard Eiland and Gary Smith (Cambridge, MA, and London: Harvard University Press, 1999).

——, *One Way Street and Other Writings* (London and New York: Verso, 1985).

——, 'Some Motifs in Baudelaire' in Walter Benjamin, *Illuminations* (London: Fontana Books, 1973).

——, 'Theses on the Philosophy of History' in Walter Benjamin, *Illuminations*, ed. Hannah Arendt (London: Fontana, 1973).

——, *Walter Benjamin's Archive*, ed. Ursula Marx, Gudrun Schwarz, Michael Schwarz, and Erdmut Wizisla (London and New York: Verso, 2007).

Berger, John, *About Looking* (London: Writers and Readers, 1980).

——, *The Look of Things: Selected Essays and Articles* (London: Penguin, 1972).

Blümlinger, Christa, 'Cinéastes en archives', *Trafic* 38 (Summer 2001), 68–78.

Brakhage, Stan, 'Metaphors on Vision', in *Film Theory and Criticism*, ed. Leo Braudy and Marshall Cohen (Oxford: Oxford University Press, 1999).

Braun, Marta, *Picturing Time: The Work of Etienne-Jules Marey (1830–1904)* (Chicago, IL, and London: University of Chicago Press, 1992).

Brenez, Nicole, and De Raymond, Pauline, 'Ritorni di immagini. Il cinema delle origini e la pratica del reimpiego' *Cinegrafie* 13 (2001), 107–14.

Breton, André, 'As in a Wood', in *The Shadow and its Shadow: Surrealist Writings on the Cinema*, ed. Paul Hammond (Edinburgh: Polygon, 1991).

Buck-Morss, Susan, *The Dialectics of Seeing: Walter Benjamin and the Arcades Project* (Cambridge, MA, and London: MIT Press, 1993).

Burch, Noël, 'Primitivism and the Avant-Gardes' in Philip Rosen, ed., *Narrative, Apparatus, Ideology* (New York: Columbia University Press, 1986).

Burdett, Charles, *Journeys through Fascism: Italian Travel Writing between the Wars* (New York and Oxford: Berghahn Books, 2007).

Burgin, Victor, *The Remembered Film* (London: Reaktion Books, 2004).

Butler, Judith, *Frames of War. When is Life Grievable?* (London and New York: Verso, 2010).

Campany, David, ed., *The Cinematic* (Cambridge, MA, and London: MIT Press and Whitechapel, 2007).

Chambers, Iain, and Curti, Lidia, eds, *The Postcolonial Question: Common Skies, Divided Horizons* (London: Routledge, 1996).

Cherchi Usai, Paolo, *The Death of Cinema: History, Cultural Memory and the Digital Dark Age* (London: Palgrave Macmillan, 2008).

Clarke, Graham, 'Public Faces, Private Lives: August Sander and the Social Typology of the Portrait Photograph', in *The Portrait in Photography*, ed. Graham Clarke (London: Reaktion Books, 1992).

Costa, Antonio, 'Landscape and Archive: Trips around the World as Early Film Topic (1896–1914)' in *Film and Landscape*, ed. Martin Lefebvre (New York and London: Routledge, 2006).

Curtis, David, *Experimental Cinema: A Fifty-Year Evolution* (New York: Delta Book, 1971).

Dagrada, Elena, Mosconi, Elena, and Paoli, Silvia, eds, *Moltiplicare l'istante. Beltrami, Comerio e Pacchioni tra fotografia e cinema* (Milan: Il Castoro, 2007).

Dalle Vacche, Angela, ed., *The Visual Turn: Classical Film Theory and Art History* (New Brunswick, NJ, and London: Rutgers University Press, 2003).

Demos, T.J., ed., *Zones of Conflict* (New York: Pratt Manhattan Gallery, 2008).

Deren, Maya, 'Cinematography: The Creative Use of Reality' in *Film Theory and Criticism*, ed. Leo Braudy and Marshall Cohen (Oxford: Oxford University Press, 1999).

Deriu, Davide, 'Picturing Ruinscapes: The Aerial Photograph as Image of Historical Trauma' in *the image and the witness: Trauma, Memory and Visual Culture*, ed. Frances Guerin and Roger Hallas (London and New York, Wallflower Press, 2007).

Dillon, Brian, 'The Revelation of Erasure', *Tate Etc.* 8 (Autumn 2006), 30–41.

Doane, Mary Ann, *The Emergence of Cinematic Time: Modernity, Contingency and the Archive* (Cambridge, MA: Harvard University Press, 2002).

Elias, Norbert, *The Germans: Power struggles and the development of habitus in the 19th and 20th centuries*, trans. Eric Dunning and Stephen Mennell (Cambridge: Polity Press, 1996).

Elsaesser, Thomas, and Barker, Adam, eds, *Early Cinema: Space, Frame, Narrative* (London: British Film Institute, 1990).

Farinotti, Luisella, 'Memoria di copertura. Il cinema di Yervant Gianikian e Angela Ricci Lucchi come catalogo dell'orrore della storia', in *Locus Solus. Memoria e Immagini*, ed. Barbara Grespi (Milan: Pearson Paravia Bruno Mondadori, 2009).

Flores, Marcello, *Tutta la violenza di un secolo* (Milan: Feltrinelli, 2005).

Foot, John, *Italy's Divided Memory* (London and New York: Palgrave, 2009).

Forty, Adrian, and Küchler, Susanne, eds, *The Art of Forgetting* (Oxford and New York: Berg, 1999).

Foster, Hal, 'The Artist as Ethnographer' in Hal Foster, *The Return of the Real: The Avant-Garde at the End of the Century* (Cambridge, MA: MIT Press, 1996).

Frazer, James, *The Golden Bough: A Study in Magic and Religion* (London: Macmillan, 1929).

Friedrich, Ernst, *War against War* (Seattle, WA: Real Comet Press, 1987).

Gianighian, Raffaele, *Khodorciur. Viaggio di un pellegrino alla ricerca della sua Patria* (Venice: Casa Editrice Armena, 1992).

Gianikian, Yervant, 'Karagoez – Catalogo 9,5', *Griffithiana* 29–30 (September 1987).

——, and Ricci Lucchi, Angela, 'Dal Polo all'Equatore', *Griffithiana* 29–30 (September 1987).

——, and Ricci Lucchi, Angela, *La marcia dell'uomo* (Milan: Edizioni Mazzotta, 2001).

——, and Ricci Lucchi, Angela, *Topografia aerea* (Rovereto: Edizioni Osiride, 2008).

——, and Ricci Lucchi, Angela, 'Tourisme vandale. Deux projects', *Trafic* 38 (Summer 2001), 63–5.

——, and Ricci Lucchi, Angela, 'Voyages en Russie. Autour des avant-gardes', *Trafic* 33 (Spring 2005), 39–49.

Gibson, Mary, *Prostitution and the State in Italy, 1860–1915* (New Brunswick, NJ, and London: Rutgers University Press, 1986).

Gordon, Robert, 'Which Holocaust? Primo Levi and the Field of Holocaust Memory in Postwar Italy', *Italian Studies* 16.1 (Spring 2006), 85–113.

Guerin, Frances, and Hallas, Roger, eds, *the image and the witness: Trauma, Memory and Visual Culture* (London and New York, Wallflower Press, 2007).

Gunning, Tom, 'An Aesthetic of Astonishment: Early Film and the (In)Credulous Spectator' in *Viewing Postions*, ed. Linda Williams (New Brunswick, NJ: Rutgers University Press, 1995).

Hall, Catherine, 'Histories, Empires and the Post-Colonial Moment' in *The Postcolonial Question: Common Skies, Divided Horizons*, ed. Iain Chambers and Lidia Curti (London: Routledge, 1996).

Hall, Stuart, 'When was the "post-colonial"? Thinking at the Limit' in *The Postcolonial Question: Common Skies, Divided Horizons*, ed. Iain Chambers and Lidia Curti (London: Routledge, 1996).

Horn, David, *Social Bodies: Science, Reproduction and Italian Modernity* (Princeton, NJ: Princeton University Press, 1994).

Hovannisian, Richard G., *The Armenian Genocide* (London: Macmillan, 1992).

Huyssen, Andreas, *Present Pasts: Urban Palimpsests and the Politics of Memory* (Palo Alto, CA: Stanford University Press, 2003).

Keathley, Christian, *Cinephilia and History, or The Wind in the Trees* (Bloomington: Indiana University Press, 2005).

Kirby, Lynne, *Parallel Tracks: The Railroad and Silent Cinema* (Exeter: Exeter University Press, 1997).

Leoni, Diego, *Prigionieri della Guerra (1914–1918)* (Valdagno: Rossato, 1995).

Leyda, Jay, *Films Beget Films: A Study of the Compilation Film* (New York: Allen and Unwin, 1964).

Löwy, Michael, *Fire Alarm. Reading Walter Benjamin's 'On the Concept of History'* (London and New York: Verso, 2005).

MacDonald, Scott, *A Critical Cinema 3: Interviews with Independent Filmmakers* (Berkeley: University of California Press, 1998).

MacDougall, David, *The Corporeal Image: Film, Ethnography, and the Senses* (Princeton, NJ: Princeton University Press, 2006).

Maier, Charles S., *The Unmasterable Past: History, Holocaust and German National Identity* (Cambridge, MA: Harvard University Press, 1987).

Mandelstam, Osip, *A Journey to Armenia*, trans. Clarence Brown (London: Redstone Press, 1989).

Mannoni, Laurent, 'The Art of Deception' in *Eyes, Lies and Illusions*, ed. Laurent Mannoni, Werner Nekes and Marina Warner (London: Hayward Gallery, 2004).

Marks, Laura U., *The Skin of the Film: Intercultural Cinema, Embodiment and the Senses* (Durham, NC: Duke University Press, 2000).

Mereghetti, Paolo and Nosei, Enrico, eds, *Cinema Anni Vita. Yervant Gianikian and Angela Ricci Lucchi* (Milan: Il Castoro, 2000).

——, and Rossin, Federico, 'Il magazzino della Storia. Incontro con Yervant Gianikian e Angela Ricci Lucchi', *Lo straniero* 110–11 (August–September 2009), 119–27.

Merleau-Ponty, Maurice, *The Phenomenogy of Perception*, trans. Colin Smith (London and New York: Routledge, 1962).

Michaux, Henri, *A Barbarian in Asia*, trans. Sylvia Beach (New York: New Directions, 1949).

Miller, Donald E., and Touryan Miller, Lorna, *Survivors: An Oral History of the Armenian Genocide* (Berkeley, Los Angeles and London: University of California Press, 1993).

Moore, Rachel, *Savage Theory: Cinema as Modern Magic* (Durham, NC, and London: Duke University Press, 2000).

Mulvey, Laura, *Death 24x a Second. Stillness and the Moving Image* (London: Reaktion Books, 2006).

Musil, Robert, *Robert Musil Diaries, 1899–1941*, ed. Mark Mirsky, trans. Mark Mirsky and Philip Payne (New York: Basic Books, 1999).

Nardelli, Matilde, 'Moving Pictures: Cinema and its Obsolescence in Contemporary Art', *Journal of Visual Culture* 8 (2009), 243–64.

Nash, Mark, ed., *Experiments with Truth* (Philadelphia, PA: Philadelphia Fabric Workshop and Museum, 2004).

Nead, Lynda, *The Haunted Gallery: Painting, Photography and Film c. 1900* (New Haven, CT, and London: Yale University Press, 2007).

Nochlin, Linda, *The Body in Pieces: The Fragment as a Metaphor of Modernity* (London and New York: Thames and Hudson, 1995).

Oksiloff, Assenka, *Picturing the Primitive: Visual Culture, Ethnography, and Early German Cinema* (London: Palgrave, 2001).

Païni, Dominique, and Hibon, Danièle, 'Marcher, monter', *Trafic* 38 (Summer 2001), 66–7.

Palumbo, Patrizia, ed., *A Place in the Sun. Africa in Italian Colonial Culture from Post-Unification to the Present* (Los Angeles and London: University of California Press, 2003).

Passerini, Luisa, *Mussolini immaginario* (Bari and Rome: Laterza: 1991).

Poggi, Christine, *Inventing Futurism: Art and the Politics of Artificial Optimism* (Princeton, NJ, and Oxford: Princeton University Press, 2009).

Rees, A.L., *A History of Experimental Film and Video* (London: British Film Institute, 1999).

Renan, Sheldon, *The Underground Film: An Introduction to its Development in America* (London: Studio Vista, 1967).

Roberts, Graham, *The Man with the Movie Camera* (London: I.B. Tauris, 2000).

Rodowick, D.N., *The Virtual Life of Film* (Cambridge, MA, and London: Harvard University Press, 2007).

Rohdie, Sam, *Montage* (Manchester: Manchester University Press, 2006).

Rosen, Philip, *Change Mumified: Cinema, Historicity, Theory* (Minneapolis: University of Minnesota Press, 2007).

Rosenstone, Robert A., ed., *Revisioning History: Film and the Construction of a New Past* (Princeton, NJ: Princeton University Press, 1995).

Russell, Catherine, *Experimental Ethnography: The Work of Film in the Age of Video* (Durham, NC, and London: Duke University Press, 1999).

Said, Edward, *Orientalism* (London: Penguin, 1978).

Schnapp, Jeffrey, 'Propeller Talk', *Modernism/Modernity* 1.3 (1994), 153–78.

Shaviro, Stephen, *The Cinematic Body* (Minneapolis and London: Minnesota University Press, 2006).

Sipe, Dan, 'From the Pole to the Equator: A Vision of Wordless Past', *American History Review* 95.4 (October 1990), 1138–9.

Skoller, Jeffrey, *Shadows, Specters, Shards: Making History in Avant-Garde Film* (Minneapolis: University of Minnesota Press, 2005).

Sobchack, Vivian, *The Address of the Eye: A Phenomenology of Film Experience* (Princeton, NJ: Princeton University Press, 1992).

Sontag, Susan, 'Fascinating Fascism', in *A Susan Sontag Reader*, ed. Elizabeth Hardwick (London: Penguin, 1982).

——, *Regarding the Pain of Others* (London: Penguin, 2003).

Spinelli, Claudia, ed., *Reprocessing Reality: New Perspectives on Art and Documentary* (Geneva: JRP Editions, 2005).

Stewart, Susan, *On Longing: Narratives of the Miniature, the Gigantic, the Souvenir, the Collection* (Durham, NC, and London: Duke University Press, 1993).

Thompson, Mark, *The White War: Life and Death on the Italian Front 1915–1919* (London: Faber and Faber, 2008).

Tobing Rony, Fatimah, *The Third Eye: Race, Cinema, and the Ethnographic Spectacle* (Durham, NC, and London: Duke University Press, 1996).

Toffetti, Sergio, ed., *Yervant Gianikian, Angela Ricci Lucchi* (Turin: hopefulmonster, 1992).

Vatrican, Vincent, 'In Memory', *Bref* 42 (Autumn 1999), 12–14.

Virilio, Paul, *Pure War* (Los Angeles: Semiotext(e), 2008).

——, *War and Cinema: The Logistics of Perception* (London and New York: Verso, 1989).

Wees, William, *Recycled Images: The Art and Politics of Found Footage* (New York: Anthology Film Archives, 1993).

Weitz, Eric, *A Century of Genocide: Utopias of Race and Nation* (Princeton, NJ: Princeton University Press, 2003).

Werfel, Franz, *The Forty Days of Musa Dagh* (New York: Carroll and Graf, 1990).

Wilkins, Ann Thomas, 'Augustus, Mussolini, and the Parallel Imagery of Empire' in *Donatello among the Blackshirts: History and Modernity in the Visual Culture of Fascist Italy*, ed. Claudia Lazzaro and Roger J. Crum (Ithaca, NY, and London: Cornell University Press, 2005).

Williams, Linda, 'Film Body: An Implantation of Perversions' in *Narrative, Apparatus, Ideology*, ed. Philip Rosen (New York: Columbia University Press, 1986).

Winter, Jay, *Remembering War: The Great War between Memory and History in the Twentieth Century* (New Haven, CT, and London: Yale University Press, 2006).

Wollen, Peter, 'The Two Avant-Gardes' in *Readings and Writings: Semiotic Counter-Strategies* (London and New York: Verso, 1982).

Yeo, Rob, 'Cutting through History: Found Footage in Avant-garde Filmmaking' in *Cut: Film as Found Object in Contemporary Video*, ed. Stefano Basilico (Milwaukee, WI: Milwaukee Art Museum, 2005).

Index

Note: Numbers in italics following the page numbers refer to images.

ITALIAN MODERNITIES

Edited by
Pierpaolo Antonello and Robert Gordon,
University of Cambridge

The series aims to publish innovative research on the written, material and visual cultures and intellectual history of modern Italy, from the 19th century to the present day. It is open to a wide variety of different approaches and methodologies, disciplines and interdisciplinary fields: from literary criticism and comparative literature to archival history, from cultural studies to material culture, from film and media studies to art history. It is especially interested in work which articulates aspects of Italy's particular, and in many respects, peculiar, interactions with notions of modernity and postmodernity, broadly understood. It also aims to encourage critical dialogue between new developments in scholarship in Italy and in the English-speaking world.

Proposals are welcome for either single-author monographs or edited collections (in English and/or Italian). Please provide a detailed outline, a sample chapter, and a CV. For further information, contact the series editors, Pierpaolo Antonello (paa25@cam.ac.uk) and Robert Gordon (rscg1@cam.ac.uk).

Vol. 1 Olivia Santovetti: *Digression: A Narrative Strategy in the Italian Novel*. 260 pages, 2007.
ISBN 978-3-03910-550-2

Vol. 2 Julie Dashwood and Margherita Ganeri (eds):
The Risorgimento of Federico De Roberto. 339 pages, 2009.
ISBN 978-3-03911-858-8

Vol. 3 Pierluigi Barrotta and Laura Lepschy with Emma Bond (eds):
Freud and Italian Culture. 252 pages, 2009.
ISBN 978-3-03911-847-2